A typical slave festival. (*Copyright: Ryksmuseum.*)

THOSE IN BONDAGE

THOSE IN BONDAGE

An account of the life of the slave at the Cape in the days of the Dutch East India Company.

By

VICTOR DE KOCK

KENNIKAT PRESS
Port Washington, N. Y./London

THOSE IN BONDAGE

First published in 1950
Reissued in 1971 by Kennikat Press
Library of Congress Catalog Card No: 76-122865
ISBN 0-8046-1368-0

Manufactured by Taylor Publishing Company   Dallas, Texas

KENNIKAT NEGRO CULTURE AND HISTORY SERIES

To
Anna, Annette and Vernon.

PREFACE

For many years past I have had the privilege of working amongst the manuscripts of the seventeenth and eighteenth centuries kept by the Dutch East India Company at the Cape. During that period I collected notes in my spare time on various subjects which deeply interested me, with the hope that one day I should have the opportunity of co-ordinating and publishing them in a form acceptable to the general public, neither leading the reader into a labyrinth of unnecessary detail nor yet omitting any of the essential facts.

For the sake of those who may wish to seek further information on any point, a selected list of sources consulted has been included, as well as a number of the more important references.

It now remains for me to acknowledge with much gratitude the kindness and assistance which I have received from all those who have concerned themselves with this work. To my wife and to my mother I feel particularly indebted; their encouragement and never-failing enthusiasm for the project throughout the years have been a constant source of inspiration to me.

To Mrs. Ethel Ferguson I am also deeply grateful: not only did she type the manuscript but in addition she suggested numerous improvements, all of which were accepted without reserve. Dr. J. Hoge unstintingly let me have a number of references which he had come across in his researches in the Cape Archives; Dr. Anna Boëseken read through the manuscript and gave helpful advice.

My colleague Miss Gienie du Toit spent much time in assisting me: both to her and to the many others — such as Dr. C. Beyers, Professor H. B. Thom, Mr. L. C. van Oordt, Professor J. L. M. Franken, Mr. William Hoal, Miss Julie te

Groen, Miss E. Anderson and Miss A. Eagar — who helped in one way or another, I extend likewise my sincere thanks.

A special word of acknowledgment is due to my friend Mr. A. C. Atkins of Kenilworth, to whom this work can be said to owe its inception; for it was he who in the first place urged me to write a book on slavery at the Cape in the days of the Dutch East India Company.

VICTOR DE KOCK.

Cape Archives,
    1 August, 1950.

CONTENTS

CHAPTER ONE On Board the Slavers	13
CHAPTER TWO Journey's End	35
CHAPTER THREE Labourers Without Hire	53
CHAPTER FOUR In Search of Liberty	71
CHAPTER FIVE Pleasures and Pastimes	86
CHAPTER SIX Education, Religion and Courtship	100
CHAPTER SEVEN Superstitions and Medicine	126
CHAPTER EIGHT The Administration of Justice	146
CHAPTER NINE Crime and Punishment	173
CHAPTER TEN The Gift of Freedom	198
PRINCIPAL SOURCES CONSULTED	225
REFERENCES	230
INDEX	238

LIST OF ILLUSTRATIONS

A Typical Slave Festival	*Frontispiece*
	Facing Page
Arrival of Slave-ship at Madagascar	32
A Method of Acquiring Slaves	33
Appeal for Help from the *Meermin*	33
Slave Quarters at "Speir", Stellenbosch	48
Selling a Slave by Auction	48
Sale of Slave Woman and Children at Surinam	49
Parade and Heerengracht in 1763	49
Pass Issued to Slave	80
Greenmarket Square in 1764	80
Slave Bell	81
Hottentots Dancing in Moonlight	81
Brandy and Tobacco for Slave Schoolchildren: a Manuscript Entry in Journal	96
The Gom-Gom: a Musical Instrument	96
The Company's Hospital	97
Malay Funeral	97
A Director of the W.I.C. and his Black Slave	160
Slaves from Angola	161
Smoking of a Pipe to Time a Flogging	161
Malay Quarter, Cape Town	176
Medical Account	176
Letter of Freedom Signed by Ryk Tulbagh	177
The *Kat* at the Castle	177

Chapter One

ON BOARD THE SLAVERS

HAD the local Hottentots at the Cape of Good Hope not evinced such an inherent and natural aversion to work of any kind, the introduction of slaves would have been unnecessary. But these happy, care-free people neither knew nor wished to know the meaning of the word toil. So long as they could slumber in front of their huts all day long and dance and feast in the bright moonlit nights, their cup of happiness was full.

To Jan van Riebeeck, founder of South Africa, this attitude of the natives was a matter of bitter regret. To him the Dutch East India Company had entrusted the difficult task of forming a victualling station on the shores of Table Bay, and the need for labourers became increasingly apparent as time went on.

Occasionally, it was true, the Hottentots fetched fuel for the cooks, scrubbed, washed or collected shells in return for a supply of bread, arrack and tobacco. Once five of them were even prevailed upon to carry a fair-sized beam to the fortress. But no amount of persuasion could induce them to repeat this performance; they were too tired, they said! In another case we read of the Europeans encouraging them with fair promises to catch some zebras, but the secretary sadly records in his journal that these natives simply "sang their old song again" and objected that the animals ran too fast, "and that they were not in the habit of taking so much trouble".[1] Kolbe relates that they were dirty in their ways, slothful and indolent, and he ironically adds that although they were capable of thinking to the purpose, they hated the effort of thought.

These Hottentots, moreover, were jealous of their freedom. Father Tachard, a Jesuit missionary who touched at the Cape in the seventeenth century, writes of a conversation he had with Governor Simon van der Stel, who told him how he had taken into his household a young Hottentot, with the object of civilizing him. No sooner had the black boy grown to manhood than he earnestly begged for his freedom. Not only was he unwilling to subject himself to "the torture of a regulated life" but he also averred that the Europeans were "the slaves of the earth" and the black men the masters. Did not the latter adhere more closely to the laws of nature, eat only when they were hungry and avoid all the hundreds of irritating conventions which bound the Europeans?

If the law of Holland had not laid down that the aborigines of its colonial possessions should be undisturbed in their liberty, Van Riebeeck would have entrapped them and made use of them as slaves. In the circumstances, however, he had to accept the decision of the directors, and he requested instead that a cargo of slaves be sent to the Cape to assist in the manual and agricultural work.

It must be borne in mind that in the seventeenth and eighteenth centuries the employment of slaves was looked upon as a necessity; the fact that men, women and children were taken away from their native habitations and separated for ever from their kindred was not considered as being contrary to the principles of Christianity. Thousands of years ago, it was argued, Moses himself made laws for the regulation and mitigation of slavery; and was not Canaan spoken of as a "servant of servants"? Even in the New Testament slavery was nowhere forbidden: did not the apostles of Christ deliver precepts for the guidance of both masters and slaves, thus sanctioning the relationship?

In the mid-eighteenth century Dutch, French and English supporters of slavery were often found quoting the words of a negro named Jacobus Elisa Joannes Capitein,* who,

---

* We are told other interesting facts concerning Capitein. It appears that he was sent by Jan Compagnie to Castle Delmina, the Dutch factory on the coast of Guinea, to preach and to teach the natives there. One of his first acts was to translate into the local language various articles of the Christian faith and several prayers, and immediately he was faced with numerous obstacles that ordinary people, with less ingenuity than he, might have found insurmountable. It was difficult, for instance, to render an abstract theological idea in a

although a slave, had been taken to Holland and provided with a sound education. Before becoming a fully ordained minister of the Christian faith he studied theology at Leiden, and there, in 1742, a dissertation written by him in the Latin language was published. In it he attempted to prove that slavery was not in conflict with the doctrines of Christianity, and, extending his theory, even suggested that a few whites should also be enslaved, by which act the Company would be rid of many useless and indolent fellows.[2]

If further proof is required to show that those Europeans did not regard slavery as incompatible with Christianity, one need but recall the prayers that they constantly offered up to the Creator for ensuring the success of the slave trade.[3] Some religionists declared that slaves were often so enthusiastic about being made partakers of the Gospel that they rejoiced in having been severed from their father's house. Other supporters, again, drew attention to the so-called humane side of the slave traffic, alleging that it was based on a desire to save the lives of those taken captive in the tribal wars.

Thus John Matthews, whose book was published in the late eighteenth century, insisted that the greater number of slaves sold to Europeans were prisoners made in such wars, and that, from the concurring testimony of many of the most intelligent natives, he deduced that these prisoners would have been put to death had their captors no other means of

---

tongue which had no exactly parallel term. So, remembering, too, the value of impressing upon simple minds the power and prestige of the Dutch East India Company, he solved the problem of translating "I am the Lord thy God . . ." by substituting "I am John Company . . ."

Another difficulty was the Commandment prohibiting work on the Sabbath Day: "Thou shalt not do any work, thou, nor thy son, nor thy daughter, thy manservant, nor thy maidservant . . ." Here was a dilemma indeed! Suppose that the slaves got to hear about this divine order that servants should not toil on a Sunday? Capitein dexterously obviated the possibility by placing the full-stop a little prematurely: "Thou shalt not do any work, thou, nor thy son, nor thy daughter."

When the Classis at Amsterdam realised what was happening they expressed their objection to such free translation, however zealously undertaken in the interests of the Company; and they requested that the book in its existing form should be withdrawn. One thing led to another, and Capitein gave up working in the vineyard of the Lord for commerce. He fell more and more deeply into debt, and died on 1 February, 1747, scarcely thirty years old, without a penny to his name.

disposing of them. "To mitigate the punishment of death by slavery or banishment," he added, "is a proof of civilization operating in favour of humanity, and every circumstance which contributes to that end should undoubtedly be attributed to the same cause." After all, continued this writer, could not a fairly close parallel be observed between the African condemned for some offence to be sold to a white man and the English felon transported to Botany Bay, that wild, uncultivated country? Was not every phase of grief and distress of the black man, parting from his native country, felt with redoubled force by the more enlightened European? It was all very well for people to say that men are by nature equal, but were there not different degrees of excellence in the human race? Was it not a fact, for instance, that from one end of Africa to the other a constant and almost regular gradation could be found in the scale of understanding, till some of the wretched beings sank "nearly below the orang-outang"?

Even Boswell, the biographer of Doctor Samuel Johnson, opposed his master on this point. Speaking of "so very important and necessary a branch of commercial interest", he said: "To abolish a status which in all ages God has so sanctioned and man has continued would not only be robbery to an innumerable class of our fellow-subjects, but it would be extreme cruelty to the African savages, a portion of whom it saves from massacre and introduces to a much happier life."

Commander van Riebeeck's first request for slaves was contained in a letter dated 25 May 1652 — barely six weeks after his arrival. The reply came, however, that none could be spared. Meanwhile their services were urgently required: the handful of European men — about one hundred and ten all told — had to work by day and stand guard by night; the Cape was becoming "an object of terror" to them, and their thoughts persistently dwelt on Batavia's inns, where they knew they could enjoy themselves as "common people are inclined to do at all times".

Five years later there were no more than a dozen male and female slaves at the Cape, all of whom were employed in private homes; only in the following year — on 28 March

1658, to be exact — did the Indiaman *Amersfoort* arrive in Table Bay with one hundred and seventy-four Angola slaves, taken from a Portuguese ship bound for Brazil; and a few weeks afterwards came the yacht *Hasselt* with two hundred and twenty-eight slaves purchased at Popo, on the coast of Guinea. From this time onwards slaves continued to make their appearance: hundreds upon hundreds annually were torn from their own countries and forced to toil for the advantage of others — strange, despondent creatures they were, full of apprehension and fear, knowing full well how few were concerned for their happiness and that, indeed, "no one careth for their soul".*

Most of the slaves from the African coast and its vicinity travelled in packets, sloops or yachts specially fitted out for the purpose: into the caboose were built large kettles with wide spouts; portholes six inches by four, protected with iron crosses, were made between decks for health reasons; wooden partitions separated the males from the females; and long chains, fastened to ring-bolts, secured the shackled captives.[4]

Each skipper, before leaving Table Bay, received comprehensive instructions for the treatment of slaves on board his ship. In addition to the usual food and fruit, he was given a supply of tamarind for the sick, pepper for seasoning the food, and a quantity of pipes and tobacco. Every day the captives had to be brought on deck while the ship was scrubbed and cleaned with vinegar. Care had to be taken that they were not allowed up there before the warmth of the sun could be felt; occasionally, too, the hatches and openings below deck had to be closed, and the unpleasant odours of closely-packed humanity dispelled by means of smoke.

The males and females were separated at meals, and certain sailors were deputed to see that each one obtained a fair share of food and water, and that nothing was wasted.[5] That these sailors, however, could not always be trusted to divide the rations impartially is evident from the remarks

---

* For Comparative Numerical Table of the European and Slave Population, see Reference No. 162.

of no less a person than Abraham van Riebeeck, son of the founder of South Africa, made during his stay at the Cape in 1676, when he witnessed the landing of two hundred and fifty-seven slaves from Madagascar. When they came ashore, he said, they received clothing, but he noticed before they were dressed that many of the women looked plump and well-nourished, a fact which he put down to the rumour that, in return for bestowing their favours upon the sailors, they were given preferential treatment. His suspicion was strengthened when he observed that the slave women parted from the seamen with a great deal of lamentation.[6]

Slaves who fell ill were given every possible attention. For hygienic reasons both men and women captives had to have their heads shaved. Sanitary facilities were provided by means of a partition placed at the mainmast. When the weather permitted, the slaves had to wash themselves in a large tub set on deck. On no account were the sailors allowed to punish any recalcitrant captives; to their own people alone was accorded that doubtful privilege. Finally, it was laid down that when they were taken on board, or when the ship approached land, all of them had to be put in irons, the women and children excepted.

Theal draws attention to a statement in the archives of the early years of the eighteenth century, which, he maintains, exhibits in a very clear light the general opinion in those times regarding negro slaves. It was made by the master of an English slave-ship bound for the West Indies which stopped in Table Bay for provisions; he asked to be treated with exceptional favour, on the grounds that his voyage had been disastrous. During the passage from Madagascar he had observed symptoms of discontent among the negroes in his ship, and so, to prevent their rising and murdering the crew, he had considered it expedient to throw the sturdiest of them overboard! "The event," comments Theal, "is recorded with no more feeling for the blacks than if they had been bales of calico."

This historian viewed as somewhat more justifiable the conduct of the crew of the English ship *Elizabeth*, which arrived at the Cape on 3 June 1719, *en route* from Madagascar to Barbadoes and Jamaica, with a cargo of six hundred slaves. The negroes had risen in revolt and had killed the boatswain and several sailors. The crew, numbering only ninety-five men altogether, suppressed the insurrection by shooting certain of the insurgents and throwing some others into the sea.[7]

The fact remains that in the days of the Dutch East India Company it was by no means unusual for those guilty of conspiracies on board a ship to be thrown alive over the side. In the sloop *Buyenskerke* of Zeeland, for instance — the vessel which brought to the Cape the news that Admiral-General de Ruyter and his fleet had sailed up the Thames as far as Chatham — the officers discovered that sixteen European conspirators aboard had planned to seize the ship and murder the crew. Four of these, without much ado, were forthwith cast into the waves.[8]

The importance of the regulation ordering that male slaves should be placed in irons can be judged from occurrences in 1765 on board the *Meermin*, a Cape packet sent to Madagascar on a slave-buying expedition. The ship called at several ports in the island, and a large complement of one hundred and forty slaves, male and female, was purchased by the supercargo at a little less than three pounds a head. As usual, the skipper had been asked before leaving Table Bay to peruse the instructions enumerating the precautions which had to be taken in order to keep the captives under control. Yet, no doubt elated by the successful outcome of his undertaking, he actually ordered that on this occasion the chains were to be removed from the slaves, and furthermore he made merry on a bottle of wine with his men, even allowing the slave women to dance and sing their native songs as an additional diversion for the Europeans.

These follies reached a climax a few days later when the supercargo handed some of the blacks a number of guns and assegais to clean. Assegais — their national weapon! Is it to be wondered at that the negroes, coming into possession once again of arms which they had been trained to use since childhood, and noting that the majority of their captors were in a state of tipsy exhilaration, should take advantage of the auspicious moment to rise in revolt?

When the supercargo returned to see how the work was progressing, the self-appointed leader of the negroes gave a loud yell, whirled round three times and then stabbed the white man in the back, killing him instantaneously.

A battle then commenced in earnest. One of the slaves pursued the skipper with an assegai, and a sailor who went to the rescue was himself fatally stabbed. During the next few hours the whole of the watch on deck were killed. Unarmed sailors who had succeeded in scrambling up to the platform on the mainmast were cajoled from their refuge on the promise of being allowed to join their mates, but no sooner had they descended than they were thrown into the sea, where their last moments were further complicated by their vain efforts to dodge the deadly assegais which were hurled at them with unerring aim. Of the twenty-five sailors left in the *Meermin* several were severely wounded. For two days none of them was permitted to go on deck. They were forced to live on raw potatoes and raw fat, an unappetising diet which was relieved by a barrel of wine, from which, according to the records, "they obtained much consolation".

At the end of a couple of days spent in these straits the Europeans resorted to a desperate measure. They ignited a quantity of gunpowder, and the terrific explosion nearly paralysed the negroes with fear. When the din had died down, they sent a slave woman to say that unless the insurgents were prepared to make peace a whole barrel of gunpowder would be set alight, and the ship and all aboard would be blown sky-high — "in de lugt zoude laten vliegen". As the slaves did not relish the prospect of such an uncomfortable end, they expressed their willingness to come to terms, and it was agreed upon that no harm should be done to the white men on condition that the ship was taken back to Madagascar. Another stipulation requested by the negroes — namely, that the gunpowder should be dumped overboard — was firmly and shrewdly refused.

After four days' sail land was sighted and anchor was dropped. In the belief that they had regained the shores of their native island, fifty-three slaves of both sexes pulled away in the pinnace and the longboat, having promised to make three fires on land as a signal if all were well, and to send back the boats for their compatriots as soon as possible. The crew of the *Meermin*, however, had in point of fact steered the ship not to Madagascar, as supposed, but to Cape Agulhas. Meanwhile, a number of farmers in that southerly part of the Peninsula, having noticed the vessel riding at anchor, had gathered near the beach to watch developments; and, as the boats approached, they saw that the blacks were well equipped with guns and swords, while the pinnace bore the mark of the Dutch East India Company. As a result of this anomalous circumstance, as soon as the slaves landed they were surrounded and, refusing to surrender, were taken captive, with the exception of fourteen who were killed in the skirmish. Twenty-four muskets, two pistols, eight swords and two bayonets were retrieved from them.

As was to be expected, the eighty-odd slaves left in the *Meermin* grew restive when neither the awaited signal nor the boats appeared, and their mood became more ugly with each hour that passed. So the sailors wrote letters describing their plight, sealed them in envelopes, enclosed them in bottles and dropped the latter overboard. These letters still exist, exactly the same as when they were borne towards land by the current nearly two centuries ago. At the time, one was picked up by a Hottentot and another by a farmer, who immediately handed it to the Landdrost. In them the writers gave details of their predicament, and added that unless three signal fires were lighted, to allay suspicion, they would soon be "Children of Death"

Shortly after the bottles had been thrown overboard one of the sailors decided he would risk swimming to the shore. Arriving there safely, he gave a prearranged signal that there were Europeans in sight. At the same time the fires were kindled. Meanwhile, the negroes had cut the ship's cable, and she was drifting gradually nearer the beach. On seeing the fires the leader of the slaves and four of his companions — still believing, of course, that they were off Madagascar — made for the shore in a little canoe which they had found. No sooner had they set foot on land, however, than they were seized by the commando, after one had been shot. It was only then that the rest of the slaves on board realised the deception, for they were close enough to witness the turn of events. They shot at the commando with their purloined muskets, and before long another battle royal was in full swing on board the *Meermin*. For three hours the negroes and the handful of Europeans contended for their lives with hand-grenades, pistols, swords and knives. Blood flowed freely, but neither side would give in.

At last the slaves were assured with "sweet words" that if they consented to submit quietly their mutinous conduct would be overlooked and they would escape punishment. This they did, and were put back into irons while the flag of the Prince of Orange was hoisted to advise those on shore of the victory. Unfortunately, however, nothing could be done to save the drifting *Meermin*. A few hours later she grounded and became a complete wreck. Every person on board was rescued; all in all, one hundred and twelve of the total number of slaves purchased reached Cape Town. In due course the skipper was brought before the Court of Justice, which found him guilty of such serious neglect of duty that he was deprived of rank and salary, and was declared unfit to serve the Dutch East India Company again in any capacity whatever.[9]

Almost from the beginning of European civilization in South Africa a regular trade in slaves was kept up with Madagascar, and small vessels were frequently sent from Table Bay to procure them. The instructions issued for the conduct of this traffic make quaint reading. "When you have arrived at Magalage," wrote Governor Simon van der Stel, "you shall send on shore a deputation to the king, who is an Arab by descent, to acquaint him with the object of your coming and present him with your credentials, translated into the Latin language . . . and requesting that the prices charged for slaves may be made more reasonable." In parenthesis he added that he did not expect much from this request, as the potentate was "an insatiable miser", and reminded the skipper that he must not omit to grease the palms of the "influential persons . . . without which nothing can be done".

As many slaves as possible between the ages of sixteen

and twenty-four should be obtained, as old and decrepit people "often in their slavery remember their more happy days and, pining away, die". The purchase of female slaves was to be avoided as far as lay in his power. The Governor also impressed upon the skipper the need for unity among the crew. Should a difference of opinion arise, he said, the minority must yield to the majority. "And, above all, God's Holy Name shall always and at fixed times be invoked for His blessing . . . If this is done, we need not doubt the good success of the slave-buying expedition."

A letter followed then, complete with the seal of the Dutch East India Company in red wax, with the Governor's signature, addressed to one or other of the numerous native chieftains. Here is one sent to Andian Mandefandangis, of Madagascar, with an impressive opening in Latin:

"Illustri Regi sive praepotenti Domino atque Principi Insulae Madagascar salutem plurimam!

How high the Directors of the Company esteemed the friendship of His Majesty your father, of glorious memory, in their voyages made to your island for slaves, when their officers and merchants were generously and kindly treated, you will most likely still remember. And we have no lesser idea of Your Majesty's generosity and civility towards our nation!

As we are desirous of making a new, fast, and permanent bond of friendship with you, we have sent this vessel to you with the request so to help the skipper and merchant on board with your counsel and assistance that they may be allowed to buy a large number of slaves, whose age and sex may be properly given, and that, as has already happened, women may not be included between for men . . .

We wish Your Majesty and all belonging to you happiness, prosperity and a long term of health . . . Most Sublime Majesty, your Most Obedient friend and neighbour, the Councillor Extraordinary of the Netherlands East India Company and Governor of the Cape of Good Hope,

W. A. van der Stel."[10]

Despite these elaborate courtesies, the job of being a slave-trader was no sinecure, as many reports of the early days prove. "By God's grace we got away from Madagascar with a whole skin," wrote Jeremias Brons in 1695, as he graphically described "some samples of the wonderful and cruel nature of King Andiaxmanatte". One of the favourite royal diversions was to invite subjects of the minor rulers in Madagascar to visit him and then, once they were merry with wine, to murder them. "He is a man, clever, strong and robust," runs Brons's comment, "with little less blackness than Monsieur du Boys, pastry-cook at Batavia, and though sometimes he has a pleasant mood, he is very strict and very much feared by his courtiers and subjects, in whose eyes and in his own he is a second Alexander, often being very tyrannous and cruel, according to the testimony of two of his chief governors — Andiamatonga and Andiasanguits — especially when drunk, which often happens, from his own drink made of honey, and since our presence, from brandy and arrack, which he drank like water. He taught his courtiers to do the same, throwing the liquor like a stream down their throats until they were nearly choked."

In exchange for slaves this redoubtable personage would take only guns, of which he had a sound working knowledge. When all these weapons had been handed over, and when the transaction proceeded to a cash basis, the king brought forward a woman who had already twice requested the white men to buy her, as she was an aunt of their interpreter. He asked eighty rixdollars for her, a sum which he gradually reduced to sixty-five. At first the traders thought the king was joking, and they offered him fifteen rixdollars, which he angrily refused, demanding to know whether they intended making a fool of him. The Europeans pocketed their money again with the excuse that their Governor would be annoyed if they paid so much. This gesture enraged the king still further. He grasped a double-barrelled pistol which always lay on his lap during these conferences, and threatened to shoot the two interpreters and the woman as well. The fury of the potentate, coupled with the fact that they were sitting in the midst of two hundred armed men, rapidly induced the traders to reconsider their decision. They paid the sixty-five rixdollars and confirmed the deal by bestowing then and there a name, "Gemma", upon their human purchase. The "brute and tyrant" Andiaxmanatte then arbitrarily imposed a price of twenty rixdollars each for boys and nineteen for girls — "so that it was not a barter but a compulsion".

Hardly were the white men out of sight of land on their homeward voyage when they were told by Princess Sara No Moya (sold to them by the king's son, her husband) that Andiaxmanatte's original intention had been to have the necks of all of them broken, and for that inhospitable purpose he had placed a thousand armed followers in ambush in a neighbouring forest to reinforce his bodyguard two hundred strong. He had been dissuaded from taking this step only by commercial considerations; his son and the two governors had cannily pointed out that such a measure would be prejudicial to future trade, and "whence then shall we obtain guns, which we so much require?"

In the course of the slave trade it was always found necessary to present gifts to influential persons, as Governor van der Stel stated, and the king himself often required a donation before giving his royal sanction to the purchase of any slaves. Then, too, courtesy demanded that the ruler's own stock of slaves should be exhausted first — at an enhanced figure! It was only after these preliminaries had been settled that the Europeans were permitted to barter guns, lead and powder, beads, common baftas and negro linen for slaves from the black traders. In later years these traders would accept only reals of eight.* The interpreter at these negotiations was usually a trustworthy slave from the Cape — one who knew the language and how to manage the slaves on board. So great was his unpopularity among his own countrymen that he ran the risk of being murdered by them, as precedent had proved on more than one occasion. The Europeans were asked always to bear in mind the intense hatred of the newly-obtained slaves for the interpreter, and therefore to afford him every possible assistance and protection.[11]

---

* For value of coins used at the Cape in the seventeenth and eighteenth centuries, see Reference No. 11.

If there were no slaves on the market the inhabitants, "with colours flying and music playing", took some of the merchandise into the interior and exchanged it there for human booty. More often than not, however, large numbers were on hand — prisoners-of-war, sold by their conquerors, or natives who had unwittingly allowed themselves to be kidnapped. We are told that when a slave-ship entered the roadstead none of the inhabitants considered himself safe, and few cared to stir out unarmed. And small wonder! Some individuals, excited by evil passions, armed themselves with assegais, hid amongst the bushes and waited till some young or weaponless persons passed by; then, tiger-like, they sprang upon their prey, rushed with them into the woods and at nightfall sold them to the traders.

When the slaves were shown to the European purchasers all of them underwent an exhaustive physical examination. They were first examined as regards their age, and then a minute personal inspection followed. Immediately rejected were those who were infirm, deformed, lame or weak in the joints, or who showed signs of bad teeth or eyesight. As soon as the negotiations were completed the slaves were brought on board, the men being chained together in pairs and sent below to the place allotted them in the hold of the vessel. The women and children were conveyed to other parts of the ship and were not shackled like the men. Leave having been taken of the ruling chieftain, the sails were unfurled and, with the first favourable breeze, the helmsman steered his vessel with its freight of unhappy human creatures towards Table Bay.[12]

Naturally the bewildered captives had their own naïve but disturbing conceptions of the white men's intentions, and their thoughts were hardly conducive to mental repose during the voyage. Thus one writer records that "we are sometimes sufficiently plagued with a parcel of slaves which come from a far inland country, who very innocently persuade one another that we buy them only to fatten and afterwards eat them as a delicacy". As a result, they conspired to kill the Europeans and run the vessel ashore in order "to free themselves from being our food" — a desperate expedient which fortunately came to nothing.

Despite the endeavours of the authorities to decrease their sufferings, the mortality among the slaves during these sea-voyages was exceedingly high. Congested space, naked bodies subjected to bitterly cold weather, scarcity of water, suicide and sickness caused many deaths among the unlucky captives. Constant warnings were issued to skippers, too, to avoid the pirates who often lurked beyond the horizon, ready to attack any ship that crossed their tracks. Thus, in 1687 the skipper of a slaver was told to be on his guard continually, "careful of your ship and arms, with your cannon, cutlasses and swords ever ready at a moment's notice . . . that you may not share the lot of the yacht *Westerwyk*, captured so treacherously by pirates . . ."

From the records it appears that the *Westerwyk* had anchored in Magalage Bay on the west coast of Madagascar, in sight of an English ship, whose chief mate came on board the Dutch vessel to buy some brandy. After having passed some pleasantries with him, the Dutch skipper went ashore to begin proceedings in slave-trading. Two days later, shortly after daybreak, the Englishman without any warning slipped cable and approached the *Westerwyk* with full sails; then, throwing grapnel on the sheet anchor of the Dutch ship, the entire English crew boarded her, every man armed with two pistols, a musket and a cutlass. The captain, "dressed in green down to his stockings", carried a bare Turkish sword when he came over. Shooting as they rushed forward, they poured into the saloon and gun-room. Some of the *Westerwyk's* crew were busy scraping the masts and yards; others were occupied in making beds in the hold — probably from planks obtained on the island — for the expected slaves.[13]

From below the half-deck the gunner discharged three guns at the pirates; the boatswain forced a spit through the grating into the stomach of one of the attackers. But the odds were overwhelming. The third officer was shot through both legs, the sailmaker through his buttock, a boy through the arm and another through the mouth and chin. The wounded were sent aboard the English ship, quarter was offered to the rest, and then the *Westerwyk*, under entirely new management, sailed away to an unknown destination.

Stirring tales of encounters with pirates and buccaneers were often related to the Governors of the Cape. The ruthless, daring, unmerciful "Brethren of the Coast" were the cause of many fears and misgivings on the high seas; almost incredible deeds of sadism and violence were attributed to them. Sailors therefore instinctively fought with great valour whenever a pirate was met, considering as superfluous the instruction which enjoined them as men of honour to defend themselves to the last.[14]

The effects of storms, whirlwinds and fire on the wooden ships can easily be imagined. In 1694 the *Merestyn* encountered twelve storms between Shetland and Rokol, and suffered much damage in consequence. During one of these tempests the chief mate and the junior mate were washed overboard by one wave and borne back again on deck by another. Calms, head-winds and adverse currents often caused much delay, and the long voyages in turn brought on scurvy and other illnesses. In view of the ever-present danger of mutiny at sea, one of the instructions issued to skippers stipulated that the quartermaster had to visit the slaves every morning to see that they had no sharp instruments concealed on them. Sometimes, indeed, the negroes were exercised in the use of military weapons, but then only under the strictest supervision. On one occasion, we read, they fought bravely side by side with their captors in a sea battle against an English fleet in the Straits of Sunda.[15]

It is no exaggeration to say that the Dutch East India Company did everything in its power to encourage the skippers to study the welfare of the slaves on board their ships. They were forbidden to carry a larger number than permitted in the Company's vessels, and a premium was paid for every slave delivered safely above half the number purchased. Special lists of the requisite victuals were drawn up and, when it became known that the English did not lose so many slaves at sea, an investigation was held to determine the reason. Hygiene, it was realised, played an important part, for when a batch of ships arrived with all aboard in good health it was stated that their satisfactory state was due in no small measure to the well-maintained hygienic conditions enforced by the skippers. Nevertheless, the heavy death-rate continued for many years: of a shipment of slaves sent to Batavia in 1733 every one succumbed on the voyage. In an effort to overcome such deplorable loss of life it was suggested that slaves negotiated for at Madagascar and destined for Batavia should first of all be brought to the Cape, where they could be thoroughly refreshed in a climate similar to their own and, when restored to health, could be sent to India with the outward-bound ships.[16]

It must be remembered, of course, that the appalling mortality among the early voyagers was not confined to the slaves, as the Europeans suffered a good deal too. For instance, when Commander Pronk arrived at the Cape with his small fleet in 1696, he had one hundred and eight-eight dead and five hundred and eighty-nine sick among the soldiers and sailors on board his ships. Mostly all, in fact, were ailing. The men's teeth were so loose that they could not bite biscuits or stale food. The new ship *Asia* arrived in Table Bay with eighty dead and fifty ill. Among the dead were all the ship's officers, the minister with his wife and child, the boatswain and the boatswain's mate. Only two of the crew had survived to bring the vessel into harbour. It does not surprise us that Capetonians so often could barely refrain from tears when they beheld the visitors "dragging along their sick limbs with sticks and crutches".

When the authorities openly expressed alarm at the great number of deaths in the outward-bound ships and the equally great percentage of sick, and asked the reason for this, they received a comprehensive reply. The chief cause, it was stated, was the lengthy duration of the voyages by the northern route, which were undertaken in very unfavourable conditions. The soldiers and sailors were put on board almost completely unprovided with necessities. Becoming wet and dirty through bad weather and through pumping water for the condensers, they went to bed at night in their damp clothes, having no change of garments, and the resultant "close and stinking atmosphere" was scarcely conducive to physical well-being generally. "One infects the other, and many, without asking whether their bodies can bear it, go and sleep in the open air during the night." This undesirable state of affairs was aggravated by the very faulty diet on board — "the unvaried consumption of salt meat and pork, and especially of grey and white peas which are the daily pot food, and by length of time become musty in the hold, whilst the beer likewise becomes sour". Such a deficiency in nourishing viands led to scurvy, which afflicted sufferers with loss of appetite, while "blue nobs and blotches cover the whole body, the gums rot, the patients become shivery and feverish, and fall into fainting fits, from which often dysentery results. They . . . take to their beds, and all germs of strength failing them, they die. This is the unanimous testimony of all the chief surgeons, given by order of the Governor . . . To prevent these diseases as much as possible, good nourishing food is required and the ships should, better than hitherto, be supplied with barley, plums, raisins, and currants, which, boiled together with a good dash of mum, and now and then some Spanish wine, and given to the men morning and evening, would be wholesome food, whilst the men should always be kept in a wholesome state of exercise".[17]

Most of the slaves brought to the Cape came from Madagascar, Bengal, the Malabar and Coromandel coasts, Ceylon and the East Indian islands, trade on the west coast of Africa being forbidden to the Dutch East India Company, according to the Charter of the West India Company. The latter Company insisted on a strict observance of its rights, and a letter was addressed to the . . . authorities which read: "You state in yours of the 2 May 1704 that you intended in consequence of the bad success of the slave-trade with Madagascar, soon to try again at Angola or the West Indies, with the hopes of better success and less danger, but as Angola is within the limits of the Charter granted to the West India Company by the States, and no one, including the East India Company, is permitted to navigate or trade there, we trust that you have refrained from that purpose, as it would otherwise cause us trouble here. For your information we send you a copy of said Charter."

As a matter of fact, the West India Company caused the Council of Seventeen much alarm and anxiety by laying claim to the Cape of Good Hope seven years after Van

Riebeeck had formed his little settlement on the shores of Table Bay. They maintained that the Cape fell within their sphere. The affair was brought to the notice of the States-General; it dragged on, however, and when the West India Company received its new Charter it was stipulated that the Cape of Good Hope should remain in the possession of the Dutch East India Company.[18]

Private persons did not participate in the slave-trade. "The inhabitants of this colony," wrote the Burgher Senate to Lieutenant-Governor Bourke, "have never embarked in any expedition to obtain slaves by conquest or barter in other countries, nor has a single individual of the numerous tribes of savages by whom we are surrounded, ever been enslaved by us, and even those who dwell within the confines of our colony are free, and are protected by the existing laws and regulations."[19]

There arose among the burghers, however, a feeling that they should be permitted to trade in slaves in Madagascar and Zanzibar, as they were of the opinion that foreigners were reaping all the benefits of this traffic. This was one of the requests made in 1779, when four delegates from the Cape proceeded to Europe and appeared before the assembly of Seventeen. Governor van Plettenberg,* however, recommended that the traffic should be kept out of the hands of private individuals, and not until the arrival of Commissioners Nederburgh and Frykenius was it decided, for reasons of economy, that the slave-trade should no longer be carried on by the Company: in the first place, it was felt that the trade was no longer profitable and, secondly, the Company was no longer prepared to keep a vessel at the Cape for the purpose of slave-trading.

In 1795 Isaac Strombom bought a little ship called the *Eliza* and asked the Council of Policy for a passport and the necessary documents, as he intended to sail along the East Coast to purchase slaves. This permission was granted, but we find another letter stating that he was waiting for the winter weather to set in, and finally a third letter saying that on account of the possible danger of an enemy invasion

---

*For a list of those who were at the head of affairs at the Cape between 1652-1795 see Reference No. 20.

he could not fly the Dutch flag, and he requested to be allowed to sell the *Eliza* to a Dane.[20]

On one occasion, as it happened, the Council of Policy sought advice from a private individual, François Duminy, in view of his wide experience of slaving expeditions. They asked him to give for guidance a detailed report of the exact requirements for obtaining slaves. In the first place, he responded, a certain amount of money was always necessary, the Spanish real being the only coin which was universally accepted; then it was advisable to take as additional inducements such articles as gunpowder, firelocks, bullets, cloth, iron pots, tin dishes, knives, mirrors, beads and brandy. He pointed out that in order to conduct with success the slave-trade on the east coast of Madagascar, for instance, where the price of a slave was usually reckoned at fifty-two Spanish reals, two-thirds of the cost should be put down in cash and the rest in gunpowder, firelocks and the other above-mentioned commodities. On the west coast of the island, however, the value of a slave was estimated as a rule at thirty-five to forty Spanish reals, and there only one-third was expected in cash, one-third in firelocks and gunpowder and the remainder in the other articles enumerated above. At Querimbo the price was reckoned similarly, though the people liked to receive in addition some table provisions, such as butter, flour, wine and dried fruits. At Mozambique the purchase price of a slave varied from thirty to fifty Spanish reals, depending on the demand, but in that place nothing was accepted but the full sum.[21]

In 1676 the Chamber of Seventeen wrote that they considered the slave-trade at Madagascar of great importance, not only to the Cape and Mauritius but also to India. "The English," they said, "appear to be well versed in this trade, and to be in the habit of supplying Barbadoes from that island; it is strange that we, who lie so much nearer, should still be unacquainted with it; it would be a most desirable thing could that trade be conducted by way of barter for merchandise, for Spanish dollars are here very scarce and dear." Their sanguine expectations were not fully realised, as time proved, for in the years which followed, when this trade had been definitely established between the

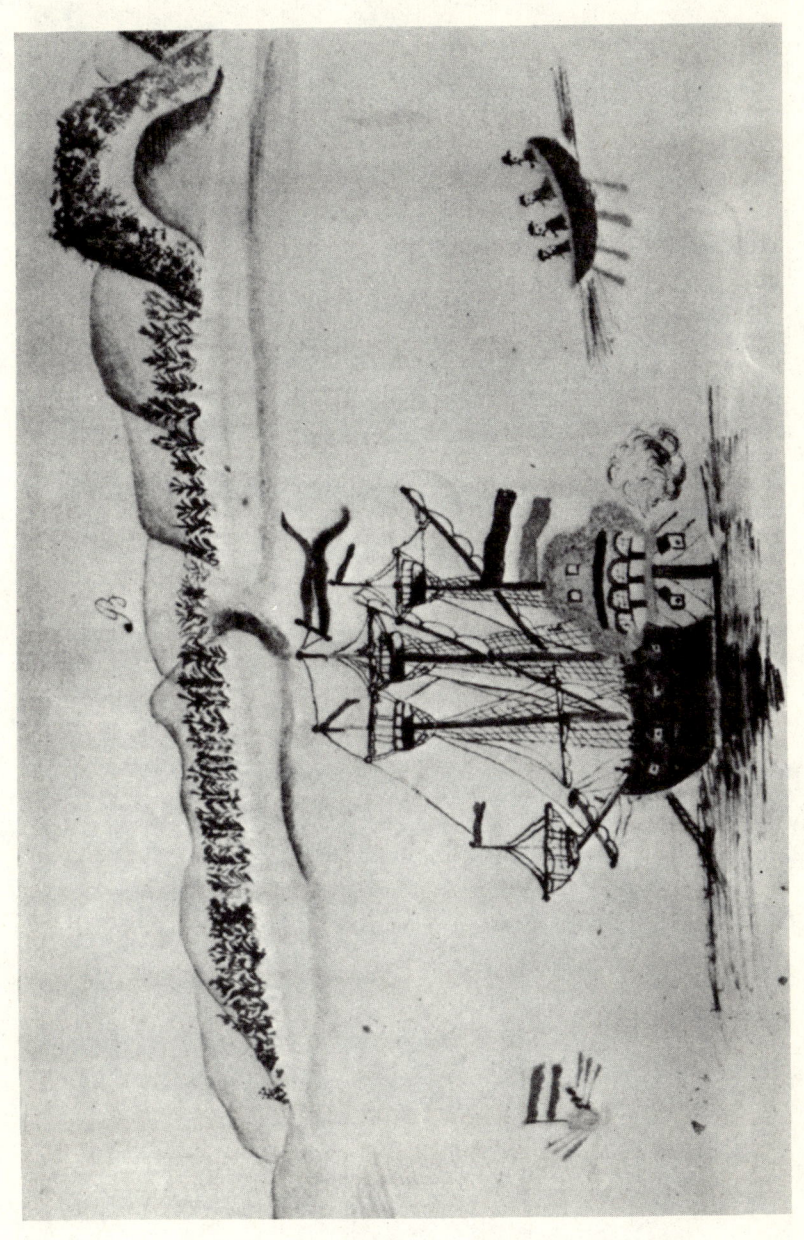

Arrival of the Slaver *Lydsman* at St. Augustine Bay, Madagascar, in 1715.
(From Original Journal in Cape Archives.)

"When a slave ship entered the Roadstead few of the inhabitants could consider themselves safe..."

Original message found in bottle thrown overboard by sailors in the *Meermin*.

(*Cape Archives.*)

Cape and Madagascar, various complaints were made: one in 1704, as we have seen, and another later on in 1771, when the Council of Policy, in a letter, described the slave traffic between the settlement and the island as most unsuccessful. In this instance, the Council consequently sought permission to obtain one hundred young slaves from Bengal — writing, they said, on the assumption that on account of the scarcity of foodstuffs there they would be able to acquire these slaves at a nominal figure.[22]

In 1721 a commercial establishment was formed at Delagoa Bay, one of the main reasons being the possibility of trading in slaves. In the beginning a few were obtained, but afterwards it was said that the Bantu were no longer willing to participate in the trade as they were firmly convinced that the Hollanders purchased the slaves for no other purpose than to fatten and eat them. To counteract this belief three natives of rank were sent on a visit to the Cape to see for themselves why slaves were needed and how well they were cared for and treated. Although the visitors professed to be pleased with what they saw the traffic did not appreciably increase after their return home. In 1730 the East India Company abandoned Delagoa Bay, after an occupation of nearly ten years. Altogether the number of slaves obtained from there did not exceed two hundred and eighty men and women, and these were generally of a murderous disposition and inclined to theft and desertion.[23]

Many slaves were acquired also from English, French and Portuguese ships, either by purchase or by capture. In one case the Company bought one hundred and ninety-four from a Portuguese vessel, and immediately re-sold them to the burghers at a clear profit of 15,188 rixdollars. Another time, owing to the scarcity of labourers, the Company permitted the burghers to buy slaves from the English ship *Joan and Mary*, which anchored in Table Bay. The burghers, however, were advised beforehand not to bid against one another![24]

With the Ceylon squadron which arrived in Table Bay in March 1677 came one hundred Tutucorin slaves. According to the letter which accompanied them hard times had fallen on Madura, and hundreds of these unfortunate beings, pressed by famine, had sold themselves as slaves. Perhaps it was a similar reason which prompted a young negro at the island of Madagascar to sail towards the white men's ship in his little canoe and hand himself over into bondage.[25]

Wouter Schouten, a servant of the East India Company, tells us that in the seventeenth century Bengal children were often sold by their parents. He himself quite unexpectedly became the owner of a youthful slave lad. It appears that one day he was approached by a heathen with the request that Schouten should purchase his son, twelve years old and practically naked. When the black man was asked why he wished to sell his child, he replied that he was too poor to feed the youngster and felt that by taking such a step he would ensure the boy's future welfare.

To Schouten's amazement, the father accepted the amount proffered with great alacrity and went joyfully on his way, completely ignoring his little son and evincing not the slightest sign of emotion or remorse at parting with him. Schouten was much upset at such callousness, but when he reflected on the absolute determination of the parent to dispose of the child to the first bidder he became comforted, and resolved to assist the lad to find happiness. So when Wouter Schouten eventually left for his fatherland he would not sell his slave. Instead, he went to a reputable burgher of Batavia and asked him to see that little Anthony was taught the buttonmaker's craft, as well as the Dutch language and the Catechism, so that in time to come he would be eligible for baptism — and, thus, for freedom.[26]

Chapter Two

JOURNEY'S END

AFTER arriving in Table Bay the slaves were counted, inspected by the Governor and provided with nourishment and a liberal supply of arrack. Despite the scarcity of labourers at the Cape, they were not put to work until they had enjoyed a thorough rest — often a month elapsed before they were sent along with some of the older hands to serve in the stone quarries at the foot of Lion's Head. Very special attention was given to those who landed here in bad health; they were placed under medical observation in the Company's hospital.[27]

Sometimes, when the hospital was overcrowded, other arrangements had to be made. For instance, the *Voorhout* brought so great a number of weak and sickly Madagascar slaves that Governor Bax decided to distribute them among the residents. This was done on the understanding that the Company would give out on loan for a full year to every needy colonist two male slaves and one female, suitably provided with clothes and covering. The hirer would be entitled to purchase monthly a *parra* (forty pounds) of rice. For every slave that died during the term he would pay to the Company, in order to share in its loss, twelve and a half rixdollars. If at the expiration of the year all three, or two, of these slaves were still alive, the hirer would be given the opportunity of drawing lots with the Company to decide who should have first choice; and after the selection had been made the Company would deliver to him, on payment of a nominal sum, any one of the remaining slaves as his property in perpetuity. All the slaves were eagerly snapped up by the residents and, twelve months later, when the latter were summoned before the Council to draw lots, they were told that it had been decided to excuse them from paying compensation for those who had died while in their employment and that any of the surviving ones could be purchased for twenty-five rixdollars each.[28]

Slaves at the Cape fell into two main classes: those belonging to the Dutch East India Company, employed on public works, and those owned by individual officials, burghers and farmers. In the days of Van Riebeeck the Company's slaves were housed in the Fort of Good Hope, from where they were later removed to a new Lodge situated outside the Castle and near the Garden. By 1669 this building was far too small and dilapidated to meet requirements, so in the following year it was completely rebuilt and made comfortable for its inmates and their children. Ten years afterwards a fire broke out in the Lodge, and soon assumed such proportions that the slaves could scarcely save their nude bodies, let alone their clothes, which had to be abandoned. The loss was not considerable, as the Company had already decided to demolish the place, but it was deeply deplored that in the conflagration a young male slave, skilled in reading and writing and possessed of a good knowledge of the Christian religion, had lost his life.

While the Company's slaves were given temporary shelter in the Castle after this disaster, a new house was erected for them on a strip of ground cut off from the lower end of the Garden. In 1680 it was completed. From time to time the Lodge was altered and enlarged, always with an eye to the health and happiness of the slaves, more especially those "who have grown old in slave work and the invalids". By 1751 the building was in such a bad state of repair that it had to be restored and extended again and, at the same time, provided with a flat roof. The Lodge, which now housed six hundred slaves, provided work for a large staff: a director, a surgeon, several overseers and some schoolteachers of both sexes. A superintendent had to call a roll at eight o'clock every night to see that all the slaves were present, and no lights were to burn, except in the kitchen, after that hour. The Lodge was then locked up and the key was delivered to the Fiscal, from whom the same official had to fetch it again at daybreak to unlock the door.[29]

Commissioner van Rheede divided the living quarters of the building into three sections: one for those who had decided to cohabit as married couples, a second for the women and girls and a third for the men and boys. Not all the inhabitants of the Lodge were slaves. The members of the staff, of course, were exceptions; mentally diseased persons were sometimes given small rooms within its walls; an attic was used to house convicts; and, in one case at any rate, a European woman who had been found guilty of aiding and abetting in the theft of wreckage was sentenced to be placed in the Slave Lodge, and to labour at the public works with the female slaves.[30]

It would certainly seem that as far as accommodation was concerned the Company's slaves were well looked after in the Lodge. An Englishman, John White, who visited the Cape in 1787, wrote that the latter was a building of considerable extent, "where the slaves, both male and female, have separate apartments in a very comfortable stile, to reside in after the fatigues and toil of the day; which is undoubtedly great, but by no means equal, in my opinion, to that endured by the slaves in our own colonies . . . they certainly treat their slaves with great humanity and kindness".[31]

When, towards the end of the eighteenth century, an attempt was made to decrease the number of Company's slaves, Hohne, the superintendent of the Lodge, submitted an interesting report. He pointed out that the Lodge contained five hundred and ninety-two males and females, of whom seventy-four were convicts. Thirty-six of these slaves were incapable of doing any hard work owing to old age or physical disability; they were responsible for cleaning the Lodge and nursing the small children. Some were in sick-beds, others were about to become mothers. There was so much to be done that many of the hale and healthy slaves did not even have Sundays to themselves. The superintendent accordingly suggested that numbers of the older convicts should be released in order to join their friends, who would willingly take care of them.

"Entirely different, however, is the position of the aged and infirm Company's slaves, of whom some are totally blind and have to be led by the arm, and others are lame and must be carried . . ." Many of them, he said, were so weak or deformed that no outsider would care to be burdened with them; in the Lodge, on the other hand, they received compassionate and understanding treatment. He himself, wrote Mr. Hohne, had often beheld with deep emotion how the younger slaves, never forgetting the days when they had been nurtured by these now aged folk, regarded them with deep affection and esteem. He added that it was always a comfort to the young to know that they, too, would be able to spend the evening of their lives in the sanctuary of the Slave Lodge.[32]

The main food of the slaves consisted of meat, fish, rice, and bread. In early years at the Cape it was imagined that these people could not subsist without rice; only after 1687 was bread occasionally substituted for it. They were given the heads, feet, entrails and other offal of slaughtered animals, as additional fare; old and useless oxen were frequently killed for them. The Company's hunters were under agreement to deliver monthly for the consumption of the slaves 2,500 pounds of meat — mostly eland, rhinoceros and hart — at a cost of half a stiver per pound. These hunters were each accorded the free use of a wagon, eight oxen and salt, but they had to pay cash for all their hunting accoutrements. Keen fishermen, including Governor Simon van der Stel, often handed over their catch to supplement the slaves' daily ration. Thus, on 11 October 1690, the Governor himself went to fish in Table Bay, and returned late that night with a sufficient haul to supply all the inmates of the Lodge.

It is interesting to notice that when occasion warranted the slaves came in a body to lay complaints regarding the quantity and quality of their food before the Governor or a visiting Commissioner, upon which the matter was immediately investigated and remedial steps taken. In one instance it was revealed that the person in charge of the provisions had defrauded the petitioners of the monthly fish ration by selling it to ships calling at the Cape.

All the visitors to the Cape testified to the fact that privately-owned slaves were well fed, as there was always plenty of food available in the colony. Most of them, indeed, were given the same food as their masters. But there were, naturally, exceptions, as in the case of one Abraham, who, while undergoing severe and prolonged punishment at the hands of his owner, called out that he would welcome death, because he had worked for long enough on an empty stomach; and he advised his fellow-slaves to take note of the treatment being accorded him so that they could lodge their complaints in the official quarters.[33]

Some detailed information is contained in a report dated 16 August 1789 concerning the slaves in the Lodge. In addition to the superintendent and the writer, it seems, there were three *mandoors* and a porter, as well as a surgeon in the Lodge's hospital. At that time eight hundred and one persons were housed and fed within the precincts, and every month the superintendent received for them the following amount of food:

5,080 lbs. rice, 31 muids flour, 5 muids peas, 11 muids beans, 1 aum wine, 25 lbs. sugar, 10 cans whale oil, 40 lbs. pepper, 57 cans vinegar.

One pound of cotton and two pounds of wax candles were added to this list. A weekly ration of bread was allowed, and a daily portion of three-quarters of a pound of fresh meat per head. This was given out, *pro rata*, to the slaves.

In addition to the above-mentioned slaves, there were one hundred and forty-five others who worked at the outside posts, and these received their rations once monthly — forty pounds of rice each and meat at the rate of three-quarters of a pound per head daily, although in this case the meat issued was not killed but given in the form of live sheep.

A list in the records affords us an accurate idea of the amount of materials issued for the clothing of Government slaves. It enumerates:

For the men: 46 pieces Kersey, 24 pieces raw linen, 60 gross buttons, 40 lbs. thread, 106 pieces gerass, 290 hats.

For the women: 282 pieces coarse chintz, 77 pieces gerass, 16 lbs. thread.

For the sucklings: 16 pieces coarse chintz, 6 pieces gerass, 1 lb. thread.

For the infirmary: 30 pieces blanketing, 30 mattresses.

Food and clothing for the nine hundred and forty-six Company's slaves cost the Company a total sum per year of approximately 48,892 gulden.[34]

A practice arose amongst the slaves of selling their clothes, and it developed to such an extent that in order to stop the abuse garments issued by the Company were marked in such a way as to be easily recognisable, with a cross in the right-hand corner of each jacket, this symbol being cut out of the cloth and then sewn on again. Drastic punishments were threatened to any Europeans found guilty of purchasing clothing from slaves: a white man after the third offence was liable to be banished from the country; and a free black or a slave in similar circumstances could be put into chains for ten years.

The food supplied to slaves was far better than that given to the convicts on Robben Island. On one occasion the superintendent of the island drew a frightful picture of the starving condition of these prisoners: "According to Council convicts are no longer to be fed on meat. They are not even able to catch a single klipfish. They have to be fed on the dead pigs and sheep which were thrown overboard from the ships and washed up here. They also feed on the sheep that die here and which have been thrown away by my orders. They go and search for and eat them. I was more than once obliged to have the pot in which they were boiling the carrion removed from the fire and emptied into the sea. The contents stink like rotten carrion, and I fear that disease may be the consequence". As far back at 1712 a request had been made for more food, and the authorities had decided then that from that date they should receive the same quantity as was given to the Company's slaves.

It was customary for the various Governors or Commanders to inspect the Slave Lodge from time to time. In 1687 the Commander wrote that he found the slaves well fed, at fixed hours and in a cleanly manner, with good bread, meat, fish and vegetables. "They are visibly growing," he appended, "and the whole world rejoices in it." Meanwhile, the sixteen European clerks employed at the Castle as scribes were finding it impossible on their meagre pay to purchase enough food for their sustenance, with the result that they often had "only a piece of dry bread to eat with a little water to drink".

Careful attention was bestowed also on the clothing of the Company's slaves. Many of these earned pocket-money on Sundays or in their spare time by labour or fishing, and were thus able to keep themselves in decent garments; others complained that they had neither change of apparel nor anything with which to cover their bodies at night. As a result of this appeal they were provided with blankets and, twice annually, with new clothes, the lining of which was frequently old sail-cloth. When, in later years, it was observed that their garments were badly made and that they therefore suffered discomfort, it was considered advisable thenceforth to order good clothing from Holland for them. Articles of dress, of course, were extremely expensive, as the material had to be imported in the small sailing-ships of those days. As early as the time of Simon van der Stel a request had been sent to the Council of Seventeen to permit the manufacture of clothes on a large scale from the locally produced wool, but this was refused on the grounds that viticulture and agriculture would be adversely affected in consequence.[35]

A French refugee had made strong hats of Cape wool; others had knitted long stockings and gloves; but these embryo industries had died out early in the eighteenth century. Not before 1782 was it once again attempted to overcome the serious dearth of such woollen stuffs as were required for clothing the slaves. A number of the leading inhabitants submitted an original plan for the production of Kersey, pilot cloth and woollen blankets. For this purpose they had obtained the services of Frederik Hyneman of Stellenbosch. With a few dissentient votes the Council of Policy acceded to the request. But the Independent Fiscal held the opinion that the colonists should rely on the factories of the Netherlands for their requirements. The memorial and a résumé of the Fiscal's remarks were then sent to the Seventeen. As no reply was received, one must presume that the Fiscal's views carried the day.[36]

Any sale of slaves by the Company to the inhabitants was advertised by notices posted on the Castle gates and at the corners of the principal thoroughfares, while a messenger, equipped with a brass plate and a drumstick, traversed the streets and loudly invited the colonists to attend. The following advertisement appeared in 1699:

> "On Saturday morning the 1st August within this Castle at 10 o'clock it is intended to sell for cash by public auction on behalf of the Honourable Court of Justice a certain slave named Alexander of Bengal, aged 16 years...
>
> The buyer must undertake to keep the slave in chains for six successive years in accordance with his punishment; only on this express condition can he be alienated or transferred to another.
>
> Those interested should come on the day and hour specified and thereby make a profit."[37]

Slaves of good character were rarely sold, either publicly or privately, except owing to the financial distress or insolvency of the owners, or by executors in the distribution of a deceased man's property. As there were no newspapers at the Cape in the seventeenth and eighteenth centuries, sales among the inhabitants were also made known weeks ahead by means of notices exhibited in conspicuous public places, giving full particulars of the nature of each sale, the date and the conditions. On the actual day the auctioneer's assistant went round the town or village, beating his metal disc at the crossroads and loudly announcing the event. Those who attended the auctions in the country districts were usually supplied with free meals and lodging; refreshments such as beer, wine, tobacco, tea, coffee, cakes, bread and cheese were nearly always served.

"I happened, some days ago," says a certain writer, "to step into one of the Vendities, or public sales, in Cape Town where, among other articles, I saw three or four slaves set up for sale. This was altogether a new sight to me. I could not without pain remark the anxiety with which those poor creatures regarded the persons who were bidding for them. It seemed as if they wished to trace the character of their future master in the lineaments of his countenance, and showed indications of joy or fear, according to the opinion they had formed of his disposition."

Another observer gives a graphic description of a private auction of slaves in a rural district: "The scene of a venditie is not unlike a country fair, and reminds a spectator of many a picture from the Flemish school. Merry revellers grouped in one quarter; sots lying drunk in another; busy dealers trafficking in one place; the auctioneer perched upon his wagon, slowly vending his tardy lots; vehicles of divers kinds around; cattle, implements, utensils, the subjects of sale, scattered about . . . a variety of dress and figure, countenances and complexions adds to the diversity of a scene to which Dutch and Negro, Hottentot and Malay equally contribute . . . It is conducted somewhat differently from a sale of negroes in Brazil, and from that of domestic slaves in the East Indies."

Many of the slaves, he records, appeared to be deeply affected by their impending separation from friends with whom they had long shared servitude. Several were bathed in tears; others lamented aloud. The slave exposed for sale was set on a table in order to be more conveniently viewed, and "was not handled and closely inspected as at a sale of imported negroes in South America, but interrogated as to qualifications and blemishes . . . The sale proceeded gravely and simply, as a mere matter of business".

When a buyer was known to the auctioneer he was allowed credit. Among the records of the Orphan Chamber numerous accounts similar to the following can be found:

2 horses	14 rixdollars.
2 mares	20 ,,
1 mare and colt	16 ,,
1 slave girl named Sophie of the Cape with her two children, Sabina and Candaza of the Cape: *Voetstoots*	383 ,,
1 bucket	1 ,,

One cannot quote any standard purchase price for slaves as they fetched extremely varying sums. At the auction of slaves in Jacob van Reenen's estate, for instance — at which his sons were buyers — Hector of Malagas went for 1,025 rixdollars, while a slave girl, Francina, was bought for only 52 rixdollars. This was unusual, for as a rule female slaves fetched relatively high prices, because any children they might bear later would automatically also become the property of the master. With the arrival of the French troops in 1781, when an expensive fashion of living became general, when money was plentiful and Cape Town was known as "Little Paris", the price of slaves soared up, increasing from fifty to one hundred per cent. We are told, incidentally, in 1790, that a tax on the importation of slaves was suggested, at a figure of ten rixdollars for every one, no matter what his age might be.[38]

It not infrequently happened that the sale of a slave was annulled in consequence of infirmities which the purchaser might discover in him after the deal had been concluded, in which event the *dedilitium edictum* of the Roman Law was observed by the Courts. The so-called "Requesten" include a letter from G. W. Hoppe, who stated that he bought a slave in a certain deceased estate, supposing, from his favourable appearance and general deportment, that he was healthy. When he took the man home, however, Hoppe found out that he was suffering in an advanced stage from a loathsome disease, and he therefore asked the Court of Justice to cancel the sale and to have the purchase price — three hundred rixdollars and one skilling — refunded to him. An interesting fact is that in cases where a man and his wife, parents and their children, brothers and sisters, and others bound to one another by the ties of close relationship, were sold in groups, the sale of any one of them could not be annulled on the pretext of an infirmity unknown to the purchaser at the time of buying, unless such a slave was restored to his former master together with the others sold with him.[39]

In the early days of the Dutch East India Company at the Cape, lots were drawn not only for life or death but also for the supply by the inhabitants of wagons for conveying produce, and even for the building of a church. The holding of lotteries for the disposal of articles, however, was strictly forbidden, on pain of a heavy fine and the confiscation of the goods. It was only at the beginning of the nineteenth century that sales took place similar to this one advertised in the *Government Gazette* — South Africa's first newspaper — on 30 January 1802:[40]

To be Disposed of by Lottery

Some handsome furniture, plate, etc., and a young female slave, African born. One hundred tickets at 10 dollars each, 30 prizes, five of which ten dollars.

The list of prizes to be seen at Messrs. Bray and Venables, where the tickets are to be purchased, and the lottery drawn.

The prizes will be left at their auction room one week previous to the drawing, and to be delivered immediately after it is drawn.

In early times public sales of immovable property were conducted by Government officials by the method known as *opslag* and *afslag*. In other words, a sale took place twice over. The article was first put up by the auctioneer in the usual manner, and the bidding went on to as high a figure as anyone would venture who had no real intention of purchasing. For this the bidder-up, as he was called, was entitled to *strykgeld* — a premium or bonus. As soon as this procedure was concluded the auctioneer continued with the second part of the sale. Thus, for example, as Mentzel explains, if a house had nominally fetched two thousand guilders at the first sale, he now asked four thousand for it, and then abated the price by, say, a hundred guilders at a time, calling out continuously: "Three thousand nine hundred!" and so on. When the price dropped to a reasonable amount someone shouted "Mine!" and the bargain was sealed. Provided that the price was beyond that of the bidder-up, the second purchaser was the recognised buyer and retained the property, while the first received only the premium.

This kind of sale was very advantageous to the seller, for a *bona fide* purchaser was in dread every moment of hearing someone else shout "Mine!" and therefore made his own bid as soon as the price descended to any sum which he could possibly afford. If the final price reached was below that offered by the bidder-up the latter had to take the property at the figure which he had bid, and received the *strykgeld*. Even the Company, when it was at last decided to sell the posts Vissershok and Gansekraal by public auction, ordered the overseer to make sure that there was enough food and drink, "en wat dies meer is", for those attending the sale, and to see that the *strykgeld*, to the amount of fifty ducatons, was paid to the bidder.

Even movable articles were at one time sold by *afslag*, but it was soon realised that the people were not accustomed to buying movables in this manner as everything went for sums far below the actual value. In the interests of all, therefore, it was resolved at the beginning of the eighteenth century to resume the old form of auction when slaves, furniture, cattle and other movable property were to be sold. Already there were people who put up their goods for sale and then refused to sell them: in fact, so much inconvenience, annoyance and ill-feeling had arisen that the Government decreed that henceforth the vendumaster should receive one and a half per cent. and the messenger half per cent. for property offered and not sold. It was hoped in this way to relieve these officials from making useless trips into the country.[41]

There is an interesting account of the auctioning of slaves, written by Semple: "In one of our morning walks about the town," he records, "observing a considerable crowd before the door of a house, my friend and I went up and enquired what was going forward, and were informed that it was a public sale of all the effects of a colonist deceased. Scarcely had we joined the crowd when the auctioneer mounted upon a chair and struck for some time upon a round plate of brass, as a signal that the auction was going to begin. Immediately all was attention. Numbers of articles were put up and disposed of, till, growing tired of the scene, we were going away; a short pause, however, and then a murmur in the assembly announced that something else than trifles was going to be produced. We accordingly waited a moment, and soon saw a black man coming forward through the crowd. 'Ah!' said Charles, 'they are going to dispose of the family slaves; let us stop a little longer.'

The first that was put up was a stout native of the Mozambique coast. His look was sad and melancholy, his hands hanging down clasped together as if they were bound and his eyes fixed upon the earth. When he heard that his lot was determined and that he was to be sold for six hundred rixdollars, he raised his eyes up heavily to look for his new master, and followed him out of the crowd without speaking a word. But we thought that his cheek was wet with tears, and perhaps we were right; for the purchaser told us with some compassion that he had been a great favourite of his deceased friend."*

From a perusal of the Cape records one soon gains the impression that the slaves belonging to the colonists were better dressed, better fed and better treated than those of the Company. Capetonians who ran boarding-houses more often than not permitted their slaves to keep tips and moneys received for liquor supplied to the guests. The farmers, again, frequently presented to those of their bondsmen who had proved themselves trustworthy and hard-working a plot of ground each, to cultivate on their own account, providing them with seed and manure gratis, and even giving them free time to do this work. When their produce was ready for sale the farmers assisted them in its disposal. Premiums were also often paid to slaves for the destruction of wild animals. With this additional money they sometimes bought extra blankets, clothing and other luxuries; generally, however, they invested the proceeds in brandy.

Firmness was always essential in the difficult task of

---

* In reviewing the various methods of selling slaves at the Cape, we certainly do not come across such a procedure as that sometimes employed in the West Indies, namely, a "sale by scramble". When this took place, all the negroes for whom the potential buyers "scrambled" bore an equal price, agreed upon between the captains and the purchasers before the sale began. According to a description given by the surgeon Falconbridge, on the appointed day the negroes were landed and put together in a large yard, belonging to the merchants to whom the ship was consigned. As soon as the stipulated hour struck, the doors of the yard were suddenly thrown open, and in rushed a considerable number of purchasers, with "all the ferocity of brutes". Some instantly laid hold of as many blacks as they could seize with their hands; others, being prepared with several handkerchiefs tied together, encircled with these the greatest number that could fit within the span: "it is scarcely possible to describe the confusion . . . the poor astonished natives were so much terrified by these proceedings".

keeping the slaves under proper control and submission. It would be dangerous, Mentzel declared, to give them the slightest latitude; a tight hold had ever to be maintained on the rein. Needless to say, there were a large number of colonists who were unable to discipline their slaves. In the records is the case of a certain owner who was not only addicted to intemperance but also showed alarming signs of "weak intellect and simpleness". He so neglected his farm that he lost all authority over his slaves. They did not in the least respect him, but committed all kinds of excesses on the property, and "during the night and unseasonable hours allured to themselves all kinds of rogues, with whom they drank and gambled, whilst in the daytime, instead of doing their master's work, they burn charcoal at the riverside, which they convey thither with the wagon and cattle of their master, selling it in his name and keeping the money for themselves". Afraid that he would soon be impoverished, and anxious that his neighbours should no longer be subjected to the annoyance of these improper actions, his relatives asked that suitable steps should be taken to prevent his utter ruin. As a result, all his landed property and his possessions were sold and the proceeds kept under the administration of the Court of Justice.[42]

Once the Fiscal himself had occasion to deplore openly the fact that so many owners treated their slaves — particularly those born in their own homes — with indiscriminate and excessive indulgence, which was frequently abused. They could see no wrong in them and, what was more, if anyone, even though holding a responsible position, delivered a slight reprimand to any of their "knaapjes", these masters and mistresses were immediately resentful, regardless of the misdemeanours which had elicited reproof in the first place. As a result, said the Fiscal, the behaviour of the slaves towards Christian people was becoming increasingly intolerable.[43]

A good idea of the clothes isued by a colonist to his slaves can be formed from the diary of Von Dessin, so ably edited by Professor Franken. We read that a slave entering Von Dessin's household at once received a blue Kersey jacket and one of chintz, a pair of Kersey trousers, a cloak, blue

Slave quarters at "Speir", Stellenbosch.
(*From a Painting by Peggy Taylor.*)

Sale of a slave by auction.

Sale of slave women and children at Surinam.
(*Copyright: Ryksmuseum.*)

Parade and Heerengracht, 1763.
(*Elliott: From Van Stolk Collection.*)

shirts, handkerchiefs, a feather bed, a woollen blanket and a sealskin which, nailed to a wooden frame, made an excellent *katel* or bunk. This information is confirmed by another diarist, who tells us that the colonists clothed their slaves with comfortable jackets of coarse material and pantaloons, and mentions that they were given mattresses, blankets, and so on. A third writer amplifies these facts in a descriptive account of a slave's costume which, he says, "generally consists of a short blue cloth jacket, a light waistcoat and loose blue trousers. On his head he wears either a coarse hat or a handkerchief tied round it like a turban, but he is in general without either shoes or stockings; the collar of his shirt is open and a blue or red handkerchief is tied loosely round his neck. Sometimes, however, you meet a slave beau: his ears are ornamented with rings, a red shawl is wrapped round his neck, a plume of common ostrich feathers waves in his hat, he treads lightly along, nodding his feathers and looking proudly round him. He is lifted above the ground, and has totally forgot that he is a slave".

As a token of their servile state many of them were not permitted to wear shoes or stockings, although Jacob van Reenen sought permission in 1782 to purchase some footwear and hats in Holland and bring them to the Cape for slaves. Mentzel, in describing the household slaves, tells us that they were "clean and neatly attired, but may not wear shoes. The bare foot is the mark of the slave. Hence at the Cape, unlike in ancient Rome, the shoe, not the cap, is the mark of freedom". A hat could adorn the slave's head only after he had learned the Dutch language. In order to encourage the blacks in this respect it was decided in Batavia as early as 1642 — ten years before the first settlement at the Cape — that no slave should be allowed to wear a hat until he could understand and speak Dutch well. The penalty for failure would be confiscation of the hat and a severe thrashing. Pascoe Thomas, too, mentions these prohibitions: "No slave is permitted to wear shoes, no man slave a hat, nor woman slave a cap." Many of the male slaves wore their hair — upon which they set great store — tied up in a twisted handkerchief like a turban, and the females wound theirs up and fixed it in position with large pins.

Those slaves who had pronounceable names were usually allowed to retain them; others were given appellations according to the ingenuity of their employers. Martin Melk, of Lutheran Church fame, owned numerous slaves, and these are some who were mentioned in his will: February, March, April, May, July, August, September, October, December, named after the months of the year; others — Samson, Goliath, Esau, Jeptha, Benjamin, Absalom, Job — had biblical namesakes; classical titles also abounded, such as Cupido, Mentor, Hector, Leander, Narciss, Jason, Titus, Coridon, Adonis and Apollo; and even geographical place-names were used — Zeeland, Gelderland, Amsterdam, Holland, Canton, Java and Swartland. Nicknames were often bestowed on slaves, some descriptive and others obviously without any significance at all: Snuffelaar, Scheel Adam, Scheele Caatje, Jan Contant. As one writer observed, regarding the classical names, "the whole heathen mythology" was ransacked to find them, and they were generally given to the slaves "in a manner not the most honourable to those deities at whose altars one half of the human race formerly bowed down. Thus Jupiter cleans the shoes, Hercules rubs down the horses, and Juno lights the fire . . ."

Many of the inhabitants employed the term "volk" when referring to their own slaves and "Coelies" when speaking of slaves in general: the expression "Coelie geld zoeken" was applied to those who roamed the streets seeking purchasers for their wares. When addressing an elderly male slave the Europeans almost invariably used the word "Paaij", meaning literally "good old man". Even the corpse of an old black beggar found in a hut in the Gardens was formally referred to as "Paaij Moor". A nursemaid was usually known as "Aia". A newly-acquired slave was often called a "Baar", a term which was also jokingly applied to a newly-enlisted sailor.

Lichtenstein throws further light on the subject of modes of address. "The Hottentot is a hired servant," he says, "and there is this great distinction between them and the slave: that the former only address their master by the title of Baas (Master) while the slaves address him as Sieur

(Lord), pronounced here Ssohr. A Hottentot in consequence takes it extremely amiss if he is addressed by the words *Pay* or *Jonge* as the slaves are; he expects to be called by his name if addressed by anyone who knows it; and by those to whom it is not known he expects to be called Hottentot (which he pronounces Hotnot) or Boy."

As far back at 1657 instructions were issued to Van Riebeeck regarding the language to be used. "With the arrival of the slaves you shall be careful that you do not import the Portuguese language with them, but prevent it by every means . . . as much depends on it. Only one mother tongue shall be employed for the slaves, who shall not be allowed to speak any other. This will in the course of years remove all anxiety."

At that time corrupt Portuguese was the common medium of intercourse between Europeans of all nationalities and native traders in the eastern seas, especially along the coastal regions where the great East Indiamen sailed. Many Cape colonists, particularly those who had visited the East, had a smattering of this language, not, indeed, as it was spoken in Portugal, but like a seaman's lingo — a hotchpotch of Portuguese, Malay, Dutch and other tongues. Like pidgin English, it lacked grammatical forms, and for this reason it was easily assimilated. Mrs Kindersley, who called at the Cape in 1765, wrote in one of her letters: "What makes it extremely comfortable is that most of them speak English; French is likewise spoken by many; so that foreigners find themselves more at home in this port than can be imagined . . . What seems extraordinary is that they (the slaves) do not learn to talk Dutch but the Dutch people learn their dialect, which is called Portuguese, and is a corruption of that language". It is interesting to note that as late as 1824 the ward-masters were ordered to explain in Dutch and in Portuguese to one slave in each house locally the meaning of certain proclamations that had been promulgated.[44]

Nevertheless, we realise the many difficulties encountered by both sections when trying to make themselves understood, and with Bontekoe we admire the resourcefulness of his friends who, in such a situation, after some deliberation suddenly shouted "Moo, baa and cock-a-doodle do" to their astonished audience, who soon produced the cow, sheep and fowls thus ingeniously requested. From the very beginning the need for interpreters was urgently felt at the Cape. Even in 1767 certain slaves were still obliged to communicate by means of signs and peculiar noises, as not a soul in the colony knew their language. Indeed, the slaves came from so many different parts that unless they learned or were already familiar with Malay, Portuguese or Dutch they were frequently unable to understand even one another. Few of them were so fortunate as Aje of Clompong, who could converse in eleven tongues.

We read that one of the reasons why the blacks from Madagascar, although cheaper than those from the East, were not at first as much in demand was the fact that they had no common medium of speech with the colonists. Sometimes, however, the slaves forgot their own native languages. It is on record that a Persian visitor once spoke to some Bengalese blacks and discovered that they no longer understood the Hindu and Bengal tongues, with the result that they had to converse by signs.

One may conclude with a description left by Dr. Sparrman of the conversational complications which arose at the Tavern of the Seas when ships of several nations came to anchor in the bay: "At mealtimes various European dialects, together with the language used in commerce with the Indians, viz. the Malay, and a very bad kind of Portuguese, were spoken all at one time, so that the confusion was almost equal to that of the Tower of Babel!"

CHAPTER THREE

LABOURERS WITHOUT HIRE

BROADLY speaking, one could divide the slaves at the Cape into four classes: the negroes, the Asiatics in general and the Malays in particular, and those born in the colony. The negroes, who were the least valuable, came from Madagascar and the African coast: of low intelligence, obstinate and intractable in disposition, they became hewers of wood and drawers of water; the females were engaged as washerwomen and in other employments requiring merely strength of limb and body. On the other hand, the Malays — one writer called the Malay the "king of slaves" — were the most active and docile, but at the same time the most dangerous; they were impatient of injury, vindictive and easily provoked. It did not take these yellow-complexioned workers long to become familiar with almost every trade or calling. As builders and house-painters they were soon in great demand. They made excellent masons, good confectioners and cooks, expert drivers and incomparable fishermen. Their womenfolk dressed tastefully and neatly and always looked picturesque in their exotic *kaparangs*,[45] bright cotton gowns, large gold earrings and golden pins skewered into the hair. It was the Cape-born slave, however, often the product of a European and a slave girl, whom the inhabitants preferred as a class.

Improbable though it may seem, there were colonists who actually did not know how many slaves they possessed: one of them, for instance, realised that the number on his farms exceeded two hundred, but he was ignorant of the exact aggregate. Another person owning well over two hundred slaves was the Governor Willem Adriaan van der Stel, who farmed on a huge scale at "Vergelegen". These included slaves whom he had purchased for his own private use, over and above the complement of Company's slaves allotted to him as Governor. Almost every colonist of rank or consequence possessed from ten to twenty, including women and children — three slaves, it was computed, being needed to perform a task which would normally be completed by a single European in Holland. As the slaves became more numerous and more easily obtainable no white man could be hired as a menial servant, deeming it a degradation to do, as he would term it, the work of a slave. Even the Netherlands women, no matter how humble their origin, once they had arrived at the Cape regarded themselves as too important for household drudgery, and soon aspired to a position in which they could direct others.

Nearly every householder maintained two slaves, who were responsible for fetching fuel from the downs and drawing water at one of the public pump-houses. Sometimes the fuel-bearer had to go many miles into the country to look for brushwood, cow-dung or stumps of trees. When he had collected a sufficient quantity he would make it up into two bundles, which were then fastened to a bamboo yoke about five feet long, one being suspended from each end. This carrying-pole was placed on the shoulder, and the slave moved off with his weights nicely balanced, one swinging before and the other behind.

At the water-pumps a good deal of rowdyism and jostling took place. One writer tells us how the stream from Table Mountain, coursing through innumerable wooden pipes (an example of which is still exhibited at the City Hall, Cape Town), was conducted to a fountain at the lower end of the town, "where many hundred slaves were accustomed to assemble, wrangling, fighting and rioting for their turn of getting water". In order to preserve the peace the Fiscal had to station two of his men there, and explained that there were no less than a thousand slaves occupied in drawing water for the people of Cape Town. Another annoying practice amongst the slaves gathered together at the water-pumps was their habit of drinking alcohol. In this many of them indulged whenever possible. From the Landdrost and Heemraden of Drakenstein came a complaint that the people of their district dared not send their corn to the mill there, as both the "knechts" — European servants — and the slaves drank to excess at a neighbouring tap kept by one of the burghers, "so that they not only remain away days longer than they ought to but also lose a quantity of the meal". These officials expressed the fear that the drunken slaves might set fire to the mill, as had actually happened some years before, causing great loss, and they asked that "no tap shall be allowed within the distance of an hour from the mill".

The slave girls born at the Cape were the favourites of their mistresses, who took pride in seeing them trim and well dressed. To these privileged abigails was allotted the duty of arranging and keeping in order everything in the home, while their leisure hours were spent in knitting, spinning, sewing and other light occupations. Sparrman describes a domestic scene which he saw once in a farmhouse, where "about ten o'clock I took shelter from the rain . . . I found the female slaves singing psalms while they were at their needlework. Their master, being possessed with a zeal for religion quite unusual in this country, had prevailed with them to adopt this godly custom . . ."

Such girls often slept at the door of their mistress's bedroom, followed her when she went to church or to pay calls, carried her psalm-book or her work-bag, held an umbrella over her head to shade her from the sun or, when darkness enveloped the little city, lighted her through the unillumined streets if she ventured out to dance or to play cards, and ministered to her comfort in winter by putting live coals in the *komfoor* or foot-warmer — a little perforated box which they placed under her feet in cold weather.

These maidservants were frequently treated more like companions than slaves; in fact, many contemporary writers averred that they shared in the general attitude shown towards members of the family, within reasonable limits. Naturally in such circumstances they had ample opportunity to study their mistress's deportment and mannerisms, and we are assured, amongst other things, that they could conduct intrigues with as much art and coquetry as the most accomplished European! A little anecdote illustrating how impartially domestic justice was meted out by a certain mistress probably sums up the treatment accorded in nearly all private households: a slave, interrogated by the Landdrost as to the woman's usage of one of her slave girls, answered "Well, if she was naughty she got a hiding, just as my mistress gave to her own children".

The household staff further comprised the cooks, the washerwomen, the chambermaid who made the beds and heated them with a warming-pan, the seamstress, the groom and the pair of slaves who carried the sedan-chair when transport was required. Then there was the female slave who brought every evening before the assembled family a tub of water for the purpose of washing the hands of father, mother, children and visitors, in that order. Sometimes these communal ablutions were extended to the feet as well. One traveller tells us that as the water served in turn for the whole company without once being changed he, who as a guest came last, felt no great eagerness to avail himself of the privilege. "To excuse myself I pretended that it was customary with me never to take off my boots till I was on the point of getting into bed; and the excuse was admitted." Finally, but by no means least on the list, the staff included those little slaves who were employed to pull their owner's young children about from place to place, lest they should "too soon discover for what purposes nature had bestowed on them legs and arms". These small servitors performed an additional duty: armed with whisks of ostrich feathers, they were stationed behind the chairs of those seated at meals so that they could drive away the flies which hovered about the table.

That most observant of travellers, Cornelius de Jong, did not hold a very high opinion of the domestic slaves. He waxed caustic about the amount of work which they accomplished and considered them lazy, indolent and miserable creatures — "the greater the number the greater the grief". Jacob Wallenberg, too, a Swede who arrived at the Cape in 1770, criticised the slaves unfavourably, as to their physique at any rate, which he seemed to think prevented their being able to undertake any arduous task single-handed. They were, he said, "as a whole short in stature and weak of limb.

I have seen four of them round a load which one boy from Dalarna at home would shoulder alone, slaves included". This physical inferiority he attributed to their irregular and promiscuous habits which began, he added, "often at the age of no more than twelve or thirteen". Certainly, though, there must have been exceptions, for we find a record of one slave complaining of another that he was always bragging of his strength: "Salomon pogt dog altoos so om dat hy sterk is".[46]

It would be no slight undertaking to give an exhaustive account of the multifarious duties performed by the slaves. Concerning the Government slaves, a list dated 1789 shows how these were distributed.[47] The Governor had sixteen; others were lent to various officials; large consignments were sent to Vissershok, Groenekloof and Gansekraal, the Government cattle farms; more of them were employed in the kilns, mills, potteries, dairies, stables, wine-cellars, hospital and bakery. Some were bookbinders, pumpmakers, thatchers and the like; some unloaded the ships, collected salt from the pans or caught locusts at Rondebosch and Rustenburg. No less than thirty-four worked in the Company's garden, although in 1708 the staff there actually numbered seventy-two men and women — a fact which caused a visiting Commissioner to complain that "not a tittle of the value in vegetables is produced for the labour of so many slaves". When special work had to be suddenly begun, such as the construction or enlarging of a reservoir, the Commander enrolled all his gardeners, soldiers, labourers, boatmen, arquebusiers, clerks and every male and female slave available.

Many of the private residents depended to a large extent for their livelihood on those of their slaves who were trained in various trades and hired out by the day or month. In one instance, Jan Hendrik Boumeester asked a slave, whom he had hired from a Chinaman, whether he would like to go to Saldanha Bay "te gaan Coelij soeken" — to work on his own account — on the understanding that he gave Boumeester six rixdollars per month. The slave was agreeable to this arrangement and obtained the necessary pass. When he arrived at the bay he found things quiet, as the roadstead was empty of ships, but he managed to earn some money by playing the violin in one of the inns and by spending part of his spare time in fishing. Contracts were often drawn up between two Europeans wherein the one undertook to instruct the other's slave in a certain craft or occupation. The soldier J. B. Rudolph, for example, guaranteed to teach a slave of Daniel van Ryneveld the tailoring trade within five years for a stipulated sum of money; another wanted his slave to learn the art of the wig-maker. A free black woman, Maria of the Cape, arranged to have her son trained as a tailor for eight consecutive years; Daniel Scheg, his instructor, had to feed, clothe and house him during that time, while she took it upon herself to mend and wash her son's clothes.[48]

One distinguished colonist even entered into a contract with a Hottentot, in which the latter agreed for forty rix-dollars to give lessons to the white man's slave in the manipulation of a wagon and six horses.[49] To those who are not acquainted with South African conditions this may seem surprising, but one must bear in mind that all long journeys were made in these vehicles; the astonishing adroitness of the Hottentot drivers, who took their white-tented wagons at full gallop over uneven, rough roads, rocks and declivities, always attracted the eye of the stranger at the Cape. In the words of a visitor, Lieutenant-Colonel Robert Wilson, "a covered wagon without springs is the usual vehicle for the most respectable families. These wagons are drawn by six, eight and ten horses. A Hottentot seated upon the fore part of the wagon on a level with and sometimes lower than the horses guides them with peculiar skill through the streets or in the worst roads, and can use the whip with such dexterity as to strike infallibly the smallest given spot . . . Whether a Hottentot coachman in England could perform the same achievements may perhaps be disputed by his brothers of the whip in that country, but it is almost certain that they could not rival his talent, nor would a French postilion be able to compete with him in the crack of his whip".

Another description appears in the pages of a diary: "Returned to Cape Town this evening noways pleased with my ride in a Cape carriage and light prancing steeds. Wonder not, my good friends, to hear me talk of eight horses driven by a stout broad-shouldered Hottentot or Malay boy; that may sound strange to the fraternity of whips in England, but I can assure them our African coachmen are superior to all I have seen in any other part of the world. They will drive you rapidly over precipices that would make a European tremble to look at and turn a corner with the greatest exactness, and what is more extraordinary 'tis very seldom you hear of any accident".

Nevertheless, possible mishaps had to be guarded against. Children were fond of playing in the wide, airy and spacious streets beneath the agreeable shade of the oaks and poplars; to ensure their safety, wagons drawn by eight horses had to be led by slaves or other persons as soon as they entered the precincts of the city, "between the outside houses and the town itself". This type of wagon was, of course, seldom seen in the far interior of the country, and when it did make a rare appearance there some amusing reactions resulted. One can picture the nonplussed expression on Sparrman's face when, in a remote part, a Hottentot, "with the greatest simplicity or as a witty and ingenious compliment", once naïvely told him that, as he had never beheld a a wagon before, he wished to be informed whether the traveller's vehicle "had grown up in the same state in which he then saw it".

Yet another writer relates how he observed a farmer bringing out a light wagon, to which he harnessed eight horses and, taking the reins in one hand and his long whip in the other, drove to a neighbouring farm in record time. The narrator remarked that these people were perfect masters of the eight-in-hand, and on an indifferently good road avoided every hole and stone with the utmost skill. "This particular farmer gave a singular proof of the dexterity in using his whip, for while we were in full trot he saw at a little distance from the road on a ploughed land a bird which had alighted upon the ground, when giving the whip a flourish, he struck the bird instantly and killed it upon the spot. In this particular case the farmer took the whole management upon himself, nor had any assistance from the slave who usually sits by the driver and holds the reins . . ."

The Council of Policy received numerous complaints from colonists who had hired out their slaves to the Company, regarding the meagre remuneration. Martin Melk once hired out twenty slaves for the construction of a new road; he was given eight rixdollars for each per month, while other burghers, for some unexplained reason, obtained only seven. While the new hospital was being erected the European workmen engaged on the task were recalled to Batavia, being urgently required there. It followed that slaves were once again rented from certain local inhabitants at the rate of only five rixdollars per month, although it was stated afterwards that as much service had been gained from them as from the Europeans. On occasions when the authorities decided to do something for the public benefit — such as the planting of trees for firewood and timber — the Governor enjoined each resident to lend a slave for the purpose, to appear personally, or otherwise to make a contribution of money with which a substitute could be hired. There is, for instance, a list in the Cape Archives containing the names of the Cape Town residents together with the number of slaves or wagons required from each person for the levelling of the parade ground.[50]

It was a common practice to send out slaves as peddlers with trays of merchandise such as cakes, oranges, biscuits, waffles, pancakes and other delicacies. We are told that ships in Table Bay had scarcely dropped anchor before crowds of black slaves arrived in small boats to sell and barter clothes and other goods, fresh meat, vegetables and fruit. Sometimes a vendor of these wares was thrashed if his sales were not plentiful enough to satisfy an avaricious owner. Various bakers protested that some of their rivals sent as many as four slaves each to sell bread on the streets; this competition was injurious to their business, and so the Council resolved to allow each baker to have only one peddler-slave, and in order to circumvent any trickery the baker's name had to be marked on every loaf. Shortly afterwards all the bakers were up in arms again; this time they alleged that private owners were using their slaves to offer bread for sale in public places. Only in exceptional circumstances were slaves allowed to work on the Sabbath or similar holy days; at such times the peddling of food or other articles was strictly prohibited on pain of severe penalties, including confiscation of the goods.[51]

As wet-nurses the slave women were unequalled, and their services in this capacity were much in demand, especially among those leaving on the protracted sea-voyage to Holland or to the East. Among the memorials of 1789 appears a letter from Hendrik van der Graaff, Captain of Artillery, which shows clearly the affection and esteem in which many of these people were held by the Europeans. The writer first of all states that, notwithstanding strenuous efforts on his part, he has been unable to find any other wet-nurse for his infant boy than a female slave belonging to the Company called Catryn. Born and educated in the house of his late father-in-law she, as well as her mother Hanna, gave to the latter so much satisfaction in her work and conduct that his collective children and heirs, from a proper sense of obligation, manumitted Hanna. The writer proposes to seek repatriation, with his wife and son, but he will be prevented from doing so if he cannot take with him a nurse on whom he can implicitly depend. For that purpose he would, by preference, choose Catryn, as his wife is very much attached to her and also because of the great care which she has hitherto shown to her nursling, and which now deserves due acknowledgment. Van der Graaff prays to be permitted to exchange a healthy male slave for Catryn, and to pay for her child the usual amount charged in order to manumit mother and offspring. He concludes his letter by solemnly promising that he and his wife, as long as they live, will provide for the maintenance of the pair, and with the blessing of God will instruct and educate both in the Christian religion.[52]

The education of slave children in suitable occupations was not neglected. Little slave girls were taught needlework, and a diarist of those times mentions how in one house the girls sat on benches in the passage busily knitting socks and bonnets and making shirts for their master and themselves. They were instructed in handwork, especially the sewing

of linen and woollen clothing, and for that reason were put
into service in the houses of the colonists. Female slaves
from Bengal or the Coast of Coromandel, from Surat and
Macassar, were much sought after because of their reputation
as skilful needlewomen. "The ladies of the Cape," says
Mentzel, "value their services because they take a pride in
fine needlework, knitting and crocheting, and are very fond
of hand-made lace. I have known some ladies who always
employed two or three women in that work only; I speak
from experience, since I have, from time to time, earned
some money in drawing designs for them."

Boys, too, were given every opportunity of learning
vocations. It was officially resolved to apprentice two or
more of the most intelligent black boys to each smith, carpenter, mason and other master mechanic, "to be taught
trades, so that they may become more useful to the Company". So we find these slaves in all sorts of employments,
as shoemakers, coopers, turners, wagonmakers, carpenters,
woodcutters, potters, wig-makers, plumbers, thatchers, tin-
smiths, tailors . . . In every trade and pursuit they were
adaptable, and many of the more frugal among them were
able in the course of the years to save sufficient money to
purchase their freedom and, eventually, to have slaves of
their own. Certainly these slaves were an improvement on
the "knechts", whom the Company hired or lent to the
colonists. These people, without the slightest compunction
or remorse, simply left their masters at the most pressing
and inconvenient times — usually when the harvest was at
hand. Besides this, the farmers were too heavily encumbered
with the high wages which they had to pay the European
servants, with the result that their profits disappeared and
their work was impeded.

Although none in authority opposed the idea of the
Company's having slaves, the policy of allowing the freemen
to become slave-owners was not favoured by the Council of
India. In 1658 they expressed their opinion that the colony
should be established and run by Europeans, "as our nation
is so constituted that as soon as they have the convenience of
slaves they become lazy and unwilling to put forth their
hands to work . . ." In 1684 they reiterated their previous

warning, and said that only a limited number of slaves would be sent, "in order not to let the colonists glide into idleness . . . and make them unaccustomed to labour".[53] But, as Theal states, labour is always in demand in countries where land is easily obtainable, where population is sparse and the products of the soil bring fair prices. It has been the case in South Africa ever since the first farmers were located on their small holdings in Rondebosch . . .

And so, pressure of circumstances proving too powerful for the dissenters, slaves were imported to serve the freemen. It is sad to reflect that there was a time in the history of South Africa when the degrading term of "slave" could have been, but was not, blotted for ever from our social system: when the attention of the authorities was engaged with the question whether this country should be occupied solely by Europeans, besides the aboriginals, or whether there was to be a mixture of races in it.

In 1716 the Seventeen dispatched a number of queries for the consideration of the Council of Policy at the Cape, to be answered individually by the members. One of the principal points was whether it would not be more advantageous to employ European labourers than slaves. It must be remembered that slavery was still in its infancy at the Cape, and with a little thought the whole organisation of slavery could quite easily have been abolished.

Has any question of equal importance ever since presented itself to the authorities? Of those men who sat in the Council on 10 February 1717 — the Governor, Maurits Pasques de Chavonnes, the secunde, Abraham Cranendonck, the Fiscal Independent, Cornelius van Beaumont, the officer commanding the garrison, Captain de Chavonnes, and Messieurs Cross, De la Fontaine, Slotsboo, van der Meer — only one had the ability, the wisdom and the foresight to look beyond the existing hour. This was Captain Dominique Pasques de Chavonnes, brother of the Governor. He refused to agree with his fellow-councillors that white labourers would be found far more burdensome and expensive than slaves. Neither would he agree that the slave was more tractable, whereas the European was liable to be rebellious, or that the latter was prone to drunkenness. His brother the

Governor had said that "as the wines and other strong liquors are cheap . . . all the common people become very much addicted to drink . . . God knows, we have been subject to this experience too much already, so that should more be added to their number we would have more trouble still", and had also stated that no white man could be obtained who would be willing to perform the more arduous kinds of toil in this climate; besides, there were no houses available and, should he be expected to do away with the slaves and make Europeans occupy the Lodge, all sorts of misfortunes and disorders would be in store.

Then Captain de Chavonnes spoke. "If this country," he declared, "were extended by European colonisation, I am of opinion that it cannot but produce anything but benefit to this land and these regions, as a more developed general trade, the increase of the Company's revenue, the inducement to discover new and more means for subsistence, may be expected to result from such a step, and the more so as the extent of the country is able to feed and carry a considerable additional number of people." He went on to suggest the type of farm servant required, and added that if the further importation of slaves were prohibited and the colonists gradually accustomed themselves to employing Europeans as farmhands, the result would be favourable to the Company, the land and the residents.

To him slavery was like a malignant sore in the human frame. He referred to the cost of purchasing slaves, the expensive voyages made expressly for transporting them and the fact that the moneys involved were lost to the country. (Exactly sixty years later Adam Smith published his "Wealth of Nations", wherein he said: "It appears from the experience of all ages and nations that the work done by freemen comes cheaper in the end than that performed by slaves". Captain de Chavonnes spoke of the tranquillity assured to the residents in being served by their own people, and compared this with the dangers and vexations which they suffered from slaves — their conspiracies, their thefts, their habit of running away and of committing atrocious crimes, their need for supervision, clothing and food. He pointed out the advantages of filling the Cape with industrious folk — men who understood horticulture, quarrying and brickmaking, and who could handle rakes, wheelbarrows, shovels and scythes — instead of a "refuse lot" of slaves, many of whom were ailing, pregnant, too young, too old . . .

Alas! his was a voice crying in the wilderness of prejudice and limited vision. Captain Dominique de Chavonnes was alone in his condemnation of slave labour; none of the other members of the Council would perceive either its lamentable consequences to the country or the necessity for a life of harder work and less luxury on the part of the burghers. Yet twenty-five years afterwards Baron von Imhoff, certainly one of the ablest and best men ever to fill the office of Governor-General, when calling at the Cape made some significant remarks regarding slave labour. "I believe," he declared, "it would have been for the better had we, when this colony was founded, commenced with Europeans and brought them hither in such numbers that hunger and want would have forced them to work. But having imported slaves, every common or ordinary European becomes a gentleman and prefers to be served than to serve. We have in addition the fact that the majority of farmers in this colony are not farmers in the real sense of the word, but owners of plantations, and that many of them consider it a shame to work with their own hands . . ."[54]

One does not need to delve too deeply into the records of the Dutch East India Company to realise that most of the labour, both skilled and unskilled, was done by slaves. To-day we can still see the work of these men of the orient in the beautiful gabled houses and the magnificent furniture which have come down to us through the centuries. Perhaps in some instances the white inhabitants of Cape Town put their shoulders to the wheel and helped them in their labours, but such cases must have been rare. We find even the first commander, Jan van Riebeeck, complaining of the aversion for work which characterised the European, who, he said, "preferred like Seigneurs to spank about with the cane in the hand and leave everything to their slaves". It would virtually appear that any European, no matter how poor, refused to associate himself with manual work, feeling that in this way he could demonstrate his superiority to the slave.

From their youth onwards such men were accustomed to give orders to slaves and to regard themselves as exalted. The very appellation "Cape burgher" was considered by them to be a grand title, it was said — an assertion borne out by the haughty words addressed by a freeman to a Company's servant in 1736: "Weet jy wel dat ik een vryman ben" (do you realise that I am a free burgher)? Earlier still, in 1663, two freemen who had come to grips with each other were forcibly separated by the dispenser, an attempt at peace-making which immediately put one of the belligerents on his dignity, for "It is not proper," he protested, "that a Company's servant should strike a freeman in that way". It was this attitude of overweening pride which resulted in indolence, as few of them would sully their hands with any menial tasks. It is slave's work, they argued; what are the slaves for?

In all fairness, we must suppose that there were, here and there, admirable exceptions amongst the owners. Some of the colonists may have echoed in their thoughts the words of the poet:

"I would not have a slave to till my ground;
To carry me; to fan me while I sleep,
And tremble when I wake — for all the wealth
That sinews bought and sold have ever earn'd."

It is at least certain that some belonged to neither extreme of opinion, such as the corn farmers owning self-supporting estates which were as complete in themselves as little independent villages, with their own slave-lodges, granaries, workshops and stables; or the lords of the magnificent wine farms, laid out in rolling vineyards and fine gardens, in Stellenbosch, Franschhoek, Drakenstein and Wellington. Such domains could hardly have been planned and developed by lethargic and uncreative people. Even if the actual hard work was left to the slaves, the supervision, direction and guidance of the Europeans in charge were constantly necessary, and continuous calls were made upon their time and energies.

It is interesting to notice that, as in the southern states of America, slavery in the western districts of the Cape had a decided effect upon the system of agriculture, which was adapted to conform to the requirements arising from this particular kind of labour. "In order to render slave labour economical and profitable under the prevailing conditions," writes Dr. M. H. de Kock, "it was necessary to conduct agriculture extensively and on a large scale. Slave labour required careful supervision and strict discipline, and such could be exercised more economically over a large than a small number of labourers. A farmer who had to direct and supervise slave labour on his farm found it more profitable to employ ten than five and to extend his operations. The economics of extensive and large-scale cultivation of new and cheap land were to counterbalance the inefficiency of slave as compared with free labour." It is an accepted fact, too, that the poor white element, which still exists in South Africa to a marked degree to this day, can in no slight measure trace its origin to the slavery of another century.

There were, however, other factors besides the prevalence of self-indulgent ease and the probability of wasted resources that made the influence of slavery profoundly detrimental. On the personal, domestic and social morality of the masters its effects were truly disastrous. In the words of the Quakers, slaves as such had "often been observed to fill their possessors with haughtiness, tyranny, luxury, and barbarity, corrupting and debasing the morals of their children, to the unspeakable prejudice of religion and virtue, and the exclusion of that holy spirit of universal love, meekness and charity, which is the unchangeable nature and glory of Christianity"

Obviously, too, one must not overlook the lot of the slave himself. It was not a happy one, particularly in the case of the farm slave, who was worse off in almost every respect than his fellows in the villages and towns. Not only did he miss all the urban amenities but he also had to endure the hardships that accompanied an agricultural or pastoral life. If he wished, he could find some bleak consolation in the fact that his master was similarly cut off from all the privileges available to a villager and a townsman. For the colonists in the interior, especially, had to make shift without many things which were normally considered the necessities of life: calabashes often took the place of cups and saucers; tanned hides were used to produce clothes and shoes; fur karosses were substituted for blankets; *katels* served as bedsteads; and the very houses — built under difficult conditions — were small and bare.

Although at the Cape, as an early writer said, even slavery wore a smile, the fact remains that the unfortunate victim of this system had scant opportunity to develop all those qualities essential to the betterment of man. He was in bondage, body and soul; he had practically no rights to claim — he could not even decide his own mode of living; if he had children he well knew that he transmitted to them the same degrading condition; he could without redress be torn away from his wife, his family, relatives and friends; he could be whipped for the most trifling offence at the caprice of his master . . . Is it then to be wondered at that so many of these slaves were "depraved and besotted"? The human creature without social rights inevitably becomes antisocial in his reactions. Wine and brandy were cheap at the Cape, and in the agricultural districts particularly wine was given to the slaves as an inducement to work. Yet it was through over-indulgence in liquor that so many of these ill-fated people were brought at last to the place of execution — an evil anomaly for which, in numerous cases, the masters cannot be exonerated from all blame.

In 1791 the Council of Policy contemplated abolishing the two Government posts Vissershok and Gansekraal, and it was then suggested that the Company's slaves should be restricted in number to four hundred and fifty; a large proportion of the group of slave women at Rondebosch and Newlands could be sold, care being taken that they were not separated from their husbands and children. The matter was revived at a later meeting of the Council of Policy, when it was decided to appoint two officials, O. de Wet and E. Bergh, to examine all the slaves belonging to the Government, to arrange for the education of others in certain specified trades and to dispose suitably of the remainder.

In their report the two councillors enumerated the many difficulties which confronted such a proposal. They pointed out that there were five hundred and eighty-two slaves and convicts owned by the Government, consisting of three hundred and fifty-eight male slaves, one hundred and fifty-one females and seventy-three convicts. Of these, only three hundred and eighty-three could be used for labour; in other words, the balance — including about seventy children — were not working. Among them were many aged, infirm slaves who were reaching their last years on earth; to take these away from their children and grandchildren and deliberately sell them at public auction — even supposing that purchasers could be found compassionate enough to "take them on their necks" — would be an act of ingratitude for past services. They should be replaced, preferably, by schoolchildren and babies who, when they grew up, could be trained as artisans. The councillors suggested, too, that fifty of the more industrious boys could be taught as follows, with the exact quota appended to each group:

> Masons 10, carpenters 10, ship's chandlers 6, blacksmiths 8, coopers 6, thatchers 2, sailmakers 2, tailors (for the slaves) 4, painters 2.[55]

After a century and a half of steady progress there lay in the shadow of Table Mountain, with its fleecy canopy of clouds, one of the most beautifully situated cities in the world — an ever-welcome sight to the travellers who arrived in Table Bay after long and tedious voyages. The broad streets were lined with rows of oaks, poplars and fir trees, which yielded a pleasant shade and contrasted strikingly with the immaculate white of the houses. Down the Heerengracht, now Adderley Street, meandered a little stream of crystal-clear water that rippled and sparkled in the rays of the sun; and on the low walls built alongside the miniature gracht bridges the Europeans as well as the Coloured inhabitants frequently came to sit during the day to hold converse. The Capetonians, who numbered chiefly Government officials, professional men, traders, craftsmen and lodging-house keepers, led a leisurely life. Even the shops were closed from one to three o'clock, while their owners enjoyed siestas. By nine o'clock everybody was in bed. It was under such conditions that the majority of slaves lived and worked, and although we of the twentieth century look with abhorrence on the deprivation of liberty and the compulsion to work without compensation, it is an indisputable fact that in many homes the Europeans followed the advice of Seneca and treated their slaves as "humble friends".

On the corn farms the mode of living was similar to that in other slave-owning countries where agriculture was practised. Under the constant direction and surveillance of the farmers the slaves toiled in the fields, while on the wine farms the work of digging and clearing the ground, of pruning the vines and gathering the grapes, of pressing and stoning, was all done by slaves, also under the supervision of Europeans. Sparrman mentions one notable exception to the latter fact, that of a slave who "had the absolute management" of a farm, which he ran with commendable efficiency. Van der Meer was one of those who preferred slave labour, as he said that European servants "for the most part arrive here poor and thirsty", and often fell back on the poor fund, whereas the slaves were obedient, "always remembering who they are with the hope that by serving well they may one day obtain their freedom".[56]

Chapter Four

IN SEARCH OF LIBERTY

MANY of the slaves had so little taste for work that they had scarcely arrived at the Cape when they began to desert, in the vague hope of either regaining the land of their birth or leading the care-free life of the natives, maintaining themselves in the mountains and committing atrocious crimes and depredations. Exactly what the desertion of slaves meant to the burghers and others two hundred years ago it is almost impossible for us to assess in its full gravity. It certainly caused them much anxiety and fear, for experience had so often taught them that unless the fugitives were caught in time thefts, burglaries and murders would ensue, highways would be unsafe and houses and buildings would be set on fire. Besides, the constant loss of his slaves plunged many a burgher into the pool of poverty in this Vale of Tears — if one may apply the words of an eighteenth-century diarist.

As soon as the authorities were notified that a slave had absconded, bells were tolled and blue flags were hoisted at the Castle and on the hills along the road to Stellenbosch. Residents were in duty bound to warn the authorities as soon as a slave had been missing for twenty-four hours. When, as often happened, a large number of slaves had conspired to run away, the ensign of the Fort would immediately collect together as many horsemen as possible and race with them inland, while the burghers of the country districts were ordered to block all thoroughfares to the interior, follow on the heels of the fugitives and endeavour to capture them. It was when the harvest smiled and the soil was decked with herbage that the open spaces and the almost inaccessible kloofs seemed to beckon to those in bondage, and they ran away by the dozen.

"The desertion of slaves," said one recorder in the early days, "which has for some time been proceeding very graciously, appears now again to become the fashion among these messieurs . . . These ignorant people still believe that they will be able to reach some country or another where they will be relieved of their bondage; alas! a too idle and fruitless conception, as they may expect nothing else than to be destroyed in a most miserable manner by hunger, the beasts of prey, or the brutal natives of Africa."

Simon van der Stel once wrote of the "terrible anxiety, painful days, and sleepless nights we pass through, for often we also are hard-pushed and threatened by conspiracies of slaves and convicts, fortunately always discovered in time by God's grace. Never, however, did the Colony appear to suffer more inconvenience from that rabble than a month ago when seven or eight slaves placed a black freeman at their head and fled inland, armed with knives, a gun, some powder and lead, etc. During the night they broke into a freeman's house and shot the hunter of the Company, who had rushed to the assistance of the owner. After having done more mischief and taken away three guns, powder, food, etc., they went away, intending to attack another freeman's house the following night and murder all the inmates, giving the arms to the slaves found on the place. In that way having largely increased their number, they decided to kill the freemen one after another and destroy the Colony entirely. They would have succeeded if the slaves of the Company and freemen and the convicts had joined them, for they are far superior in number to the whites and would have made it sufficiently hot for us, but the Commander having been informed in good time of their plans decided to smother the monster in its cradle. All the passes were occupied by the Company's servants and freemen, the conspirators were surrounded on all sides, and in a river thickly covered with rush and trees they fought four hours desperately against six of the freemen and were only overpowered after having killed one of the latter. Three of the ringleaders were killed fighting to the last . . ."

Van der Stel ends his letter by saying that in these circumstances it was considered too dangerous to give firearms to slave herdsmen — "hence last year a placcaat had been issued forbidding it, even knives included".[57]

There were several reasons, of course, which contributed to the desertion of the more adventurous slaves, beyond the natural wish to return to their own habitat or to live unencumbered by toil and obligations. One was harsh treatment on the part of their masters and mistresses, coupled with severity of labour, as in the case of a young Dutch boy and two slaves who fled together into the interior to seek a new environment. After an absence of some days they came back, "having missed the bread basket", and stated in extenuation of their misdemeanour that they had to work too hard under their masters and that they were daily treated to blows. "This, however, will not serve as an excuse for these scoundrels," wrote the secretary with an implacable air, "but rather as an aggravation of their offence as a warning to other eager imitators."

From a general survey of the records, it becomes quite obvious that the chief cause for the abscondence of slaves is that summarised in the words used by the master gardener when he reported a large-scale flight which had been contemplated: "They said that if they stayed here they would remain slaves and be obliged to work". Ample proof of their dislike of even a nominally servile condition was evinced one morning when it was found that a male and a female slave — an old couple who were no longer able to serve but who were nevertheless well cared for — had walked away together to seek their freedom. On another occasion the diarist expressed surprise when a runaway slave was brought back: "He looked well nourished, healthy and not badly dressed, so that one does not know what has induced him to abandon his master and a good kitchen and exchange them without a doubt for a worse condition".[58]

Many of the slaves — and more particularly the light-coloured ones — deserted with the return fleet or in the foreign ships that came to anchor in Table Bay, and once having arrived in Holland they wrote to their former companions here of "the vast difference between liberty and slavery and about the Fatherland, making them also anxious to escape". Any such letter would be entrusted to an obliging friend, and it is not unlikely that the envelope might bear an inscription of the type often used then by Europeans, expressing the pious hope that God would guide the intermediary safely over the tempestuous seas . . . "Met vrind die God zijn Lydsman zy over de Woeste zee". Once a skipper of a Dutch East Indiaman announced that his men had discovered a raft, made of three doors tied together, drifting near his vessel. He was accordingly ordered to keep a watchful eye by day as well as by night, for the Capetonians had a "strange suspicion" that a stowaway might be lurking in an English vessel also anchored in the bay. Next day the Dutch skipper proceeded on board the English ship on the pretext of visiting the captain, and he subsequently reported that during the previous night a slave had arrived at the vessel on the raft, "certainly an act of great daring to entrust himself for such a long distance to the fickleness of wind and weather to which, especially at this time of the season, we are almost every moment exposed".[59]

In the imagination of many of those held in bondage the sea represented a means of escape. Once Robert Semple, *en route* to Plettenberg Bay, hired a slave guide from one of the farmers. This man, a native of Bengal, told a woeful tale of having been enticed, when thirteen years old, on board a ship and having been conveyed in it to the Cape, where he had ever since languished in slavery. He expressed vehemently in broken Dutch his rage at this misfortune and seemed confident of one day regaining his freedom. When asked how he could ever hope to escape, he raised his right hand toward the sea and cried "there, there", to show to what quarter he looked for deliverance. Strangely enough, the first slave to have arrived at the Cape was himself a stowaway, found on board the *Malacca,* which anchored in Table Bay on 2 March 1653. As he had deserted from his master in Batavia, it was decided to employ him in the Company's service in the settlement until the owner could be informed. But Abraham, as he was called, gave little satisfaction to Commander van Riebeeck: "In consequence of ill-health," the latter wrote, "the man was unable to earn half his food," and he suggested that the slave's master should be made to pay half of the food money!

It is not surprising that from time to time the authorities at the Cape did everything in their power to discourage the visits of foreign ships in Table Bay, by making their stay as uncomfortable as possible to "these very unwelcome guests". We even find Van Riebeeck apologising for his liberality to some English captains by stating that the oxen supplied to them "seemed likely to die". One of the reasons for the dismissal of a later Commander was the fact of his "kind reception and caresses bestowed upon the French" during their sojourn at the Cape. He let them — as the record runs, in a singularly mixed metaphor — "pluck all the ripest pears" instead of "allowing them, as we have often directed, to drift upon their own fins".

Sometimes the Cape authorities found themselves in a cleft stick regarding these matters as, for instance, in the case of a Danish ship, the *Ganges,* which called in at Table Bay. A letter which they wrote to the Council of Seventeen at that time speaks for itself: reprimanded for not having gone on board the vessel and removed the slaves of certain free burghers who had hidden there, they pointed out that experience had taught them that such errands never met with success, as when the captains of the ships were not inclined to return the stowaways — Europeans or slaves — these deserters could conceal themselves in such a way as to elude recapture. The only alternative in the case of the *Ganges,* they continued, would have been to refuse the Danes water or provisions or to prohibit them from leaving, but such a course would have caused the Danish captain to apply with exaggerated complaints to his principals, and so the Council of Seventeen itself would have been inconvenienced.

Co-operation, however, was not always withheld by the ship's captains. In 1783 the Council of Seventeen wrote that they had been informed that a black man had managed to board a French ship in Table Bay, by posing as a deserter from a Portuguese vessel and by asking for a passage as a sailor. When the ship was at sea it was found out that he was a slave who had escaped from his master. The French, therefore, took him into custody and enquired what further measures should be taken. For various reasons the Council replied that they could set him free, although as far back as

1636 a placcaat was in force to the effect that any slave discovered stowing away on board a ship had as punishment to remain in bondage for life.

In 1746 a dark gentleman by the name of Valentyn Vis came to the Cape from Batavia, having been sent there as a convict for some misdeed or other. One can well imagine the surprise of the local officials when they recognised him as a former slave of the Company who had fled some years before to Holland and had there entered the Company's service. Three years previously a sailor who stepped ashore in Table Valley was instantaneously identified as Thomas of the Cape, a slave who had disappeared at an earlier date. So many of the inhabitants and slaves managed to escape overseas from time to time that it became necessary to send a small vessel to accompany each departing foreign ship to the end of the bay, so that no deserters might board her from boats in the open sea.[60]

Slaves and Hottentots were often guilty of sheltering fugitive slaves, notwithstanding the rigorous interdicts periodically issued against this practice. One frequently reads of the punishment of slaves for not having advised their master when they became aware of the intention of a fellow-servitor to escape. In 1713 a Javanese "Guru" was sentenced to death for inciting slaves to desert, and also harbouring and arming them. In many cases Hottentots joined the runaways in attempts to rob the white people, and the rest of the tribesmen refused to give up the slaves despite the reward offered of merchandise equivalent to the price of an ox for each absconder brought back. Sometimes, when hard-pressed, they would surrender the malefactor with the request that he should not be punished. In one instance the Commander concerned agreed to this stipulation, probably because it was realised that the defaulter would be of great use in holding intercourse with the natives of the interior, as now, through association with them, he understood their language.

We find, too, a case in which a burgher was severely chastised for having given refuge to a female slave of the Company, "that this evil may once for all be suppressed as it has been existing for such a long time". In fact, the freemen accorded shelter and assistance to fugitives, both servants and slaves, to such an excessive degree that the Council of Policy decided to force them to declare on oath that henceforth they would not render the least aid or sustenance to such vagabonds or give them any sanctuary either directly or indirectly, but that on the contrary they would do their best by every possible means to capture them and deliver them to justice. Two members of the Council were first deputed to confer with the principal and most influential of the settlers, in order to obtain their opinion regarding the wisdom of demanding this oath from every resident in the colony. In their ensuing report the two deputies said it had been pointed out to them that such an oath, especially among the ordinary folk and their servants, would be taken much too rashly, as through misguided compassion it might later be broken, and that, besides, some "through forgetfulness and disregard of what they might supply to such needy fugitives, not even fathoming the bottom of their conscience, might make themselves perjured and infamous". As a result of this report the authorities resolved to leave the matter in abeyance and merely to have the placcaat against the offenders carried out.[61]

It was the far-seeing Jan van Riebeeck who originally issued orders that runaway slaves who returned voluntarily should not be punished. He well knew, as did his successor, that "on the dry sandhills the cook could not cater", and that the realisation that they could come back with impunity would encourage them to retrace their steps "and with the prodigal son to say 'Pater! peccavi!'"

The position became so serious at the beginning of the eighteenth century — so many of the Company's servants as well as slaves, Englishmen and other foreigners had escaped to the wilderness and the mountains, where every attempt to apprehend them had failed — that the Council decided to act on the Fiscal's proposal to clear the colony of all such pernicious people by pardoning them and publishing a general amnesty, excluding the incendiaries, murderers, burglars, cattle-thieves and highwaymen. One has only to scan any of the criminal record books of those days to appreciate the feelings of the secretary who wrote so fervidly of the "frightfully cruel, unheard-of, horrible and barbarous murders" perpetrated by many of these fugitive slaves — outrages, he said, "which make the hair of a rational being to stand on end and his entrails to shudder and freeze . . ."

Too much liberty allowed to the slaves by their owners was one of the chief reasons to which the authorities attributed the prevalence of desertion amongst these people. In 1708 a placcaat was issued instructing every Company's servant and the burghers that whenever they sent slaves some distance with messages they should provide each one with a letter signed on the day of his departure, containing the name of his master and particulars of his destination. For the benefit of any owner who could not write, a lead penny was to be given instead to each slave, engraved with his name on the one side and the Company's mark on the other. These coins could be purchased at the Castle. Even a slave employed as a cattle-herd, and thus obliged to go into the fields, had to be supplied with one of these tokens — with this distinction, that on the one side, in addition to his master's name, the letters S.W., meaning *schaapwagter* (shepherd), were inscribed. It was also decided that when any slaves were apprehended and were found to possess no passes, those who had arrested them were to receive the usual rewards, payable by the owners. In 1760 an almost identical placcaat appeared, because the problem of abscondence had become so bad that the authorities exacted the handing over of daily notes from even those slaves sent to gather wood, who had to pass the sentry and give him the notes when they returned from their errand.

The eighteenth century had scarcely dawned when eight male and female slaves determined to desert from the service of their owners and proceed to Madagascar. Self-appointed captain and leader of the band was Augustyn of Batavia; then came Titus, Little Aaron and Large Aaron of Cochin, Large Marie of Madagascar, Small Marie and Anthony of Bengal, Jannetje of the Cape, and two tiny infants. To meet the requirements of their journey they collected bayonets, knives, loaves of bread, a large cheese, a bottle of brandy and some clothes. After remaining in the kloof beyond the ridge of Devil's Peak for seven days, they went on their way. At Salt River they came across a slave shepherd sleeping in the veld. Taking counsel among themselves as to how to steal some sheep for their sustenance with the minimum of trouble, they decided on the simple expedient of killing him. When he awoke and looked about for his flock, Augustyn suddenly seized him by the hair while Large Aaron pulled his feet from under him. They then bound his hands and stuffed a handkerchief into his mouth to prevent his making any noise. After these preliminary precautions, Augustyn cut the throat of the helpless victim, tore out his larynx and threw it on the ground. From his pockets the slaves then extracted a small white bag containing money, which they divided in shares, and crept away stealthily through the bush.

A little farther on they encountered a European carrying a gun on his shoulder and accompanied by two dogs. Quietly the four adult male slaves sharpened their knives on a flat stone and approached the man, whom they asked for some water. He led them to a fountain, and gave Augustyn a pipe of tobacco at the latter's request. Suddenly, however, the quartet attacked him violently and threw him to the ground. The European begged for his life, promising to let them go and not to attempt to capture them. But they forced the handkerchief into his mouth, hacked and cut at his throat with their knives, ripped up his abdomen, took out the entrails and cut off his left hand. These bloodthirsty measures were adopted in order to give the impression that he had been killed by a wild beast.

While the murderers were lifting the dead man by the legs, mutilating the body and smashing the bones, Small Marie was an interested and co-operative spectator. Clapping her hands with joy, she cried out words of encouragement in Portuguese to the ringleader: "Tyn bon, tyn bon, Augustyn! tyn bon!" A short distance away from the corpse the party at last sat down in the veld, where Augustyn cut and ate some Hottentot figs. Jannetje, noticing that blood still dripped from his knife and hands, said "Fie, Augustyn! Why do you not wash the knife?" and received the unexpected reply, "Maski, I wish to drink that blood also, for then I become strong."

The intention of these fugitives, as has been seen, was to proceed to Madagascar, and they planned amongst themselves that Augustyn would be the "King" and Big Marie "Queen". Their hopes, however, were never fulfilled, for they were caught and thrown into the Black Hole at the Castle: four of them, including the "King", were subsequently broken alive on the wheel, and the "Queen" was strangled at a pole. Klein Aaron and the babies were the only ones who escaped punishment. Kolbe, who witnessed the execution, stood amazed at the fortitude of the culprits. On other occasions, he said, when he had seen criminals undergoing the terrible punishment of having their limbs broken, they had screamed with pain. But from these people he heard not the slightest sound, and when they were taken from the cross alive and tied with a rope back to back on the wheel, they still uttered no word except to ask for water to drink, calling in the Portuguese language "Ago, por bebe".[62]

Another notable case occurred in the year 1714, when sixteen slaves banded together with the object of marching to the land of the Portuguese. One of them, called *Cnap een Deuntje*, established himself as head of the gang and chose three sub-captains with the impressive names of Courage, Hannibal and Caesar. They stole a number of muskets, made their rendezvous in a thicket near Wynberg, and decided to take an oath that they would die rather than be captured alive. Then they smeared sixteen slices of bread with blood. Each man was asked to eat the slice dealt out to him and to vow that he would remain loyal to his comrades in all circumstances. Early next morning the band set out towards a Hottentot kraal, where they murdered a Hottentot woman and clandestinely took a few head of cattle. Soon after this episode they were encountered and challenged by a group of soldiers, and a battle ensued. While being pursued, one of the fugitives, faithful to his oath, drew a knife and cut his own throat.[63]

Even the personal slaves of Van Riebeeck nearly succeeded once in killing a number of Europeans and running away with some draught oxen; in fact, had it not been for one of the Commander's servants, his Guinea slaves, "strong, daring fellows", and the "equally courageous" female slaves would have seized a boat on the beach and escaped in it, searching for their own country by sailing

Pass issued to slave, 1762.

(*Cape Archives.*)

Greenmarket Square, 1764: showing a sedan chair, a prisoner returning from a flogging, fruit sellers and water-carriers.

(*Elliott: Van Stolk Collection.*)

Slave bell at "Meerlust".
(*Elliott Collection.*)

Hottentots dancing in the moonlight.
(*Kolbe.*)

along the coast. Fortunately the aforementioned white servant was a powerful, dauntless and determined man, who soon managed to get the better of the miscreants.[64]

Another occurrence in the time of Jan van Riebeeck, barely eight years after his arrival in Table Valley with his little party of followers, might have resulted in the death of the Commander and his companions. Twenty-nine men, of whom fifteen were slaves, conspired to kill the crew of the *Erasmus,* a richly-laden vessel lying in the bay, after that to slaughter the men at the Schuur, and finally to scale the Fort and murder everyone within it, "the smallest child included". They planned then to proceed to the above-mentioned yacht, to seize her and so to make their departure. Luckily for all concerned, the surgeon of the Fort, William Robertson of Dundee, discovered the plot and at once acquainted Commander van Riebeeck with its details. The majority of the conspirators were immediately arrested, whereupon they confessed that their original scheme had been to march overland to Angola, but that when the *Erasmus* arrived in Table Bay they had changed their ideas and had resolved to appropriate that vessel.

The attestations taken at the time make interesting reading, particularly the account of how the ringleaders had tried to persuade others to join them. One, on being asked whether there were really a possibility of reaching the territory of the Portuguese, had answered that he wished it were as easy to become King of England as to travel through the country. Another had said that he "had given the devil his life and soul for the purpose" . . . Many of the European conspirators were Scots and Englishmen, and as a result of this plot the Council decided to send everyone of these nationalities to Batavia, in order to cleanse the Cape as much as possible of "rubbish" — "omme soo veel doenlijck dese plaetse van alle oncruijt te suijveren" — with the exception, of course, of the surgeon, who received a reward. The plotters were punished, some on the spot and the chief offenders at Batavia, whither they were sent for trial.

As a master was held responsible for any damage done by his slaves, and as he was liable to lose any one of them condemned by the Court of Justice for the commission of a crime, it was generally recognised that the most sensible course to adopt with an incorrigible slave, impervious to correction and persistent in running away, was to send him to auction in the hope that he would be sold to a new master who might find him more amenable to discipline. On one occasion a burgher at Stellenbosch wrote to the Government about his slave David, aged thirteen, who for four or five successive years had made it a habit to absent himself for a few days at a stretch. The writer said that he had employed every method likely to be effective in the case of such a youngster; that, however, instead of improving, the little vagabond continually ran off and hid on the neighbouring farms. He was caught setting fire to the veld, too, and as the complainant did not wish to be put to any useless expense for this unserviceable slave, and as he feared that if he got loose again he might do more serious mischief, and furthermore as it appeared to lie in his nature to abscond, the owner begged the Company to accept him for nothing.

Very often the plans formulated by these runaway slaves were most ambitious. In 1690, for example, a band of them arranged to obtain a large number of adherents, to murder and burn whomever and whatever came in their way — and to carry off the wives of the French refugees as slaves for their own womenfolk, before proceeding to Madagascar! It was usually an extremely difficult feat to root out these depredators, as they were so well acquainted with every cavern and recess of the numerous mountains; sometimes, indeed, the Government was forced to send commandos equipped with hand-grenades to drive the rogues out of the caves. In one case, every member of a certain commando ordered out was warned to observe the utmost secrecy, as it was a well-known fact that the particular gang they were hunting had their comrades and correspondents who kept them constantly informed of the plans made to seize them.

Large rewards were offered for the capture of fugitives both white and black, dead or alive. We read of permission being given to Jacob Joubert to go among the kaffirs to take some slaves who were in hiding there; for every one recovered he was to receive twenty-five rixdollars, and if the owner of the slave refused to pay this sum the Company would assume the debt, and the slave as well. As much as one hundred rixdollars was sometimes held out as a prize for the capture of the leaders of the various gangs.

At Cape Hangklip a large number of fugitive slaves lived in comparative luxury and security. They were not only well provided with guns, powder and lead but they also had their own fishing-boat. Not all the slave deserters, however, were in a position to supply themselves with food and sustenance, and hunger was their greatest obstacle, often causing them to return to the Cape, where — as a journalist remarked sarcastically — the executioner and the Caffres were always willing to prepare a merry welcome feast for their backs. One must also remember that usually great stamina was required to keep up the pace set by some of the fugitive leaders. Many of those following dropped out through fatigue, and were subsequently found by the Hottentots or the Europeans, famished for want of food and thoroughly exhausted — probably agreeing wholeheartedly with another journalist who said that the foolish conception of obtaining liberty "must end in smoke and misery". One recaptured absconder caused consternation amongst the Europeans in the little settlement when, being asked how he and his fellow-deserters had expected to survive away from their masters' care, he replied that they would have depended on Hottentots' flesh!

Most of the runaway slaves were able to subsist on wild berries and Hottentot figs, vegetables such as carrots, turnips and pumpkins stolen in the fields, quinces, apples and other fruit filched from the orchards, tortoises and porcupine roots; at low tide they could collect among the rocks on the shore shell-fish such as mussels, periwinkles and ear-shells, crabs and crayfish. Fish was available, too, and we read of one slave who made a fishing-line from the bark of certain bushes, having furnished himself with hooks before he left.[65] Sheep, oxen, cows and even horses were killed and eaten. There is a "droster's" cave near the top of Simonsberg, a 4,600-foot mountain near Stellenbosch; those slaves fortunate and nimble enough to reach such well-nigh inaccessible caverns were able to establish themselves in comparative safety, to grow their own vegetables and to keep their own sheep and cattle; if they had the additional good luck to secure guns, powder and lead with which to kill game, there was little to worry them. Those less successful, however, were often so feeble from lack of nourishment that they could not walk. Mention is made in the records of a fugitive slave who was actually found grazing on the veld; hunger had reduced him to seeking the resources of the beasts of the field.

A unique case of desertion on the part of a slave girl is described in the diary of Mrs. Duminy. This girl, she wrote, was in ill-health and had therefore been taken by her mistress to the Warm Baths at Caledon. After a few days she disappeared, and was later found hiding in the bush by Mrs. Duminy's own maid, who thereupon brought her before that lady. Mrs. Duminy asked the ungrateful maidservant why she had been so wicked as to run away from such a good mistress, and received the surprising answer: "My 'nonnie' is not pretty; she is ugly!" Nevertheless, she persuaded the girl to behave herself and to make use of the baths until her mistress (who had left soon after she had decamped) sent for her. And when, some days afterwards, slave boys came to fetch the defaulter, she wrote to the latter's mistress asking her to forgive the girl and not to beat her.

Such a letter might well have been inspired by that which was written by St. Paul concerning the slave Onesimus, who had robbed and deserted his master Philemon. From Colosse, where Philemon resided, the slave had made his way to Rome and, coming under the ministry of St. Paul, was converted to Christianity. So high an opinion had the apostle of the character of his convert, says the Reverend William Wright, that he entrusted him with his Epistle to the Colossians, as well as a letter to his former master. This letter, for tenderness, address and elegance, has probably never been surpassed:

> ". . . I beseech thee for my son Onesimus, whom I have begotten in my bonds: which in time past was to thee unprofitable, but now profitable to thee and to me . . .
> For perhaps he therefore departed for a season, that

thou shouldest receive him for ever; not now as a servant, but above a servant, a brother beloved, especially to me, but how much more unto thee, both in the flesh, and in the Lord?

If thou count me therefore a partner, receive him as myself.

If he hath wronged thee, or oweth thee ought, put that on my account; I, Paul, have written it with mine own hand, I will repay it . . ."

Chapter Five

PLEASURES AND PASTIMES

LIFE at the Cape in the seventeenth and eighteenth centuries was never as dull and monotonous as some writers would have us believe; such amusements as dancing, horse-racing, music, games and cards were thoroughly enoyed by the early colonists, and also by their slaves. Those were the days when cock-fighting — the sport of blood and feathers — had thousands upon thousands of adherents. It is one of the oldest sports — if not the oldest — in the world. We are told that more than two thousand years ago Themistocles, the famous Grecian soldier and statesman, when moving with his army against the Persians, observed two cocks fighting desperately. The great soldier stopped his troops and, summoning them before him, inspired them by calling their attention to the valour and intrepidity of the little feathered warriors. As a result of the ensuing victory of the Greeks, cocking became their favourite pastime; and it was one which gradually spread throughout every country in the world.

Malays were always devoted to cocking. In the eighteenth century they carried their love for the game to so great a degree that it became quite a common sight to see a number of them, each with a gamecock under his arm, taking up a position at some corner or other, where they would patiently await the appearance of a rival with whom to contend. Small wonder that one or two early visitors remarked that the most picturesque spectacles they beheld at the Cape were the battles fought by Indian gamecocks.

The regulations drawn up in the year 1779 by the authorities at Batavia may still be seen in the Cape Archives.

Among other things, it is stated that a licence for a gaming-house would be granted to an applicant on the express understanding that he exhibited outside his premises either a wooden cock or a painting of one. The lessor would not be allowed to gamble, but he could demand a certain percentage of the profits. He had to pay particular attention to the "heeling" or the proper fastening of the spurs so as not to prejudice the chances of either bird; and on no account could he sell any strong liquor on his premises.

The local slaves had no gaming-house: their cockpit was a natural depression in the ground; their place of rendezvous more often than not the stone quarry on the slopes of Lion's Head. "The Malays are great gamesters and generally spend the Sunday in cock-fighting and other amusements of the like kind, at which they stake considerable sums," writes a diarist, "and the Fiscal's officers, I am informed, license the place (the Quarry) to a certain set who collect a trifle from every Malay who fights a cock or otherwise makes use of this privileged spot." He adds that instances have been known when the abandoned wretches, infatuated with the sport, have through a continual run of ill-luck lost their all, and as a last stake have set their wives and children upon the hazard of the battle.

Another visitor to the Cape describes how, the clemency of the weather having invited him abroad, he rambled at random till he at last found himself in the middle of a crowd of Malay slaves who, having formed a circle, were enjoying the pleasures of a cock-fight and had bets depending on the match. The avid expression of their countenances and the warm interest of the onlookers excited his curiosity. The conflicts were obstinate; the birds, armed with artificial spurs, were seldom separated till one of them received the mortal blow. "Among this class of slaves at the Cape," he says, "a wild gambling spirit is universally predominant, and is carried to such an excess that not only do they cheerfully risk every farthing they possess, but the very clothes upon their back . . ." The police often disturbed them when they were assembled for that purpose, but the slaves had friends posted to signal and give warning of their approach, "that they may betake themselves in time to their heels".

Unfortunately they were not always particular about the way in which they made their escape. Chevalier François Duminy once wrote to the Council of Policy complaining of the conduct of the many slaves who congregated in the street behind his house every Sunday "and other holy days", in order to gamble at a cock-fight. What really annoyed the memorialist was their habit of jumping over the wall and into his garden as soon as they were pursued by the vigilant "Dienaaren der Justitie".[66]

The most ardent supporters of cocking were those men who came from the island of Java, and they carried their enthusiasm into even the country places. Professor Pearce, in describing "Meerlust", the magnificent estate on the Eerste River granted to Henning Huysing in 1701, draws attention to the fact that a short distance from the homestead is an interesting relic in the form of a dovecot with enclosed courts on either side which, it is said, were used for cock-fighting. It does not need much imagination to picture the scene at such a cock-fight: the heroic little birds sparring with heads stretched forward and feathers ruffled, avoiding many fatal blows with lightning-like movements, pecking, ripping, fighting . . . One can visualise, too, the eager faces of the spectators, the greedy look in the eyes of the gamblers, the hushed, tense, excited expectancy of the group who watched while the battle of death was being fought . . .

In the days when South Africa was still in its infancy, inns and taverns of all sorts were to be found dotted about Cape Town. Quaint signboards, some bearing paintings or drawings in chalk, dangled above the doors. Many of these inns were the rendezvous of respectable burghers and inhabitants, while at others soldiers and sailors gathered together to celebrate their arrival on *terra firma* after having faced all the hardships of a long voyage. How these jolly fellows ever found their way back to their ships remains a mystery: even when the kettledrums were sounded throughout the valley as a signal to go aboard, many of them decided "om nog eens gestooft te worden"; and they repaired again to the nearest tavern, leaving devastation and desolation in their wake. There was a regulation which stated that forty-eight hours before the muster day a skipper should hoist flag and pennant, loosen the foretopsail and fire a gun to give notice to all on shore — and if any of the crew allowed the ship to leave without them they were to be thrashed by the Caffres, put in irons and banished to hard labour on Robben Island for six months, forfeiting at the same time three months' wages. But even this had no effect. The Orang Bharu, or "verdant greens", as those proceeding to India were called — no doubt with the same implication as our own modern metaphor "green" in the sense of "callow" — were rough customers enough, but they were angels compared to those returning from there, the Oranglammen — Cape Oorlam — the men of wide and actual experience. These were wild and obstreperous — terms which, for that matter, could be applied to the English and the French sailors as well.[67]

Whenever the return fleet sailed into Table Bay, complete uproar followed. On one occasion, when there were not yet even two hundred souls living at the Cape, we read of the visitors calling out along the streets: "What are you doing in this cursed country — this land of famine? Come with us . . . Whoever likes to go, let him get into the boat: Amsterdam, Zeeland, Rotterdam, Hoorn, Delft, Enckhuysen . . . Fall in for the Fatherland; the ships are ready to sail!" They trod underfoot and crushed all the vegetables in the Garden; drove the gardeners away with knives and stones; burned the Company's boat, a sampan, as well as wheelbarrows and other such objects that came within their reach; carried off pigs, fowls, ducks, doors and window-frames; pulled from the ground the pole to which the placcaat was affixed and threw it at the Provost and his soldiers; persuaded more than a quarter of the full quota of residents to stow themselves away in the ships, and merrily ended a busy and boisterous day by setting upon the settlement's one and only policeman and chasing that discomfited official from house to house.

A traveller tells us that many times he witnessed Dutch sailors falling helter-skelter into sloops and other craft, hotly pursued by "innkeepers and alehouse wives", who in ringing tones demanded the moneys due to them. Sometimes — nay, often — the soldiers and sailors returned to their ships in sodden solemnity or high hilarity wearing neither jackets nor shirts, shoes nor hats. These articles had been assiduously removed from them by fairweather friends, being among the stakes which they had gambled away at the local inns.

A word is perhaps not out of place here about the above-mentioned innkeepers and those who kept lodging-houses at the Cape in early days. They earned a bad name amongst their customers for their acquisitive habits, which were neatly summed up in a remark made by the skipper of a Cape-bound East Indiaman in 1773. In reply to a question put by a bookkeeper, this captain said: "Gy moet wel voorsigtig weesen, want zy bestaan aardig aan de Caab en vallen wat aan de greijpende kant, daarom word 't ook de Caab de Greijp genaemt" — literally, they are on the grabbing side at the Cape, and that is why it is also called Cape Grab.*[68]

This, then, was the roistering and unruly company in which slaves of both sexes drank and gamed when, in defiance of the most stringent placcaats, they continued to frequent the taverns. It was by no means unusual for irate burghers and their tired wives to lay their grievances before the Fiscal. In vain they tried to woo slumber, they declared; the noise which emanated from the inns was unbearable. One night in 1771 several slave-owners decided to make a combined search for some of their slaves who were missing. They found them at 1 a.m. gambling by candlelight in a Rondebosch tavern. Only one of the ten culprits concerned had a pass, and all of them had been drinking heavily. The innkeeper was fined 150 rixdollars and had his licence permanently suspended. Strangely enough, the slaves always

---

* Another amusing anecdote has been left to us by Captain Carmichael, who wrote an account of Sir David Baird's expedition. He says that when they arrived at the Paarl they found the people prodigiously civil. Every door was thrown open for their reception, and several of the inhabitants carried their kindness so far as to send even to the Parade to invite the newcomers to their houses. "Some of our speculators," he observes, "ascribed this marked hospitality to fear, while others, inclined to judge more favourably of human nature, imputed it to general benevolence of disposition. Those who suspended their opinion on the subject had the laugh at the expense of both, when, on our departure next morning, the true motive was discovered in the amount of their bills."

gambled for money, though where they acquired it remains a mystery. In one case, during a single night's gaming a slave won no less than 16 rixdollars from some of his fellows.

According to a placcaat of 1658, Europeans discovered gambling with these people rendered themselves liable to be thrown into a dark hole for eight days, on a diet of bread and water. In the criminal proceedings for 1684, we read of some white men drinking Spanish wine at the house of a Capetonian, together with a number of the Company's slaves. After the wine had flowed for some time, the Europeans and the blacks began to play with dice — "speelen met de dobbelsteene . . . in de wandelinge genaemt tossen" — and then switched their potations to brandy. Within a short while a fight broke out, and we are given in the records a vivid pen-picture of an inebriated European chasing a slave towards the Slave Lodge at the point of a dagger.

During week-days, and even on Sundays after divine service, large numbers of the colonists repaired to the taverns to listen to the strains of violins, flutes, hautboys, trumpets, harps and other instruments played by the slaves. Lichtenstein mentions two additional musical instruments in use at the Cape, one "a guitar, made in the country, of African ash-wood. This is a favourite instrument among the colonists, and is almost always to be seen in the houses of substantial people". He refers to the second in the course of an account of his visit to a household residing near Swellendam: "There was an apartment in the house appropriated solely to the performance of divine service. In it was an organ, on which one of Muller's daughters played very well. It was built in the place itself by a person of the name of Hoddersum, who was still living at the Cape Town . . . continuing this trade, and gaining a very good livelihood by making harpsichords . . ."

Some of the tavern-keepers bought only those slaves who were familiar with the use of some musical instrument, and we find the owner of a False Bay inn admitting that he kept a slave boy for the dual purpose of fishing from the boat and playing the violin at the tavern. In his diary Von Dessin relates his pleasure at learning that a Madagascar slave whom he had purchased as a cook could perform on the flute, the hautboy and the French horn. As far back as 1676, when Abraham van Riebeeck — the second child of European parentage to be born at the Cape — arrived in Table Valley on a visit to the land of his birth, he was entertained at the Governor's residence by a black steward and another young slave who played the harp and the lute. Their execution was masterly; both of them had a nice ear for music, "voornamentlyk in de loopjes ende in de praeludia, die hij meesterlijk speelde, dog hij speelde nooijt uijt noten, maer al van buyten".

Many other visitors to the Cape spoke of the beautiful music dispensed by the slaves. Augusta de Mist, for example, mentions how she called at a farm in the country and how intrigued she was on hearing a band of slaves playing there. Nature, she says, was their only music-master. She adds that in Cape Town itself she knew several private families whose slaves were musicians. This fact is borne out by other writers as well, and further confirmation can be found at Hope Mill (now the Normandy Hotel), where there still exists a raised dais or gallery at the upper end of the dining-hall, on which the slaves used to sit and provide music during meal-times for the delectation of their masters.

In this respect one is reminded of an amusing episode in the travels of Monsieur le Vaillant. He had many caustic remarks to pass about the manners of a certain "lordly vine-dresser" on whose Constantia estate he and a friend were invited to make a brief stay. Le Vaillant resented the ostentatious grandeur and the air of stately superiority with which he and his fellow-guest were received, and one can easily imagine the French traveller's additional annoyance when they were served at dinner with the common *vin du pays* — local wine — while the "petty potentate" had the impudence "to drink himself, before our eyes, some choice Bordeaux, which his slaves poured out for him . . ." That night in their bedroom Le Vaillant and his friend made plans to retaliate for their host's discourtesy, and "to inspire wisdom into the inflated brain of this African Jupiter". But how great was their astonishment when they awoke in the morning to be greeted with a most admirable concert playing under their windows! "Delighted with the enchanting sounds," he narrates, "we endeavoured to guess their cause. We asked each other how it could happen that this satrap, the night before, should have shown himself so haughty, and now display the most refined attention? We concluded that either his rudeness was the affair of a day, or that, being sobered by a night's rest, he hastened to obliterate from our minds the negligence with which we had been treated. Our conjectures and our praises were of short duration. The concert was intended for the amusement of our host, and not for ours; and this was not the first time that it had saluted the walls of his palace. This great man was accustomed to be thus awakened every morning; and he retained, for the express purpose, fifteen slaves particularly skilful in musical execution."

Young and old in the colony had a passion for dancing, and here again the slaves were the musicians. There was a time in the 1730's when the English country dances were much in vogue at the Cape, and were very gracefully performed; waltzes, minuets and quadrilles were great favourites. Balls were frequently given, and it was customary for the Governor and other distinguished personages to hold such functions once a month. These events, of course, were considerably enlivened when the Dutch East Indiamen anchored in Table Bay. In their own social stratum the slaves themselves were very enthusiastic dancers. One visitor to the Cape, after attending a "rainbow ball" — to use his own phrase — remarked that he was agreeably surprised to notice with what decorum the slave girls and others "composed of each different hue in this many-coloured town" conducted themselves, and with what striking success they imitated the manner, conversation and dancing of their mistresses.

These facts were confirmed by another writer, who described the rejoicings, feasts and dancing so dear to the hearts of the slaves, and the hours of nocturnal merriment spent in celebrating the birth of a child to a slave mother. It was on these occasions, he said, that the blacks showed themselves off to the best advantage: "The women display much taste and even elegance in their dress, nor are their dances wild, irregular or unaccompanied with proper music". He added that, faithful mimics as they were of the white inhabitants, they exhibited "an easiness of motion, and a justness of ear, which never fail to surprise and please a European unapprised of this circumstance".

When Lady Duff Gordon came to the Cape she was told of the extraordinary musical gifts of the Malays, and such a scene as she graphically portrays must have been witnessed repeatedly in the days of the Dutch East India Company. She says that at a certain ball held in Cape Town, where the music provided was very poor, the problem was solved by the timely arrival of two bricklayers — a Malay and a negro — one of whom could play the concertina and the other the tambourine. "The handsome yellow man took the concertina which seemed so discordant, and the touch of his dainty fingers transformed it to harmony. He played dances with a precision and feeling quite unequalled, except by Strauss's band, and a variety which seemed endless. I asked him if he could read music, at which he laughed heartily, and said music came into the ears, not the eyes."

Lichtenstein describes how Mr. van Reenen of Klavervalley entertained a company with a concert performed by his slaves. "They played first a chorus," he says, "and afterwards several marches and dances upon clarinets, French horns and bassoons. The instruments were good, and there was great reason altogether to be pleased with the performance, though much was wanting to render the harmony complete. They afterwards played upon violins, violincellos and flutes, upon which they performed equally well." He adds that it was not uncommon to find the same thing among many families at the Cape, and that there were men in the town who gained their living by instructing the slaves in music, though neither master nor pupils knew a single note, playing instead entirely by ear. "This practice receives great encouragement from the natural inclination that the slaves, particularly the Malays, have to music, from the passion for dancing that prevails among the young people of the colony, and from the advantage the gentlemen find in having them at hand on all occasions of festivity. I know many great houses in which there is not one of the slaves that cannot play upon some instrument, and where an orchestra is immediately collected together, if the young people of the house, when they are visited in the afternoon by their acquaintances, like to amuse themselves with dancing for an hour or two. At a nod the cook exchanges his saucepan for a flute, the groom quits his curry-comb and takes his violin, and the gardener, throwing aside his spade, sits down to the violincello."

William Hickey, who visited the Cape in 1777, became aware of the musical talents of the slaves in somewhat unusual circumstances. During his stay he was a member of a party which climbed Table Mountain, under the direction of Colonel Gordon of the Cape garrison. About half-way up, he recounts, they stopped for rest and refreshment, and "I thought we were suddenly got into enchanted ground, such celestial sounds burst upon our ears. It seemed to come from the air above us, and consisted of the sweetest harmony I ever heard. Our surprise was increased upon Colonel Gordon informing us that what we imagined came from a complete band of instrumental music proceeded from nothing more than two flutes played upon by his servants, whom he had sent forward for the purpose, but that the peculiar sweetness and melody arose from the situation of the spot where they had performed, which was surrounded by echoes innumerable". Nor was this all. At the end of the climb, Hickey adds, a meal was spread in readiness for the party, with "comfortable camp stools to rest our wearied limbs upon, whilst a pair of excellent French horns yielded us increased pleasure".

Up till quite recently one could find traces of what was once a centre of entertainment with the Van Breda family, who lived in the beautiful homestead "Oranjezicht". A short distance from this residence, within a pleasant garden, stood a raised bandstand, with low stone walls, in which area an orchestra of thirty slave musicians performed on fiddles and flutes for the benefit of visitors. We are told that the hospitality of the Van Bredas was a matter of so much consequence that it was customary to hoist a flag at the homestead to indicate when the family was "at home".[69]

The Hollanders, incidentally, as is well known, always

had a great fondness for bells, and we therefore cannot be surprised to find Commander Wagenaar asking the Directors to send two bells to the Cape, the one to be hung at the Schuur to call the slaves home with the cattle and also "to enliven the farmers who live in that lonely place, and which could in time serve to collect all the inhabitants to hear divine service . . ."

Often on a Sunday afternoon the slaves could be seen dancing with their own womenfolk or with Hottentot partners; sometimes, indeed, they would pool their rixdollars to hire a wagon in order to spend an afternoon at the seaside or at one or other of the dancing-houses in the country. Clavichords, zithers, mouth-organs, trumpets, clarions, drums and even "een instrument dat men een ravekinje hiet" were amongst the musical instruments employed by the slaves. Some of the latter were actually named accordingly: thus we find an old slave bearing the title of "de Harpeslager", i.e. the Harpist. The above-mentioned term "ravekinje", incidentally, is rendered with a slight difference elsewhere, in the memoirs of Borcherds. He gives us a picture of the slaves in their own quarters, indulging in gossip, enjoying their supper round a fire, or listening to the music of the "ramakienjo", as he calls it — a contraption with three strings stretched over a calabash which acted as a sounding board — and says that usually one of their number was an expert player of this instrument. There was also a one-stringed instrument known as the *gom-gom*, much in use among both the slaves and the Hottentots; Kolbe describes it as bow-shaped and made of very hard wood. Not all the music-makers in the colony were slaves, of course; many of the Europeans were equally accomplished performers. How vividly one can visualise the scene in a little gabled tavern at the Cape in 1724, when a soldier was softly playing the violin, and suddenly a voice broke in: "Keerel, indien ik zoo speelen kon, zoo gaf ik je een stuk van mijn ziel . . ." (Fellow, if only I could play like that, I would give you a part of my soul).[70]

During the time of the Dutch East India Company, New Year's Day was generally kept as the most important annual holiday. When that day dawned, it was the custom to fire

Original Journal of 17 April, 1658, regarding brandy and tobacco given to school children: "is mede belast na 't eijndighen elck een croesjen brandewijn en 2 duijm taback te geven".
(*Cape Archives*.)

The Gom-Gom — A musical instrument played by the slaves.
(*Elliott Collection*.)

The Company's Hospital. (*Elliott Collection.*)

Malay funeral.
(*By Courtesy of the Parliamentary Librarian.*)

seventeen cannon from the Castle, which were answered by those of the ships at anchor in Table Bay. The approach of each New Year usually found the farmers of the interior and their slaves inspanning their white-tented wagons and making all preparations for a journey to Cape Town — a trip which took them over rough and uneven roads, formidable mountains and perpendicular precipices down which vehicles and cattle sometimes fell headlong. Nevertheless, it was a journey which had many compensations. Even if the rate of speed was seldom more than twenty miles a day, did not that very fact afford the travellers ample opportunity of seeing the beautiful countryside through which they passed? And once they had reached Cape Town these sturdy, taciturn farmers evinced great eagerness to join their urban relatives and friends. Soon the youngsters could be observed with the little slave boys at the quaint gracht bridges, or alongside the streams of limpid water that wound down the valley; here they would play ball and racket, marbles and ninepins, or spin tops, trundle hoops, fly kites, slide on skates and walk precariously on stilts . . . It was habitual, too, for many families to permit their slaves to enjoy the day with their own kind. During such a celebration they would don their best attire, bent on passing the whole holiday in mirth and pleasure.

One of the most cherished privileges accorded to the people of Cape Town was visiting the incomparable Garden of the Dutch East India Company. Jan van Riebeeck had established it as merely a vegetable garden for the garrison and the fleet; Simon van der Stel succeeded in developing it into a recognised beauty-spot of the Cape. "Whatever the ancients have said about the gardens of the Hesperides, with their golden apples, or those of Alcinous, Adonis and Epicurus, or of the Hanging Gardens of Babylon . . . and of many others, which have been so highly lauded, can in no way compare with this matchless garden," wrote Valentyn. Here along the shady avenues and pleasant paths — to this day one of the chief charms of the city in the summer season — the Capetonians ambled. Unfortunately, for a period in 1753 it became necessary for the Council of Policy to prohibit all slaves from entering the Garden, with the exception of those who were in charge of children; even then, these children had to be satisfied with only the main walks or lanes for their pleasure and exercise, and were not permitted to go into the fenced parks and squares, much less to wander into the paths between the flower-beds. Those slaves who accompanied their masters and mistresses were also allowed into the Garden, on the understanding that any one of them found damaging the trees would be publicly scourged. Great attractions in the Garden were the menagerie and the aviary which stood at the upper end of the avenue. In the former were harts, elks, zebras and many other animals, and the latter contained birds of almost every South African species.

Hickey's memoirs contain some flattering remarks about this pleasure-spot. "In the mornings and evenings," he says, "we walked in the Company's gardens, which are well stored with curious plants, the choicest fruits and vegetables. There is also the finest menagerie in the world, in which are collected the most extraordinary animals and birds of every quarter of the globe."

In the year 1708 a most uncommon sporting event took place at the Tavern of the Ocean. One Sunday — 11 November, to be exact — Governor Louis van Assenburgh startled the conservative burghers by departing from his usually staid habits and inviting the Company's officers and the more influential citizens to repair after divine service to the Castle, where he endeavoured to entertain them with a fight between bulls and dogs. Unluckily no details are available; the journalist who made the entry in the records concluded it with nothing more than a brief remark to the effect that everybody was well treated by the Governor. One may feel assured, however, that amongst the most interested of the spectators were those slaves who had contrived to be present in one capacity or another.

Improbable though it may seem, fighting with knives was considered an extremely exhilarating pastime by the seventeenth-century sailors of the Company. We learn that in Batavia it vied in popularity with the boxing matches in England and had its fixed rules and regulations — although the height of fun was really reached only when a general rough-and-tumble mêlée developed between soldiers and sailors. Naturally, the authorities at the Cape looked askance at this perilous diversion, and severely punished the offenders. A sailor, for instance, who was found guilty of engaging with a soldier and inflicting on his opponent two cuts in the face, one on the right and the other on the left cheek, in such a manner that the wounded man bled profusely and fainted, was brought to the place of execution, bound to a pole, thrashed and finally given two cuts in the face similar to those suffered by his victim.

Another case occurred in January 1717 when a sailor, lounging drunkenly in the doorway of the "Kaizer's Crown" inn, observed a friend a little distance away who, not unlike himself, had walked with Bacchus. Suddenly a bright idea struck him: he suggested to his friend that they should fight a duel, and whichever of them survived the conflict should bury the deceased. The notion appealed to the other, and arm-in-arm they made their unsteady way, each with knife in hand, to the garden at the back of the inn. At a certain point the sailor cried out: "Stand fast, we are far enough!" "Stand it shall be," came the answer. Then the fight commenced in earnest. On the following day both were buried; the one had been killed in combat, and the other was hanged.

The slave was never slow to imitate the example of the European. Despite the stringent placcaats issued forbidding the sale of any sharp implement to him, his "love of the little knife" caused the authorities much vexation of spirit; and when, in later years, duelling took such a prominent place among the fashionable follies of the day, a diarist wrote that he would indeed be greatly surprised if the slave did not in the near future also demand to settle his differences with the pistol!

Chapter Six

EDUCATION, RELIGION AND COURTSHIP

ONE can well imagine what our modern coloured parents would say if their children, on coming home from school, informed them nonchalantly that the teacher had given each pupil a glass of brandy and some tobacco. Yet in the days of South Africa's infancy parents looked upon this occurrence with approval — one can almost say they became a little envious now and then!

Soon after the arrival early in 1658 of the first large batch of slaves, preparations were made for the establishment of a school for the little heathens, where they could receive instruction in the Reformed religion, and learn to speak the Dutch language; and on 17 April of that year we find an entry in the journal to the effect that a school had been opened on that date for the education of slave children. The teacher was Pieter van der Stael, brother-in-law to Jan van Riebeeck, a pious sick-comforter who was given the appointment "especially as he reads Dutch correctly".

On the day of its opening, and for many days thereafter, the Commander was a constant visitor to the school, as he desired to see discipline maintained and everything placed on a satisfactory basis. He told the teacher to give names to those children who had none, and to see that all of them were properly clothed; "and that the slaves may be encouraged to attend and hear or learn the Christian prayers, it is ordered that everyone shall receive, after school hours, a glass of brandy and two inches of tobacco".

One can picture these small black pupils, wide-eyed and vaguely puzzled, listening to the exhortations of their pious instructor, singing psalms, repeating the Catechism and sundry prayers, and vainly trying to say their ABC. Perhaps their young minds wandered occasionally to former days when they were still in their native land, far away on the west coast of Africa; or to their relatives and friends there who were at that very moment living in liberty, with never a care in the world; or even to their little Hottentot playmates who were patiently waiting for them to come out of school. After a short while these scholars realised at any rate two things about their present circumstances: firstly, that the new language was very difficult to understand; and, secondly, that the school benches were uncomfortably hard. So gradually they began to absent themselves from class — first individually and then collectively. It is recorded that on one occasion a large number of children played truant and were found, after a prolonged search, hiding in a cave at Hout Bay.

By 1663 the white population had so increased in number that it was decided to open a school mainly for European children. On the arrival of Ernestus Back, the successor of van der Stael, instructions were issued regarding the amounts that could be demanded as school fees. On the opening day there were seventeen pupils, four of whom were slaves and one a "Hottentoosie". These non-European children were to be taught without charge — *Pro Deo*, as stated in the Resolution — but half a real was asked for lessons given to each child of a burgher, provided he could afford it, the Commander himself determining which parents were able to pay the fees.

There being at that time practically no distinction made between people on account of colour, the co-education of white and black children could not have been looked upon with any degree of disfavour. These youngsters did well, and in the following year the Governor could write saying that there were now twenty-nine pupils all told, and that many of the slave and Hottentot children could repeat the Lord's Prayer. But then the schoolmaster was banished to Batavia, his place being filled in the meanwhile by the Fiscal, pending the appointment of another suitable teacher. This was a soldier by the name of Daniel Engelgraaff. Unfortunately he died a few years later, but under his care the pupils had increased in number, and nothing occurred until his death to interrupt his work.

In the meantime steps had been taken to provide the children with an appropriate schoolroom — a loft, which had often been required for the storage of grain, or for the accommodation of sailors when ships came sailing into the bay. Certainly in the early days everything was done to encourage the slave children to attend school regularly, and when it was found that Alexander Carpius, a temporary sick-visitor and teacher, showed great application to duty, especially to the instruction of the Company's slave children, the Council of Policy were so pleased that they raised his salary very considerably. In 1676 a movement was set afoot to establish a separate school for these children of the Company, but from various facts that emerge from the records it is obvious that this segregation was not based purely on colour prejudices — in fact, the Council resolved that the cleverest among the black children could attend the European school.

Slave education at the Cape received a tremendous stimulus as a result of Commissioner van Rheede's visit to the Cape in 1685. He set aside a part of the Slave Lodge to serve as a school for the Company's slaves under twelve years of age. There these pupils were to be taught to repeat the Catechism and certain prayers, and to learn the principles of Christianity, as well as to read and write and to conduct themselves respectfully towards their superiors. Slaves over twelve years old were to be allowed two afternoons in the week for the purpose of being instructed in the Christian religion. All the slave scholars had to attend church services twice on Sundays, accompanied by their teachers, and in the afternoon when the sermon ended they had to recite in public the Heidelberg Catechism. A mulatto named Jan Pasqual of Batavia was appointed schoolmaster for the slaves, and as schoolmistress for the girls Margaret, a slave woman who had been freed, was selected.

Certainly as the seventeenth century progressed the slaves showed a greater inclination to learn. Some of them, having acquired knowledge, on their own initiative were eager to pass it on to those of their companions who were eager to be taught. We can imagine the pride of the teacher when, one Sunday in 1686, the congregation was edified by the ready and apt answers made to questions on the Heidelberg Catechism, put by the minister of the Holy Word to the Company's slave children, both boys and girls, who were said to give equal satisfaction in their school to their male and female instructors and their superintendents.

Detailed regulations by the Lord of Mydrecht for the slave school may still be seen in the Cape Archives. Translated, they read as follows:

Rules for the Schoolmaster

(1) He is to manage to be at school at eight o'clock in the morning, and in the afternoon till four o'clock.
(2) He will hear the lessons twice daily.
(3) He will teach the children good Christian principles and manners, and not to tolerate any vile or evil talk.
(4) He will not allow any other slave or Dutch children in the school.
(5) He will follow the pupils to church on Sundays, and question them on the Heidelberg Catechism every Wednesday and Saturday.
(6) He will teach them to sing psalms and to write, and let them say their ordinary prayers every day.
(7) He will allow no European children in the school.

Rules for the Children

(1) They are on no account to be kept away from school by their parents.
(2) They have to show respect to their teacher, as well as to the Commander and other officials whom they might encounter in the street or other places.
(3) They have to learn their lessons; in fact, the minister has to visit the school twice a week to see whether satisfactory progress is being made.[71]

Unfortunately, within less than two years of his appointment the teacher of the Lodge School, Jan Pasqual, was accused of immoral conduct with his pupils, and was taken in custody to the Castle. Another person of colour was put in his place.

Governor Simon van der Stel, at a Council meeting held three days before Christmas in 1687, spoke of the necessity of education, especially among the "rough and coarse inhabitants". He decided that in order to encourage the children, both white and black, to absorb the Christian principles and to learn their school work, a prize should be given on Christmas Day to each of them after undergoing a test. The free children were to receive prizes varying from silver pens to money, and all of them were to be awarded sweet cakes, "but of different sizes". Nor were the slave children forgotten; in order to stimulate their interest in their studies, each of them was to be given a sweet cake. At the same meeting, it was resolved that among the children of the inhabitants all boys between nine and thirteen years of age were to be exercised in arms on the parade ground — a practice in which the slave schoolboys were never allowed to participate.

As the years went on, the number of pupils in the little slave school in the Lodge grew ever larger, and in 1717, when an alteration in the Slave Lodge became necessary, four divisions in the new building were specially set aside for educational purposes. One apartment was allotted to the teachers, one to the boys, one to the girls, and the fourth was used as a schoolroom. Soon after this date the habit arose of entering in the records every month the names of deceased slaves. For various reasons, the mortality among the children of the Lodge school during the three months from December to February, 1737 to 1738, was unusually high, eleven having passed away.

The precedent set by Van Rheede of having suitably qualified slaves to act as teachers to the children in the Slave Lodge — boys and girls to be taught by instructors of their own sex respectively — was followed, and these teachers were generally people who had been baptised, had been taught the Dutch language and had been instructed in the principles and practice of the Reformed faith. Dr. P. S. du Toit, author of *Onderwys onder die Kompanjie, 1652—1795*, gives us a list of the teachers at the Slave

Lodge. They received some small remuneration from the Company, even though they were slaves, with the result that they were able to apply for their freedom and also to pay the required fee.

Among the teachers mentioned in the records is Presuma of the Cape, who received her freedom after four years' service as teacher of the girls at the Lodge school; and Jan van Manda, who was baptised and spoke the Dutch tongue, and who, after being granted his freedom, continued teaching the slave boys. In 1751 a slave, Christoffel Stents of the Cape, applied to be manumitted. According to his request, his age was forty-nine years, of which he had spent nineteen serving as schoolmaster in the Lodge school, yet only seven years previously another teacher had been freed from his duties. From the evidence, Dr. du Toit asks the question whether it cannot be accepted as a fact that there were more than one teacher at the Lodge at the same time. We know that in 1779 eighty-four slave children were attending the Lodge school; forty-four of them belonged to the Company and lived on the premises, and forty were owned by colonists.

In the same year a thorough investigation was made into the running of the Lodge school, and in consequence the emoluments of the teacher were increased, as it was reported that he had found difficulty in maintaining a livelihood with his wife and family; then, too, the investigators were concerned with the educational welfare of the slave children who were taken away from school at an unsuitably early age. As a result, it was arranged that the children should remain at school for a longer period.

Strange though it may seem, the instruction issued by the Lord of Mydrecht that no slave children whatsoever should be admitted to the general schools in Cape Town was certainly not obeyed; in fact, right throughout the eighteenth century such children belonging to the colonists attended the general school. And together with the white and black youngsters of the colonists there were also a large number of half-breed and free black children in attendance: in other words, there grew up a class of non-whites whose education was in no way different from that given to the Europeans. The following is a complete list of the general schools in Cape Town in 1779, showing the number of children attending each:

Teacher	Boys	Girls	Slave Children	Total
Meyer	37	34	6	77
Mellet	24	30	8	62
Dureng	34	20	2	56
Knoop	49	62	25	136
Joosten	42	56	17	115
Wydeman	40	55	3	98
Redelinghuys	46	51	5	102
Jacobse	18	16	16	50

Thus we find in these schools altogether 696 children; and, besides these, there were in the Lodge school 44 Lodge slave children and 40 burghers' slave children, a total of 84.

Even in the country districts — Drakenstein, Stellenbosch, Roodezand, Zwartland and Swellendam—schools were established, and it is highly probable that these were attended by non-European as well as European children. Many farmers in the interior hired private tutors, and several of the more enlightened ones stipulated in their contracts with these teachers that instruction should be given to the slave children in their possession, besides their own children. A large number of these farmers were themselves unable to write, but were determined that their sons and daughters should not grow up illiterate, and this laudable attitude was often extended to their slaves as well. It is interesting to note that some of these farmers had to represent their signatures with crosses, not knowing even how to sign their own names. But imagine, in one instance, the consternation on the face of poor old Johannes Myburgh, who, after attaching his signature to a contract in which he hired as schoolmaster a certain Hardewich Fleck, saw the latter gentleman make a neat cross in the place where he, too, should have placed his signature!

RELIGION

From the earliest days of slavery at the Cape the conversion to Christianity of those in bondage was always a cherished aim of the Dutch Government, whose invariable policy it was to raise the status of any slave who embraced the Christian faith. Slave-owners who were themselves not Christians — "Moors or other heathens", as they were defined in the placcaat — were strictly forbidden to hinder their slaves from becoming Christian converts, on pain of their being ceded to Christian masters at reasonable prices. Although proclamations were made prohibiting all public worship, except in the Reformed Church of Holland, it appears that many of those slaves who professed religion were followers of the doctrine of Mahomet — perhaps in some instances encouraged by their proprietors, who preferred to entrust to slaves of that persuasion the access to their wine cellars, on account of the sobriety which their faith inculcated. Certainly, however, the Dutch East India Company looked on all those who deviated from the tenets of the Calvinist creed with deep disapproval; their attitude towards any who wished to worship in accordance with the rituals of the Church of Rome, for example, was one of contempt and obstruction.

In his own home, of course, everyone was at liberty to worship God in any manner which he chose. Lutheran chaplains frequently led services and administered the sacraments in private houses in Cape Town, but they would not have been allowed to ring a bell to call the congregation together. The only exceptions to this rule occurred in the years 1749, 1751, 1752 and 1753, when clergymen of the English Episcopal Church were granted permission to conduct services in the Dutch Reformed Church building in the town. And not until 10 December 1780 was the first service held in the Lutheran Church, which was then publicly opened for divine service.

Mentzel tells us that some of the slaves who were brought from the Portuguese territorial possessions had been baptised in the Catholic Church, and the records contain references which support this statement. In 1685, for instance, the Council of Policy felt compelled to refuse the request of a Company's slave to go on board the French ship *La Royale,* in order to practise his religion there with the priest. Priests who arrived in Table Bay in French or Portuguese ships found that their activities were kept under surveillance. Not only were they prohibited from having meetings for the celebration of worship according to Roman ritual but also, when it was discovered that despite their promises they were holding Mass for some of the inhabitants with whom they lodged, proper sentries were placed over them. A half-breed, banished from Batavia because he had there endeavoured to seduce many freemen to the Roman belief, was arrested because of his apparent intimacy with the French priests. Another person, a free black, Manual Perera by name, who owned a large number of rosaries, crucifixes and various images, threw them all into the sea, as he was afraid of being held up to ridicule — "omdat die religie hier niet was en een ander daarmede de spot niet en soude drijven".[72]

In spite of the precautions taken by the authorities, it is evident that a very small percentage of the inhabitants were of the Catholic persuasion; some of them, finding themselves victimised by the Company, suddenly developed "a sincere affection and love for the Reformed religion". Others, like Etienne Barbier, preferred to conceal the fact that they were Catholics. That interesting Cape character, the Reverend Engelbertus Franciscus le Boucq — a clergyman who, whilst reading his sermons, made use of allegations and applications intended for certain persons who were not to his liking, "to the dissatisfaction and the very slight edification of most of his hearers", and then, with a sword on one side and a brace of pistols on the other, wandered through the country, escorted by two slaves armed with heavy sticks shod with iron — was of French descent, had been educated for the ministry of the Roman Catholic faith, and had been a monk in the abbey of Boneffe in Belgium before finally becoming a Protestant.

In the days when the Cape was still an embryo colony, before it had progressed sufficiently to justify the appointment of a fully-ordained minister, sick-comforters were enrolled to provide for the religious needs of whites and blacks — to minister to the colonists "by visitations, exhortations and consolations". Like those of all other persons in the employment of the Company, their duties were strictly specified, and swift retribution followed if they acted beyond their orders. In one case a sick-comforter took upon himself to address the people in his own words instead of reading a printed sermon as he was expected to do. The ecclesiastical court of Batavia got to hear of these "irregular proceedings", and a strongly-worded letter was immediately sent to Commander van Riebeeck. It did not please them, they said, to learn that the sick-comforter had transgressed the limits of his office, "conducting the service in the manner permitted only to a minister . . . He ought to know that he may not strike his sickle in another's harvest, nor may he usurp those functions which do not as yet belong to him".

During the whole régime of the Dutch East India Company an intimate relationship existed between the Church and the State, and the ecclesiastical court which was established had the direction in the first instance of all educational institutions. In the beginning we are therefore not surprised to find the sick-comforters as schoolmasters and the curriculum confined almost entirely to religious instruction. Seventeenth-century conceptions of religion were very different from those of to-day; absentees from public prayers, for example, could easily discover that they had been deprived of their wine ration for six days, or, if that did not produce the required salutary effect, they might be forced to labour in chains at the public works for a year.

Marriages and baptisms were usually solemnised by ships' chaplains who arrived in Table Bay. As a matter of fact, the question as to whether the children of heathen parents should be baptised or not was one which received a great deal of attention in early times; indeed, as Theal points out, in some of the Company's possessions this problem could not be set at rest; congregations were rent asunder and the strife extended even into families, creating bitterness between the nearest relations. It had been the custom at the Cape for chaplains to baptise all slave children, whether half-breeds or pure blacks, who were brought to them for that purpose, at the same time warning the owners that it was their duty to have such children educated in the Christian principles. But there was such division of opinion on the matter, and consequent unpleasantness, even among the members of the Council of Policy, that it was decided to apply to Batavia for an authoritative ruling. The reply, dated 25 January 1664, was read out to the Councillors. The Church authorities in India and the fatherland, it stated, had decided in the affirmative, provided that those responsible for the upbringing of such children undertook to have them educated in the Christian religion. This practice had been observed for a long while in India and by the Company itself, for whose baptised slave children schools had been organised. "We are instructed to follow the same rule," the letter continued. " The late Reverend Johan van Arckel, the first established clergyman here, obeyed this order, and during five months baptised all children that were brought to him, whether they were of Christian or of heathen parentage. The oldest of the Company's children were afterwards sent to school to be instructed in the knowledge of God. Mr. Johannes de Voocht, the present acting clergyman, is following the same order."

Some while before the burning question had been thus settled, an incident occurred which set the Cape in an uproar. It appears that after the congregation had finished listening to the sermon, one Sunday in 1661, a child of European parentage was presented and baptised. Then a slave woman walked up to the font with her infant in her arms, but before the minister could dip his fingers into the water up rose the chaplain of the ship *Weenenburgh,* who was present at the service, and in no uncertain terms objected to the baptism of the slave child, stating that he was better informed on the point than any other person there, and that the practice in vogue was wrong. The Governor, who was also present, remained silent, and the officiating clergyman refrained from performing the ceremony. Next morning, however, the Council met, and it was unanimously resolved to adhere to the orders received from the authorities, and to instruct the minister to baptise the rejected slave child on the following Sunday, together with any others who might be brought forward to him for that purpose, for, they said, "it is our desire to preserve harmony and peace in ecclesiastical as well as in political matters at this place".

Ten years later the matter came up for discussion again, when the Church Council suggested that the custom of baptising black children whose parents were heathens should be altered. It was the view of the local Church authorities that if children of heathen parentage were presented for baptism, the rite should be deferred and the parents instructed in Christianity, in order to be baptised at the same time. Children of mixed blood, however, should be baptised without delay. The Council of Policy simply referred the Church Council to the orders from Batavia, and there the argument rested. But in October 1721 it was revived once more in a discussion in the Council of Policy, following on a combined attack against the practice by the ministers of the Cape, Drakenstein and Stellenbosch, who used as a thesis their conviction that the children of heathens did not truly believe in the Lord; that they made no profession of such a faith and were not in the least sensible of what took place about them; and that they were not helped in these respects by their parents, who were merely ignorant unbelievers.

As before, it was felt that the attitude taken up by the ministers was in opposition to established custom, which had prevailed at the Cape since the 1660's; it was also contrary to the opinions and arguments of the Classis of Holland. In the same year (1721), however, various changes in connection with baptism were made in the colony: thenceforth no slaves were to be allowed to stand sponsors at the font, or *in loco parentis*. It was noticed, too, that "to the great annoyance and disrespect of the Europeans" the children of free blacks and of slaves were generally better dressed, when being baptised, than those of the white inhabitants; a decision was therefore made that these non-European infants should no longer be permitted at the font with such adornments as worn hitherto. In fact, the ministers even suggested that slave children and illegitimate babies should be baptised at another time than that appointed for Europeans.[73]

This question of baptism, as has been seen, was a bone of contention among the people for many years, and the instructions issued periodically were too often ignored. In 1683 the authorities at Batavia said that they would prefer Christians to present for baptism any children born of non-Christian parents, but that these sponsors should bind themselves to educate them as their own, to teach them diligently and at the proper time the Christian doctrine, and, in the event of their being slaves, to manumit them. A note was added to the effect that adult slaves should not be admitted to baptism or communion before they had been suitably instructed and found capable, on examination, of giving the reasons for their faith.

The Lord of Mydrecht himself emphasised his order that children of slaves and unbelievers should be more thoroughly educated in the true faith by presenting on his own behalf to the holy sacrament of baptism a four-year-old child. But it is very evident that the people became chary of well-doing, as the conversion of slaves to Christianity fell more and more into abeyance in the eighteenth century; and when the order came in 1770 — an order which was designed to advance Christianity — that slaves professing the Christian religion should not be sold, either in public or in private, or alienated in any manner whatsoever, many owners, who naturally stood to lose their rights over their slaves in such case, avoided co-operation and saw to it that the latter were not baptised.

Years later, in 1792, the Church Council of Stellenbosch came to the fore again with a further query regarding baptism. Since the inception of slavery at the Cape, it had been considered wrong to retain any baptised slave in bondage, and in view of this opinion the Church Council enquired whether owners who permitted or encouraged their slaves to undergo the ceremony would thereafter be obliged to emancipate them. The matter was referred to the Church Council of Cape Town, and that body replied that neither the laws temporal nor the laws spiritual prohibited the retention of baptised persons in slavery: this local custom, it was added, strongly supported the practice of conversion; if the reverse were the case, many masters would naturally be reluctant to agree to the baptism of their slaves, and so the progress of Christianity would be impeded.[74]

There can be little doubt, however, that the average colonist, left to himself, would have attended to the religious needs of his slaves: certainly one knows that many of the farmers living in the country districts encouraged these blacks to attend the domestic morning and evening prayers; and we must always bear in mind that the great majority of the early settlers were God-fearing and worthy people. Lichtenstein, for instance, speaking of one of the field-cornets, says that this man "made a great display of his piety. Every morning early, all his children, his slaves and his Hottentots were assembled for the purpose of devotion, which consisted of singing psalms, in reading a long prayer and a chapter from the Bible. He did not even forgo this ceremony during our stay, though at most places where we had been the bustle occasioned by so large a party of guests, was considered as reason sufficient to dispense with the customary religious exercises".

If, as Theal states, the colonists gradually began to hold the view that slavery was the proper condition of the black race, we cannot wholly blame them. "Other days, other ways", runs the old proverb, and, besides, there were two inexorable factors working against the baptism of the slaves: the behaviour of the blacks themselves, which often left much to be desired, and the indisputable fact that, as Professor MacCrone points out, slavery became no longer merely a form of cheap labour but an institution, in which the slave was not simply an unpaid servant but a valuable piece of property belonging to an owner.

COURTSHIP

Slavery at the Cape in the days of the Dutch East India Company was regulated by the laws made and promulgated by the Governor and the Council of Policy; the Statutes of

India, in as far as they were not contrary to the existing laws of the Council of Policy; and the Roman law, in as far as it was not contrary to the laws of the Council of Policy, the Statutes of India or the spirit of jurisprudence.

Slaves had none of the rights and privileges which distinguished the state of the free in civil society: among other things, they could neither marry nor claim the right to dispose of their children. The Roman laws, however, admitted as a principle that although slaves did not partcipate in the Civil Law, they had a share in the laws of nature: although they could not form a valid marriage contract, they could legally cohabit as married people. But the breaking of the faith of such cohabitation among slaves could not be punished as adultery, because no marriage could exist among them. Are you a Christian and not a heathen or a slave? — was the question put to everyone who appeared before the Matrimonial Court. But even the profession of Christianity gave no sanction to the marriage of the slave.

As early as 1671, Commissioner Goske had suggested that the girls in the Slave Lodge should be paired with male slaves. In later years Commissioner van Rheede, Lord of Mydrecht, decided on a proper separation of the sexes. First of all, those who had voluntarily determined to live together as man and wife were given separate quarters in the Lodge; with the threat of many punishments they were advised to remain faithful to each other and to beware of unchastity. The boys and girls were placed in different quarters, while unattached males were located on the eastern side of the Lodge and unattached females on the western side, thus preventing the one section from interfering with the other during the night. Any male slave who developed an affection for a female slave could give the authorities the name of his beloved, when suitable arrangements were immediately made to have them paired and sent to the appropriate quarters.[75]

The number of male slaves at the Cape always exceeded that of female slaves, roughly in the proportion of three to one. In 1791, for instance, there were 11,026 adult males and only 3,687 females — a majority of 7,339 males. This disproportion of the sexes resulted in a good deal of miscegenation with Hottentot women, who since the days of Van

Riebeeck had evinced great fondness for the slaves. One recalls the complaints of the Europeans at that time, when they saw the native women enticing away their slaves by offering them roast tortoises and other delicacies.[76] These women were far from handsome — "a tawny, swarthy sort of people . . . certainly the next to beasts of any people on the face of the earth", says one traveller, while Thunberg describes them as being short and slender, with prominent cheek-bones, flat noses, protuberant mouths, peaked chins, crooked backs and pot-bellies. They also had the unfortunate habit of besmearing themselves all over with "suet or other oleaginous stuff which . . . causes them to stink so that one may smell them at a considerable distance to windward" — one of the main reasons, probably, why intermarriage between European men and Hottentot women was rare.

The natives of the interior were very sceptical about the authenticity of the light complexions of some of the slaves, and, indeed, of the Europeans themselves. Once a group of Bechuanas, encountering in a remote country area a party from the Cape, surrounded one of the "altogether white slaves" (geheel blanke slaven) and practically forced him to submit to being washed by them, as they simply could not credit that the colour of his skin was natural. They still believed that all the white people were really brown in colour, like themselves, but had daubed their skins white with some kind of paint. Certainly some of the slaves must have been very fair-skinned; even in the *Government Gazette* references appear in advertisements to "white African slaves".[77]

Fortunately for the slaves, the Hottentots — if one can take Captain Cowley's word — were very free and easy with their wives. He tells us that any slave who desired the company of a "Hodmandod's" wife had merely to offer her husband a stick of tobacco, three inches in length. Not only would this ensure the husband's consent, but also the object of the slave's affections, humble and submissive, would be actually delivered by her complaisant spouse. Unlike the Hottentots, however, the slaves would not tolerate infidelity. In the eighteenth century, for example, we find a Hottentot girl swearing to a slave that she could not possibly love another man while he was alive. The slave believed her and was happy. But shortly afterwards he discovered her in a compromising situation. "Doe doen myn hart seer," he said, so he pushed her lover aside and thrust a knife into her stomach.

It must be borne in mind that many of the female slaves from the East Indies were not unattractive. Some, indeed, were handsome, particularly the mulattos, whose "black eyebrows, hazel eyes, ruddy complexion, and well-moulded limbs merit the delineation of the ablest painter or the chisel of the most accomplished sculptor".[78] Even Sparrman, the Swedish naturalist, was not blind to the charms of a female slave who, during the course of one of his excursions, obligingly pointed out to him the shallowest places in a brook which he had to cross. He says, however, that though for the service she seemed to expect "some amorous kind of acknowledgment", he was forced to disappoint her, as she had "had the misfortune to meet with a delicate as well as a weary philosopher".

When one couples the fact that some of these slave girls were attractive with the further fact that white women were extremely scarce at the Cape — so scarce, indeed, that orphan girls sent out were literally snatched up by ardent swains, and European women stowaways who landed in Table Bay were soon persuaded to change their life of singleness and adventure for that of matrimonial bliss — one cannot be surprised to read occasionally of a colonist's marrying a slave girl. Three such marriages took place in Van Riebeeck's time — all to Bengalese women; in the second case, the sick-visitor Pieter van der Stael transferred his female slave Maria of Bengal to Jan Sacharias of Amsterdam, on the express condition that he married her immediately after her emancipation.[79] A year later we find in the official records a reference to "the black wife" of the freeman Jan Sacharias, but this was not meant discourteously, as in the very early days cases of lawful marriage between Europeans and blacks were not looked upon with disapproval. Once a slave girl had been emancipated she was allowed the same privileges as a European, and was respectfully styled, for example, "the virtuous damsel Catharine Anthony of Bengal".

Not only did white women dislike the idea of leaving Europe for a remote settlement such as the Cape of Good Hope but also, even if they did contemplate taking the step, we can imagine their horror on reading accounts like, for instance, Mr. Christopher Frycke's story of his visit to Cape Town in the latter part of the seventeenth century. These would have deterred the most venturesome woman — provided that she was credulous enough to believe some of the absurd tales which were spread. Frycke declared that as he was walking along the shore of Table Bay he caught sight of "a servant maid, who was come to fill a little tub with sand: as soon as she saw me, she cry'd out to me as loud as she could, Maridi fini Senior: Oh Sir! Pray come and help me! I ran full speed towards her to help her, and when I came up to her, she shewed me a dreadful long Serpent, that had just then been devouring a young Hottentot, and had swallowed him up all but the Legs, which still stuck out of his Mouth".

This, he said, had put the maid into a great consternation, and made her afraid that she should be his next prey: "And truly being much in the same Apprehensions myself, I betook myself to my heels". When the maid saw him flee, she gave a great shriek and began to run too. Some Hottentots, hearing all the noise, came hurrying towards them, and as soon as they saw what was the matter "they got themselves ready to catch the Serpent". Frycke stated that they brought out some long ropes, threw them with wonderful dexterity about its middle and, "drawing the ropes, some at one end, some at another, as hard as they were able, they held him so fast that I expected they would have cut him in two. All the while the Serpent hiss'd in a fearful manner, and twisted itself strangely, but could not slip away. At last came some of the Men with great poles with which they knocked him on the head". Such travellers' tales were hardly an inducement to European women to see the Cape for themselves!

It was Commissioner van Rheede who decided to prohibit marriages between Europeans and emancipated slave girls, although he had no objection to wedlock between a white man and a daughter of a European and a slave woman, if the intended husband were of good character. A slave, or even an emancipated black, who had carnal connection with a white woman was liable to the death penalty — " it being a detestable thing that a heathen should amalgamate with a Christian, and contrary to divine and human law". Fortunately few such cases are on record — the much-quoted one of a young married woman from Zeeland and her paramour, the slave Titus, being the best-known. Cupido of Bengal not only admitted having had criminal connection with his master's daughter but also confessed to similar misconduct with another European female, both before and after her marriage, "thus adding to his offence the greater crime of adultery". He was sentenced to be hanged and burned under the gallows. Any slave who attempted to violate a maiden would, of course, receive similar punishment.[80]

Despite all attempts made at legislation, only a small percentage of children born at the Cape of slave mothers were black, the remainder being half-breeds. Sometimes these female slaves caused a nine days' wonder in the colony. Consider, for example, the following startling declaration made by the journalist in 1714: "Here lies a matter for natural philosophers to ponder. To-day our reverend minister baptised twins, of which the one was fairly white and the other perfectly black". He added that both the parents were black. On an earlier occasion a predecessor of this journalist reported a similar case, which he explained to his own satisfaction in these words: "The female slave of a certain burgher was this day delivered of twins, the one procreated by a negro and the other by a Hollander; a rare occurrence, and being a different (verscheijden) conception, we could not omit mentioning it".[81]

Slave women were very proud when their children proved of lighter colour than themselves. When Thunberg arrived at the Cape in 1772, he noticed that there were already a few families living who were descended from black mothers for three generations back. He says that the first generation proceeding from a European married to a tawny slave remained tawny but approached to a white complexion; the children of the third generation, mixed with European stock, were quite white and often very handsome.

So loose were the morals of many of the slave women that early visitors to the Cape almost invariably referred to the fact. Notwithstanding stringent efforts made to maintain order in the Slave Lodge, soldiers and sailors of different nationalities could be seen entering that abode every evening, where they misspent their time with female slaves. Even the soldiers at the Castle and some of the residents "had so far degenerated from the fear of God" that organised meetings were held at which they and the female slaves feasted together in inns and other places, and were guilty of all sorts of irregularities, "Yea! they even go so far as to undress themselves completely, and in the sight of everybody on the public roads and places . . . dance with each other and commit all kinds of shameful things . . . each acknowledging his concubine or mistress, living with and supporting her, so that the descendants or illegitimate children of female slaves fill the Lodge of the Company and the slave quarters of private owners. It is a blot on the Netherlands and other Christian nations".[82]

As these were considered "matters of very evil consequence", it was decided to uproot the shameful abuse; everyone was interdicted from attending meetings where female slaves congregated; from that date any European discovered in the Slave Lodge was to be tied to the pole which stood there and soundly thrashed. Apparently, however, these corrective measures availed but little; scarcely four years later the Lord of Mydrecht viewed with grave alarm the state of affairs existing among the slave women at the Lodge. Their cohabitation with European soldiers and sailors, he said, was so overt and well-known that it was regarded as an accepted practice.

As far back as 1660, no less a person than Jan van Riebeeck was accused of tolerating such cohabitation. According to the declaration made, a certain sailor publicly said that the Commander had come to his farm "Bosheuvel" and had asked Barend Waende, who lived there, if any of his men had been responsible for the condition of certain pregnant female slaves on the property. Barend had answered "No, Sir", and Van Riebeeck then came to the point. "Barend," he enquired, "did you have any hand in this affair?" Barend replied "Yes, Sir," and the Commander advised him to go to the Fiscal, as it was a matter of little importance and, after all, it was to the benefit of the Company! There was, however, probably no foundation for such an accusation, as we find in the records that on one occasion Commander van Riebeeck, accompanied by Peter Potter, arrived at night at the dwelling of Gunner Willem, whom they discovered lying alongside a female slave of the Commander, named Maria. In the court case which followed, it was pointed out that concubinage was expressly forbidden, and the gunner was severely punished.[83]

In the Lodge alone, the Lord of Mydrecht found thirty-two boys and twenty-six girls who were the children of European fathers and slave mothers. These unfortunate children, he told the Governor and the Council, could on no account be kept in bondage as they had no share in the fault of their parents, and, "being indisputably children of our own nation, cannot be made slaves". He issued regulations for their instruction, until the males had attained the age of twenty-five and the females that of twenty-two, when they could claim freedom as a right, under an obligation to repay one hundred gulden each for the expense of their education. Special attention was to be paid to the teaching of various trades, so that they would be able to maintain themselves in freedom, and would become attached to the land of their birth.

The Commissioner, an upright and humane man, was obviously much distressed at what he had seen. It was his wish that a different attitude should be adopted as regards the slaves, "for they are the Company's own people, not hirelings; they cannot quit the service of their master when tired, but are bound, not only for all their lives, but for those of their children and descendants. The better we make them, the fitter will they be to perform their duty, the more will they love their masters, and the more faithful will they prove to our nation. They are heathens, ignorant of the true God; and we — in whose power are their bodies — we may almost say, their lives — are Christians. It would be a shame to us, whose part it is to take good care of our irrational domestic cattle, if we permitted men to run wild, and left them in a worse condition than when in their fatherland ... How do we know what God, in his mercy, has determined as to these people, and what will foreign nations not say to our shame, if we allow them to live together by hundreds, like brutes, in utter licentiousness ... ?"

All that happened in 1685. Forty years later, we find two sailors discussing the Cape while on board their ship. "There is a fair wind blowing," said one. "Soon we shall be at the Cape, and then you will be able to have a good time with the black women — if you have the money."[84] Apparently, then, not all the sailors who sang the old sea-chanty

"Ik ben zeeman in mijn hart,
Ik walg van landvermaken;
Zelfs in d'armen van mijn vrouw
Hoor ik de masten kraken"

were really so eager to hear the creaking of the masts as they tried to make out. To some of them a visit to the Cape of Good Hope was merely an opportunity to entertain the dusky slave girls at the inns, even if the proprietors, as alleged, made their charges "without having the fear of God before their eyes"!

But we must not imagine that it was only the slave girls who were inclined to immorality. Take the case of a certain European woman, for instance. Many complaints reached the ears of the Church Council regarding her behaviour, with the result that towards the end of the year 1778 it was decided to send her to three spinster sisters by name Colyn, to whom they paid four rixdollars per month for her keep. From time to time they had cause to warn the young lady, and when she ran away from the house the councillors resolved to avoid further scandal, and to give an object lesson to others, by tying her with a chain to a block. Once she broke loose, but was brought back and chained again. Nine months later she was released, as her custodians believed that she had by this time reformed. Some years afterwards she was again guilty of bad behaviour and became pregnant, so the deacons of the church threw up their hands in despair and gave her up as a bad job.[85]

It was a generally accepted principle in Roman Law that children not born in legal wedlock must assume the state of the mother; the immediate effect of this was that any seventeenth-century burgher could live for years with a slave girl and then, should he tire of her, he could sell the mother and also the children whom he had procreated by her. After all, the children followed the condition of the mother and were therefore their father's slaves. Gradually, however, changes were made to the advantage of the children and to the prejudice of the father, and at last it was stipulated that the mother, as well as the offspring begotten by a master with her, should never be sold, whether the estate were solvent or insolvent, but should be emancipated after the death of the master.[86] Slaves who lived together as if in wedlock, however, were liable to be separated by the caprice of their master, or by sale for the satisfaction of his creditors. According to Mentzel, private owners usually made no objection if their female slaves lived with European men. He points out that the master benefited in two ways: the cost of upkeep of the slave was reduced through the presents she received from the man, and her children were the master's property, since the offspring of such a union were themselves slaves. These slave children, he adds, were found useful at a very tender age, and cost little to bring up. They were better mannered, better educated and more amenable to discipline than imported slaves, and in many cases became skilled artisans.

In the archives one often comes across complaints from half-breeds regarding the treatment received by them at the hands of the white men with whom they had lived. Jannetje Bort, emancipated female slave of the Company, begotten by a European father, repeatedly wrote to the Commander and Council to the effect that under promise of marriage she had borne the sergeant of the Castle four children, and that he would not contribute anything towards their support. Each time the father was cross-examined on the subject, and was earnestly admonished to abandon his wicked ways. But he stubbornly refused to provide proper maintenance for the children, and took little heed of the reiterated admonitions; the result was that Simon van der Stel ordered him in round terms to keep his concubine, and told him that he would never be allowed to marry any other woman than the complainant.[87]

Obtaining a female companion for a slave was often quite a problem, especially among the poorer class of slave-owners. On one occasion a slave, Cupido of Malabar, not only complained to his mistress that he disliked having to wear trousers — an unheard-of thing in his own country, he said — but also expressed annoyance at the apparent lack of interest shown in his domestic happiness. He had worked for three years now, he declared, and it seemed that "Nonje" had no intention of buying a "meijd" for him. Many owners hoped to avoid jealousy and quarrelling among their bondsmen by refusing to accommodate female slaves on their premises. Sparrman tells us of a conversation which he had with the manager of a farm, who lamented the fact that his employer excluded his slaves from commerce with the weaker sex, "which sweetens life, and renders its cares supportable". Even though these very slaves were kindly and familiarly treated and, according to Sparrman, were better off than many servants in Europe, they remained lonely and apathetic. Furthermore, in the manager's opinion, there was a pecuniary disadvantage. "The chief of my master's income," he explained to Sparrman, "arises from the breeding of horses. Could we keep female slaves here, he would get still more by the propagation of the human species; and indeed, a female slave who is prolific is always sold for three times as much as one that is barren."

The same writer states that the Bugunese slave girls were extremely constant in love, and exacted the strictest fidelity from their lovers. He mentions also the case of a young male and a female slave who were passionately fond of each other but could not obtain their master's consent to allow them to live together as man and wife. The lover, he says, was seized with a singular fit of despair; and having first plunged a dagger into the woman's heart immediately afterwards put an end to his own life. On the other hand, another eighteenth-century writer begs his readers not to imagine for one moment that the slaves regretted separation from one another; he maintains that they formed new connections with the greatest facility, and the knowledge that their children were the property of their masters removed all anxiety.

In a proclamation of 4 September 1775, it was ordered that the offspring of slaves and Hottentot women born in the service of inhabitants, in which they had remained during the first one and a half years of their lifetime, should continue to work for such inhabitants until they had attained the age of twenty-five years. Hottentot mothers were to be at liberty to remove their children under eighteen months old. These bastard-Hottentots sometimes made good labourers — certainly better than the pure-bred ones, who, when employed as shepherds or cattle-herds, spent most of their time lolling on the ground, asleep in the sunshine.

Kolbe writes that the Company's slave women were always freed from work from six weeks before to six weeks after their confinements. The most unrestrained licentiousness prevailed almost without exception among them, and in order the better to indulge their passions — and, incidentally, to enjoy in due course the above-mentioned holiday — they manufactured a love-potion of wine and eggs, to which they added sugar, saffron and cinnamon. Small wonder, he exclaims, that no fewer than two hundred children were running about the Slave Lodge.

Many a privately-owned female slave, once she attained the age of fifteen or sixteen years, received the visits of some lover by whom she became a parent. "Her second child, and so on, has another father, and probably one of different colour." Often these unhallowed births were far from discouraged or kept concealed from her owner and his family; we even find a man like Dessin kind-heartedly sending his slave girl to a place where she could be given proper attention during her confinement, and providing her with swaddling-clothes and other garments. Not all masters, however, were willing to admit into their homes the children born thus. In one case, the prison authorities informed a certain widow that her female slave Amarantia, who was lying in chains for some misdemeanour which she had committed, had given birth to a baby, and asked the mistress if she wished to take over the child. The widow refused, and the Government, nothing loth, proceeded to choose a name for the infant and entered it in the book as having been accepted as the property of the Company.

CHAPTER SEVEN

SUPERSTITIONS AND MEDICINE

IN the seventeenth and eighteenth centuries, Europeans and slaves were prone to attach the most ominous significance to particular objects and events. The majority of people all over the civilised world in those days harboured many crude superstitions: they had no doubt whatever that spirits walked abroad at night, that various localities were haunted and that evil persons were possessed by devils. Many of them, too, believed in witchcraft, in magic cures for diseases and in love philtres.

That shrewd adventurer Christopher Schweitzer describes the infatuation which, in 1680, he unwittingly inspired in a certain "long-ear'd" widow of Colombo. From the very day when he entered her lodging-house she treated him with marked civility: in fact, "her entertainment grew in time kinder and kinder; and then it broke out in some preliminary interrogations, why I would not settle there? Why I would not marry? and many things of that kind; at last it came to a close application, and to a plain offer of herself, if I would marry". At first Schweitzer was tempted. "When I considered her on one side, as to her fortune," he says frankly, "I must confess she did not altogether displease me." But this qualified approval was more than tempered by his dislike of several of the lady's physical features. Her ears worried him: "though they were richly set out with gold, they look'd but hideously, being longer than my hand"; the first factor was highly desirable; the second deplorable! Then, too, her figure was not at all attractive, while her hair, "which she would besmear every day with oyl made of Coco-nuts, and then wind it up on her head", reminded him forcibly of the long-tailed horses in his fatherland, a comparison that was hardly conducive to romantic feelings. All these facts together "were so far from raising any passion for her, that they were a preservative against it, so I e'en left her as I found her".

Nevertheless, the reluctant swain tried hard to reconcile his fastidious distaste for her person with his natural inclination for material gain, a prospect by no means to be lightly dismissed; and a little later on we find him approaching his enamoured landlady with surely one of the most extraordinary compromises ever presented to woman. If she would cease oiling her hair, and would moreover allow her ears to be clipped into shape, he declared, he would seriously consider matrimony. The lady's fortitude was not Spartan enough to induce her to accept this offer; she preferred, though regretfully, to lose a potential husband and retain the offending ears in *status quo* instead. So she shook her head and said in a doleful manner that she would die first. She bore her over-exacting cavalier no ill-will, however, and when he left she magnanimously pressed upon him an abundance of fruit and spices. Here again, though, the cautious fellow was taking no chances. As soon as he was out at sea he threw the whole load of her gifts overboard, "for fear some trick or philter should have been play'd with them . . ."!

Another widow sold one of her slaves when she fancied that he was to blame for the otherwise inexplicable defection of all her beaux, who suddenly became reticent and shy and hurriedly left her premises one by one just as they were on the point of proposing marriage to her. She insisted that the slave had bewitched her suitors.

In a case which came before the Court of Justice in 1773, a slave who had experienced some difficulty in his courtship was convinced that his problem would be solved if he placed near the bed of his coy beloved some parings of the finger-nails of one of his friends, a man who had the reputation of being able to "tover" (bewitch). Any individual accredited with this power was never *persona grata* with the authorities. Early in the eighteenth century, among a number of suspects pardoned by Governor-General van Hoorn, was Maria of Macassar, old and blind, formerly the female slave of a Batavian merchant. It appears that she had been banished to the Cape twenty-two years before, on the charge of having woven spells round her master. "Being poor and blind, she now wishes to return to her people to find her food and her end among them . . ."[88]

In several instances, Hottentot women suffered at the hands of slaves who believed that through their agency they had been bewitched. One Anthony confessed that he had dragged such a woman from her hut, and had beaten her with his kierie so violently as to cause holes and heavy wounds in her head and on the arm. He had taken these steps because for a considerable time he had endured a permanent pain in the stomach, and other Hottentots had told him that this woman could practise magic and had focussed her attention upon him. When another offender was asked why he had killed a female Hottentot, he explained that four people had died in quick succession through her baleful influence, and he had prudently decided not to be a possible fifth! At the request of the Court he described how the deceased Elsie had set to work: she went to the bedside of a sick person, blowing, sniffing, wringing and rubbing her hands, and so casting her spells upon the patient that he could not avoid death.

This power of performing supernatural acts was often claimed by slaves: in 1695 one ran away from his master and tried by every conceivable means to persuade others to follow him, adding as an additional and stronger motive that he could so bewitch them that they would be neither seen nor caught. A second troop of fugitive slaves took with them a small square card on which had been scratched with a pin certain Malay words; they firmly believed that it would protect them not only from wild animals and illness but also from all sorts of other dangers, including that of being caught by their pursuers. A further example of the credulity of the slave is the answer given by a bondsman when he was asked whether a certain person named Pantry had not imprinted in him many Moorish beliefs and superstitions; he replied piously that he had an abiding faith in Pantry, whom he had always regarded as a holy man.[89]

The appearance of a comet had a most disturbing effect

SUPERSTITIONS AND MEDICINE 129

on everybody at the Cape. "Its significance is known to the Lord," Van Riebeeck wrote of the "strange star with a tail" which manifested itself on 17 December 1652. Exactly twelve years later, when another comet was seen, Van Riebeeck's successor issued a placcaat exhorting the people to cease their uncontrolled and godless mode of living, and to attend every Sunday at the Fort to offer up prayers "to the great and jealous God, praying that He may ward off the punishment that hangs over our heads, of which we are warned by the long-rayed star — a terrible sign of vengeance which threatens us nightly from the heavens . . ." Simultaneously, Commander Wagenaar decided to deport one Ernestus Back, the sick-comforter and teacher who had fallen into a state of drunkenness and licentious conduct, as it was felt that God had given a personal warning of His righteous wrath to come if that worthless and incorrigible man were not ejected. Consequently, in obedience to the divine displeasure so impressively demonstrated, Back and his family were hurriedly bundled on board a ship leaving for Batavia.

This last-mentioned comet created much consternation among the visiting sailors as well. Wouter Schouten, who happened to be calling at the Cape at that time, tells us that these men testified to having seen a star with a tail, which later disappeared. This they all considered as a premonition of many hardships and perils which they would have to endure on their impending voyage to the fatherland. In 1682 another of these awesome celestial phenomena terrified the colonists. Its advent coincided, very suggestively, with heavy rains and an insect pest which destroyed the crops! "What will happen when the comet has sunk right down," wrote Simon van der Stel in profound trepidation, "God Almighty alone can tell."

An irresistible tendency to believe in signs and portents of one kind or another is one of the oldest of human characteristics. Here and there traces of it can be found in our own archives. The folk at the Cape used to say that when on Saturdays or Sundays many sea-winds blew and misty dark clouds banked up, such weather usually brought vessels into the bay. This was at least a familiar and recognised theory: but imagine how puzzled both whites and blacks must have been one day when two doves, with no accounting for the fact at all, were seen falling to the ground from the parapet of the Governor's house in the Castle, and, after fluttering about a little, were found to be dead without any perceptible evidence of injury. Speculation was rife, and many regarded the incident as an omen of disaster. "It certainly gives the augurists something to talk about," sagely commented the recorder of the event.

Once, when a number of slaves escaped, a pistol carried by a member of the party fired accidentally, wounding one of them in the finger. This unexpected explosion was looked upon as such an inauspicious sign that the deserters voluntarily returned without delay to their master's house, fearing human punishment, which would at least take an orthodox form, less than some incalculable supernatural retribution! On numerous occasions, too, the Devil became the scapegoat for offences committed by the slaves, who blamed him for inciting them to perpetrate the most horrible crimes; one sinner actually went so far as to lay the responsibility for his wrongdoing on "a party of small devils" who collectively urged him into it. Even among the Europeans the Devil played an important part. A survivor of the wreck of the *Grosvenor* relates in his narrative how he and some of his fellows discovered one of their crew lying upon his face in the sand, dead, with his right hand cut off at the wrist. This fact was fraught with the most sinister significance, as they all remembered that his favourite adjuration in life had been "May the Devil cut my right hand off if it be not true!"[90]

In connection with medicine and the art of healing, particularly, many popular beliefs were held without sense or reason, not at the Cape alone but universally. Only two hundred years ago, a very fashionable physician in Edinburgh tried to cure some of his patients by prescribing "the juice of twenty wood-lice squeezed through a muslin bag, twice a day". His remedy for a whitlow was even more crude and unscientific: "Stop the finger into a cat's ear," he advised, "and it will be whole in half-an-hour"! Theal tells us that the medical practitioner at the Cape in the early days — the "chirurgijn", as he was called — was more often than not a copying clerk or a soldier, with no other training than that of an assistant in a hospital. If he had any aptitude for the duties of a surgeon, he was promoted to that office; all he required was a slight knowledge of medicine and some skill in dressing wounds.

There is an interesting description given by Dr. Sparrman of a Cape physician whom he met in the 1770's. He says that this "African Aesculapius" scarcely knew the names, much less the virtues, of the divers herbs laid before him. Conversation lagged between them, and at length the traveller changed the subject to that of commerce, upon which it immediately became more brisk and fluent, a fact which caused him little surprise, "for this worthy physician's income depended more upon merchandize than upon Apollo and the Muses; and it is much the same case with the rest of the faculty at the Cape, to the great prejudice of the sick in particular as well as to that of natural knowledge and the art of medicine in general".

Perhaps, however, the apathy of this medico was excusable, or at any rate understandable, on certain grounds as described by Lichtenstein in a reference to a young itinerant physician "who was established at Swellendam, but who occasionally travelled about the country to sell medicines to the farmers, carrying them in a little chest. They consisted chiefly of doses of emetics and cathartics, and above all, of the Halle medicines so much in repute here, and which are made up in abundance by the apothecaries at the Cape Town. He confessed that his principal trade consisted in the sale of these, and asserted that nobody could subsist in this country by the ordinary course of practice, since there was not a colonist who had not rather be his own physician, and would only in cases of extreme necessity send for assistance". The lack of interest shown by some of the doctors, therefore, was probably merely a reflection of the public indifference to their ministrations.

The surgeons showed what amounted almost to an obsession for the expedient of bleeding their patients: they would "let blood" from the veins of nearly every person with whom they came into contact professionally; one "chirurgijn" even tied a cloth round his patient's neck and then opened the vein under the tongue "to give him some relief". The application of leeches (horrible blood-sucking worms) to the sick was a still more popular medical measure. If a child had the whooping-cough, a worm or two would be carefully affixed behind his ear; if he had a headache, half-a-dozen of these little parasites would be set to work on his temple. And if this failed to alleviate his sufferings, there was always, as a last resort, the Spanish-fly, used for raising blisters.

One cannot be surprised that many of those held in bondage preferred to seek medical advice from other slaves! The criminal records of 1760 contain an interesting letter written in the Bonese language by Oepas, a slave at Stellenbosch, asking September, a shepherd, to heal him of his illness, with which he had been afflicted for two months without having been cured. "Have pity on a fellow-Bonese," the writer implores. "We are all children of Boelo-Boelo in Sanja-l." September, it appears, acted as medical consultant to many of those slaves who came from the south-west peninsula of the Island of Celebes. In one case when a slave was injured in the hand, September cleaned the wound by first of all licking it and then washing it with fresh water.[91]

Even the Europeans did not always disdain to seek medical aid from slaves and other coloured people. One eighteenth-century traveller states that the Javanese had both male and female physicians, who were alleged to have effected some very surprising cures by means of their knowledge of the medicinal and vulnerary herbs; he adds that they sometimes enjoyed a wider practice among the Europeans in Batavia than those doctors "who have been regularly bred, and come over from Europe". In 1742, a Cape colonist was treated by a slave named Augustus, and perhaps we may conjecture that the man who said "Ik laboureer braaf aan de jigt kan knap te paard rijden", and the one who wrote that he found himself "den meesten tijt aen den onlijdelijcke pijnlijcke colicq bed leger leggende", also turned eventually to the black man for medicaments.

Much faith was placed in the curative powers of various herbs. From the Bantu a good deal was learned concerning the value of certain medicinal plants; from their own experience and observation the Europeans and their slaves became acquainted with the use of many more. *Buchu* for diseases of the bladder and as an embrocation; the *truidjie roer my nie* as a gargle and lotion for sore throats and affections of the gum; wild garlic for lung complaints; *heuningtee* as a restorative; *bitterwortel* for colic; *dagga* and raw fat for pains in the eyes; aloes for stomach trouble; so-called *davidjies* as an emetic and a purgative: these were a few of the more popular herbs employed to relieve the sufferings of both master and slave in the early days.

Sparrman has an interesting story to tell about the aloe plant. He says that its medicinal value had long been unknown to the colonists, even though there had always been in the service of the Government a number of negro slaves who were not similarly ignorant of its properties, having learned the method of its preparation as well as its value at their birthplace on the African coast. "But bowing as they did beneath the yoke of slavery, they would rather at any time have seen a dart pierce the hearts of their tyrants, than be instrumental in procuring them any additional knowledge or wealth of what kind soever; by which, on the one side, the pride, avarice, and power of their masters, and on the other side, their work, as well as the number of slaves employed would be increased. For this reason, the use of the aloe was for a long time kept a secret among the slaves; who, indeed, made a point of conscience of not revealing it, till one of them, called Goree, discovered it to a colonist . . . who had, through this discovery, obtained an exclusive privilege for the delivery of a certain quantity of aloes to the East India Company, and had given up to Goree the inspection of the whole work. It is likewise after the name of this slave, that the aloe plant is still to this day in Africa most commonly, if not solely, called the Goree-bosch."

As far back as 1694, an emancipated slave who was on trial for seduction confessed that a slave woman had explained to him how his victim could have procured an abortion. She had even pointed out the necessary herb, and had told him how the sap was to be extracted and used.[92] On another occasion we read of a runaway slave who, when pursued, tried to commit suicide by cutting his throat with a knife; when he realised, however, that he had eluded those on his trail, he healed the wound by the application of leaves from the olive-tree. The stories of the efficacy of all these herbs and simples we can accept as true, in part at any rate if not in full. But we must remain completely mystified by a prescription which old Dr. Schabort of Drakenstein recommended — namely, roasted "hartebeest hoorn"! Apparently he kept a sort of private hospital, for we can still read an account rendered by him for treating a sick slave, whom he looked after at his own place in Drakenstein for three days in 1733.

The snakestone (*slangesteen*) was often used in cases of snake-bite. A specimen was shown at Tulbagh to Dr. Thunberg, who stated that these stones were sold at such a prohibitive price that few of the farmers could afford to purchase them, although they were held in great esteem. The snakestone was imported from the Indies, especially from Malabar, and it cost, according to Thunberg, between ten and twelve rixdollars. It was round, convex on one side, of a black hue with a pale ash-grey speck in the middle, and tubulated with minute pores. Kolbe saw the snakestone applied to the swollen and inflamed arm of a child who had been bitten. It adhered closely to the puncture and did not fall off until it was saturated with poison; it was then soaked in milk, which turned yellow, and was finally replaced on the wound until all the poison had been drawn out.

Thunberg also describes its use by a colonist who had been struck in the leg by a *ringhals* snake. Unluckily this man was several miles away from his farm when the mishap occurred, but, having bound up the poisoned limb tightly, he sent a slave to fetch his horse with all possible speed. On his return home he became semi-comatose, so that his wife could scarcely rouse him, and he went suddenly and totally blind as well, a condition which persisted for a fortnight. The wound was washed with salt water, the patient drank quantities of milk, and then the "serpent-stone" was applied. Gradually he recovered, but for years afterwards he still suffered pains during any change of weather, and at times the wound broke out anew completely.

SUPERSTITIONS AND MEDICINE

Thunberg's statements regarding the price and the popularity of the snakestone can be verified in the official records; towards the close of the eighteenth century Pieter du Preez sold one for ten rixdollars at Swellendam; and in the inventory of the estate of Governor van Assenburgh a snakestone is mentioned among his possessions. The same writer tells us that the blood of the turtle was much extolled as an antidote against the bite of serpents. The colonists dried it in the form of small scales or membranes and carried these about with them, so that if any one of them was bitten he could immediately swallow a couple of pinches of the substance, and could also apply a little of it externally to the injury. A Hottentot in like case went at once in search of a toad, with which he rubbed the wound and thus effected a perfect cure. The account book of Dr. Bergh, dated 1708, includes an interesting item supplied to one of his patients: "*schlangen houd*: two gulden". Snakewood is defined as an East Indian climbing plant with a bitter taste, supposed to be a remedy for the bite of the hooded serpent.

The Europeans by no means despised the methods of the Hottentots in treating snake-bite. In 1658 the journalist at the Castle reported that "a man of the *Harp,* busy working in the Liesbeeck River . . . was bitten by an adder on the side of the foot, which began to swell very much and to become inflamed, but when brought into the Fort and doctored by the barbers, the swelling decreased and also the fainting fits. We hope for the best. The Hottentots know of efficacious and immediate remedies, but none of them was at hand, otherwise we should have employed them, having had sufficient proof of what they can do".

That the blacks themselves did not always reciprocate this confidence, as regards the Europeans' curative measures in general, is illustrated by an unusual case worth quoting in full:

"A son of the burgher councillor, Elbert Diemer, about eleven years old, was this morning in the Hospital, where, with a Hottentot boy of about the same age, he had been eating a watermelon. After that they began pelting each other with the skins; this play, however, ended seriously on the part of young Diemer, who drew a knife from his pocket and stabbed the Hottentot in his left breast, and then ran away, without anyone knowing whither. Truly a sad misfortune for the parents. If that happens in the green wood, what will it be in the dry?" The little wounded Hottentot was taken to the surgeon, but later it was discovered that he had escaped — or had been removed by other Hottentots, most likely believing that with their own natural knowledge they might better cure him.

Many inhabitants of the Cape, of all classes, found that health could be restored at the Warm Baths, Caledon. It is recorded that Commissary Cnoll, for example, who was afflicted with "a heavy and depressing hoarseness, accompanied by a hard feeling both on the left and right sides and also in the belly", after two immersions in the waters of the *spa* startled the attendants by producing "a noise in his chest like the sound of a pot of stew or starch boiling on a fire", and within fifteen days of this curious but apparently salutary reaction made a full recovery. Ailing slaves were often sent to Caledon, where a separate bath was placed at their disposal. There is pathos in the story recounted by Sparrman of a young Madagascar slave who had a chronic ulcer in his leg. A surgeon at the Cape had given him up as incurable, and now he was trying to regain his health at the Baths. He told the traveller that once before, when he was in a state of freedom in his native country, he had had the same infirmity, but then it had been cured in a few days by means of the bark of a certain tree, bruised between two stones and laid on the part. He added that he knew the tree very well and had seen its bark used with equal success by many of his countrymen; but that since his arrival in Africa he had looked for it in vain.

A smithy at the Cape, Matthys Greft by name, gained local fame for the healing virtues said to be contained in his plasters for the breast. He never charged any fees, and when he died he took his secret with him. He had not divulged it even to his slaves — those unfortunate human guinea-pigs on whom he had always first of all tested the plasters. We read also of a Bugunese slave who had achieved many cures in the colony, notably that of a female slave suffering in an advanced degree from the effects of the virulent *geitje's* bite;

unluckily he, too, went to the grave without disclosing the nature of any of his remedies.

In describing the medicines made up at the apothecary's shop in the Heerengracht, Captain Cook probably hit the nail on the head when he expressed the opinion that the method of administering to all patients indiscriminately out of two or three huge bottles, full of different preparations, "suffices to convince us that the fresh air of the land and fresh provisions here, contribute much more to the recovery of the sick than the skill of their physicians".

The first hospital nurses appointed in South Africa were slaves — both men and women — who had to pay every attention to the comfort of the sick by moving and lifting them, making their beds, cleaning and washing the mattresses and blankets and generally helping the invalids. Originally only three male and three female slaves were enrolled, but their ranks were augmented from time to time until in later years sixteen male slaves, but no females, were assigned to assist the convalescents. Simultaneously the matron who had been installed to superintend the slaves was dismissed, as it was felt that the office was entirely incompatible with the status of a woman.[93]

In 1656, during the time of Jan van Riebeeck, the first hospital was built. Needless to say, this establishment left a great deal to be desired. In close proximity to the cattle-sheds and the smithy, it stood within the precincts of the Fort. Constructed of planks and thatched with reeds, it was buffeted in winter by the north-west winds, while in summer the odour of rotten seaweed from the neighbouring beaches rendered it almost uninhabitable. The second hospital at the Cape was erected during the governorship of Simon van der Stel. He selected for its site the ground between the upper ends of the present Adderley and St. George's Streets. This comparatively immense building, which was commenced in 1697 and completed on 24 October 1699, was designed to admit five hundred patients without crowding and seven hundred and fifty in an emergency. The third and last of these institutions to be raised was situated in the vicinity of the Castle and was large enough to accommodate one thousand four hundred and fifty persons, with quarters for the medical officers and attendants, and spacious store-houses. The foundation stone was laid by Governor van Plettenberg on 2 November 1772. In 1781 the French regiment of Pondicherry was quartered in a wing of the building, which was demolished in 1903.

From time to time helpful suggestions were made for the greater comfort of the invalids. For instance, it was noticed that on Robben and Dassen Islands and also at Saldanha Bay the pastures were so good that cattle having run there a few months became as fit as could be wished, and consequently a plan was mooted that periodically a large number of these animals should be sent to those places, "for the benefit of the ships and the poor sick, the chief thing to be borne in mind at the Cape, and the reason why the Company bears the heavy expenses there". The mental wellbeing of the patients, too, was not overlooked. In a letter received at the Cape from the authorities, we read: "Your regulations for the hospital we approve of; they have been drawn up with much care, and are practical. We expect a good result from them. It would likewise not be unserviceable if the minister or sick comforter, when sometimes visiting the sick, encouraged them with an edifying and comforting word, as the care for the salvation of the soul is . . . as necessary as that of the body".

There was at least one instance in which a ship was used as a makeshift hospital, as the following record shows: "The *Swarte Leeuw*, employed for a long time as a hospital for convalescents, we found . . . to be so leaky and rotten that, in order to lighten her, we took out her 28 guns; afterwards on inspection she was declared unseaworthy, and . . . we decided to sink her before the wharf . . . The *Standvastigheid* has taken her place".

Usually, however, the reverse was the case, and it was not uncommon for ships from the fatherland to burden the hospital with hundreds of indisposed people. In 1695 there were close on a thousand crippled, maimed, sick and injured folk inside its walls. In that year, four ships arrived one day with two hundred and seventy-three dead and four hundred and six ill, "endangering the safety of the vessels and causing a heavy loss to the Company, as the men cost much money and are with difficulty to be had". Often the pottery, the kraal, private houses, lofts, tents and even the Slave Lodge were utilised for the overflow.

How well the slave nurses discharged their duties can be gathered from an entry in the journal which records that, after a vessel called the *Delfshaven* had entered Table Bay and yielded up the customary batch of incapacitated persons, some of these convalescents began within a short time to show themselves in the streets and to walk abroad in fine weather, while others, whose legs were still weak, crept about on hands and feet out-of-doors, or were carried into the open air. They had one and all enjoyed the refreshments as well as the nursing at the hospital. Slaves of both sexes who took ill were also admitted to the institution and received the same rations and attention as were given to the Europeans —at any rate until the authorities realised that this encouraged the idle ones to feign sickness, when it was resolved to reduce their daily portion of one pound of meat to half that amount, although the quantity of vegetables was to remain unchanged.[94]

In 1713 a terrible calamity fell upon the country. In March of that year the small-pox made its début in South Africa, having been introduced by means of some infected clothing from a visiting ship. These garments, the property of certain of the ship's personnel who, though now recovered, had suffered from the disease during the passage from India, were sent to be washed at the Company's Slave Lodge. The washerwomen who handled it were the first to be smitten, and of the five hundred and seventy slaves of both sexes and all ages belonging to the Company, nearly two hundred were carried off within the next six months. From the slaves the contagion spread to the Europeans and the Hottentots. Theal gives us a graphic description of the event: "In May and June there was hardly a family in the town that had not someone sick or dead. Traffic in the streets was suspended, and even the children ceased to play their usual games in the squares and open places. At last it was impossible to obtain nurses, though slave women were being paid at the rate of four to five shillings a day. All the planks in the stores were used, and in July it became necessary to bury the dead without coffins. For two months there was no meeting of the Court of Justice, for debts and quarrels were forgotten in the presence of the terrible scourge. The minds of the people were so depressed that anything unusual inspired them with terror . . . the very clouds and the darkness of winter storms seemed to be threatening death and woe. During that dreadful winter nearly one-fourth of the European inhabitants of the town perished, and only when the hot weather set in did the plague cease".

Forty-two years later this pestilence broke out again, having originated in similar circumstances. It followed on an epidemic of scarlet fever in a severe form which raged at the Cape in April 1755, and it reached such virulence that from May to September about one thousand persons of European birth and about as many slaves succumbed to it. The Company itself was so short of slaves that the Batavian authorities sent some — all of whom had already experienced small-pox — to replace those who had died at the Cape. So many slaves in the Lodge were laid low at the time that the Governor requested the surgeons to investigate the conditions under which they were living, and to ascertain whether anything could be done to aid them.

In a signed report the surgeons stated that they had examined the one hundred and eighty victims of small-pox in the Lodge, but to their sorrow had found that only about a sixth part of that number were likely to survive, as the rest were all stricken with the most dangerous kind of confluent disease. Meanwhile, however, proper medical attention was being accorded them; their food and clothing were entirely adequate; the nursing and care given by other slaves were laudable; and the apartment in which they lay was spacious and large, and so constructed that when the air was warm it could be ventilated or, when rough weather came, could be closed to prevent the intrusion of wind and cold. These surgeons reported also that the epidemic had for some time prevailed only in and around certain small houses situated along the beach, and had at first sprung up among the slaves. As some of the owners in Table Valley had no suitable accommodation for their slaves and were consequently obliged to domicile them in their homes, while others had only extremely limited space in which to house them, it naturally happened that when one slave became infected the sickness soon spread.

As a result of this report two temporary hospitals were established: one for poor Europeans, supported by the board of deacons, and the other for blacks. To the latter were sent all slaves attacked by the epidemic, at the expense of one shilling and fourpence per day each, which amount was to be paid by their owners.[95] Those who recovered were employed as nurses. Slave-owners who did not immediately advise the hospital authorities of any outbreak of disease among their slaves rendered themselves liable to a heavy fine. Even after the warm weather had set in and the violence of the scourge had abated, householders were warned to open the doors and windows of all houses under their charge, and to have the bedding used during the sickness thoroughly cleansed and aired.

So much was learned from experience during these two outbreaks that when the dreaded disease again manifested itself in 1767 only one hundred and seventy-nine Europeans and two hundred and fifty-one slaves died. In the cash book of the Burgher Council for that year we find a long list of inhabitants from whom payment had been received for the maintenance of their slaves who were in the hospital. On the credit side of this book we notice that payments were made to a surgeon for attendance on these invalids, rent was paid for two houses used as a slave hospital, and fees were given to a maternity nurse for having tended the women among the stricken slaves.

It has been said that in olden times it was a dangerous thing to be ill, an expensive thing to die and a ruinous thing to be buried. Certain it is that in the seventeenth and eighteenth centuries people were obsessed with the idea that their relatives and friends should be given as splendid funerals as possible; a large and imposing ceremony, they contended, was a proper mark of respect to the dead. Those were the days when *huilebalken* and *tropsluiters* were employed. The former were professional mourners who were paid to weep copiously at funerals. Their tears flowed easily; their sobs and their sighs as they followed the procession, and their wailings at the graveside, made up in volume what they lacked in sincerity. The office of the *tropsluiters* was merely to lengthen the funeral cortège. They were hired for two reasons: firstly because a large gathering was regarded as a token of esteem to the deceased, and secondly because kinsmen and friends liked to see a long row of people behind them, on the assumption that the nearer they were to the corpse, in precedence, the greater was their distinction.

After a body had been laid to rest, it was the custom that those attending — many of whom had probably travelled some distance to be present — were invited to return to the house of the newly-departed to partake of refreshments. The mourners were regaled with coffee, beer, wine, brandy, pastry, sausages, poultry, tobacco, snuff and so on. Sometimes the glass went round with such insidious rapidity that mourning turned to merrymaking. This strange custom, by the way, was practised in other lands too. We read, for instance, of the funeral of the mother of Forbes of Culloden, in Scotland. Long before the time came for the company to follow the hearse to the cemetery, every person was three sheets in the wind. However, with torches flaring and coronachs sounding, the mourners set out in due course for the kirkyard. Imagine their surprise and consternation when, on arriving at the graveside, they discovered that they had left the corpse behind!

The Hottentots and the slaves, always faithful imitators of the Europeans, greatly admired this habit of entertaining friends at a funeral: in the records of the Court of Justice, we find Jacob Dikkop sending for two casks of wine with which to treat those who attended a certain funeral. And when Adam Tas heard of the death of Henning Huysing's farmhand, he dispatched forthwith to Stellenbosch, for the bearers and those who followed the body, some wine, a ham, three fat quarters of roast mutton and three loaves, "so that they might make merry withal". In his diary he mentioned that there had been a fair attendance; that some of the food had been left over; but that the wine had given out — "so Arij has been buried in tolerable good sort".[96]

Slaves, once they had obtained their freedom, made

SUPERSTITIONS AND MEDICINE

arrangements, in the event of funerals, to have these ceremonies as ostentatious as possible. Take the case of Manual of Macassar, for instance, the account for whose funeral expenses in 1718 we find filed in the records of the Orphan Chamber. Manual was at one time the slave of Jan de la Fontaine's mother-in-law, and when he died Jacob of the Coast received forty rixdollars as compensation for the trouble he took in attending to all the details of the interment. Amongst the items of expenditure appear the following:

	Rds.	Sch.	Stivers.
Coffin	10	—	—
Pipes and tobacco	1	3	2
Tea and sugar	—	6	—
Candles and linen	1	3	3
Half aum wine	6	—	—
300 cakes, cracklings and rasped bread	3	6	—
12 paid mourners	—	6	—
Grave shroud and bier	—	3	—
Gravedigger	1½	—	—
Undertaker	4	—	—

According to an old Indian placcaat, a freed slave who had no children was required to leave one-quarter of his estate to the person who had given him his freedom. In the case of Manual, we read that Mrs. de la Fontaine received a sum of money out of the estate, as her mother, the slave's quondam mistress, had already passed away.

One writer recorded that — unlike the natives of Malabar and Mozambique, who expressed their sorrow at the graveside in a most vociferous manner, often seeming "to begin and end in concert" their noisy grief — the Malays mourned their deceased friends in dignified and pensive silence. This attitude was actually the more sincerely sorrowful one, for whereas the other slaves soon recovered from their woe "the Malays alone extend their care and seem to cherish their grief. On the third, seventh, tenth, fortieth and hundredth day, they again assemble round the grave, pour sweet-scented waters upon it, and strew over it the choicest flowers. They bid the earth lie lightly on the breast of their former companion, and for the last time mingle their tears together over him. Having thus performed the last duties of friendship and affection, they return and feast together, well assured that their friend is happy".

We learn that when a soldier or a sailor died in hospital, it was customary to sell his effects by auction, the money gained thereby being laid out on his burial. In general the corpse was sewn up in a cloth and carried away in a hearse; but if the possessions of the deceased — after the best part of them had been embezzled! — still brought in a small sum of money, a coffin was provided for him. And if what the defunct had left behind him realised a yet larger sum, it was expended in wine at his funeral — assiduous care being taken that nothing should remain for his relatives and heirs! For urgent reasons, incidentally, it was considered necessary that neither the superintendent of the hospital nor his assistants should be allowed "to profit by any testamentary dispensations of the sick, unless it be a few bits of clothing or a trifle".

During the small-pox epidemic, the surgeons declared, observation had taught them that both fresh meat and newly-baked bread drew to themselves very strongly all foul humours, and it was therefore regarded as desirable to abolish the custom of offering to those who came to pay their last respects even the smallest piece of cake in the house of mourning.[97] At the same time residents were also interdicted from selling, hiring or lending slaves the usual black clothes in which to attend funerals. In the previous year the slave code of Governor Tulbagh and his Council had been published; one of the clauses prohibited the presence of more than twenty slaves at the burial of a companion; the number was to be regulated according to the rank of the owner of the deceased. And, in accordance with the spirit of the Sumptuary Laws, by which all undue display was forbidden, a European slave-owner was not allowed to dress his slaves in mourning clothes when a member of his family had passed away.

When it was noticed that slaves were carelessly interred — many of them being barely covered over — and that the people generally employed as undertaker whomsoever they liked, regulations were issued and special gravediggers appointed. None other could thereafter be engaged, unless in extraordinary circumstances. These gravediggers, more often than not, were widows. A woman thus bereaved was sometimes permitted on compassionate grounds to work for remuneration, especially if she had numerous children to support — in other words, in a case "when the cradle has for some years never been at rest in the family, and the coffin never been required".

Chapter Eight

THE ADMINISTRATION OF JUSTICE

AS the seventeenth century was drawing to a close, there arrived at the Cape of Good Hope a Chinaman who had been detected in the perpetration of an unnatural and abominable crime, which in the ordinary way would have earned him the death sentence. "The mildness of our laws, however," it was said in a letter which accompanied him from Batavia, "requires that no one shall be executed or condemned unless he personally confesses to the crime of which he is accused." The prisoner, although tortured, had made no avowal; it had therefore been decided to banish him for life. The infliction of torture as a means of eliciting evidence from a witness, or of obtaining the confession of an accused person when the proof of his guilt was conclusive but he would not acknowledge it, was never looked upon as anything but a normal factor in judicial procedure. The records of the seventeenth and eighteenth centuries contain numerous references to the consignment of both white and blacks to the "pyn kaemer".[98]

As in England, the rack was the favourite engine of torture. It consisted of a large frame upon which the body was gradually stretched until, sometimes, the joints were dislocated. Another method employed for extorting confession was that of affixing a heavy weight to each of the examinee's big toes, fastening his wrists together with a rope passed over a beam in the roof, hoisting him up and then allowing him to dangle in mid-air. Other instruments of torture and death included the gibbet, whipping- and strangling-posts, the cross and the wheel upon which limbs were broken, the wooden horse, the strappado — a device for pulling up the victim to a certain height and then letting him fall so that his bones would be fractured — the headsman's axe, thumbscrews, the pillory, stocks, branding-irons and, for whipping, ropes' ends, split bamboo-canes and the sjambok.

The use of the cross and the wheel is described in some detail by Mentzel: lightly lashed to a double wooden cross, an ill-fated sufferer would be beaten with a heavy iron club on his arms and legs until they were broken. "In some cases the *coup de grace* is then administered by a blow on the chest with the same instrument; if this is not done, the wretched man may be stretched by chains on a wheel, notwithstanding his broken limbs, and linger on in agony until death releases him . . ." Riding the wooden horse was another form of punishment — reserved for soldiers and sailors — frequently mentioned in the records. This contraption consisted of a wooden horse's head attached to a sharp-edged body on high legs, and on it a culprit was forced to sit for days on end, with ponderous weights suspended from his feet. It was a cruel ordeal which often permanently disabled the man. His awkward posture made him the butt of unfeeling taunts, and he would be plied with all sorts of questions, such as would he be good enough to deliver a letter on horseback?

In 1782 a burgher was condemned to be taken to the place of execution and handed over to the executioner, who would then blindfold him, make him kneel on a mound of sand and chop off his head. This sentence having been carried out, it was disclosed in an entry in the journal that the hapless man had been decapitated by means of a machine constructed locally for such a purpose and set into operation, presumably as an experiment, for the first time. We must infer that the secretary approved of the innovation and felt a certain patriotic pride in this home-made guillotine, for he added, after his record of the event, that he had made a sketch of it.[99]

An offender sentenced to be scourged was tied to a post with his hands fastened above his head, and the lashes were laid on the back and shoulders. The executioner inflicted the first stripe, his chief assistant the next few; form and precedence having thus been observed, the remainder were given by the Caffres. Certainly there would have been little chance at the Cape for anything so ludicrous as the occurrence in an English village related by the poet Cowper in a letter to the Reverend John Newton, and quoted in the book *Old-Time Punishments*. It appears that during a fire at Olney, England, in 1783, under cover of the general confusion a man stole some ironwork. The pilferer was apprehended, tried and condemned to be whipped.

"The fellow," wrote Cowper, "seemed to show great fortitude; but it was all an imposition. The beadle who whipped him had his left hand filled with red ochre, through which, after every stroke, he drew the lash of the whip, leaving the appearance of a wound upon the skin, but in reality not hurting him at all. This being perceived by the constable, who followed the beadle to see that he did his duty, he (the constable) applied the cane, without any such management or precaution, to the shoulders of the beadle. The scene now became interesting and exciting. The beadle could by no means be induced to strike the thief hard, which provoked the constable to strike harder; and so the double flogging continued, until a lass of Silver End, pitying the pitiful beadle thus suffering under the hands of the pityless constable, joined the procession, and placing herself immediately behind the constable, seized him by his capillary club, and pulling him backwards by the same, slapped his face with Amazonian fury." And so, the poet concluded, the beadle thrashed the thief, the constable the beadle and the lady the constable — the thief being the only one whipped who suffered nothing.

Usually it was necessary only to take the accused into the torture-chamber — *ad actum proximum,* as was said — to obtain the desired confession. The very sight of the wicked-looking appliances awaiting him more often than not persuaded the prisoner to repent and make a true admission of his crimes. But there were exceptions, of course. A slave named Fortuyn was suspended in the air three separate times, with first a twenty-five pound weight and then one of fifty pounds attached to each big toe; but he would not confess, although he died as a result of the excruciating pain. Two sailors were more fortunate: arrested for burglary, they denied the crime and were sentenced to be brought *ad*

THE ADMINISTRATION OF JUSTICE

actum proximum and then, in the event of no confession, to the full torture "according to the custom of the country". Nevertheless, they persistently refused to avow their guilt, and as the charge could not be proved against them they were set free.[100]

An interesting case recorded in the archives is that of a European accused of having killed a black man. On 18 March 1707 he was threatened with torture, as he continued obdurately to deny the charge. In the presence of nearly all the members of the Court of Justice he was escorted on the following day to the torture-chamber, but he could not be induced to confess the whole of his guilt. Three days later he was condemned to the full torture; still he would not commit himself. Next day fifty-pound weights were hung from his toes, "but though he confessed a little, he confessed nothing of what was required"!

It not infrequently happened that accused persons admitted their alleged guilt when the instruments of torture were applied, only to retract their admissions as soon as the ordeal was over. But the authorities frowned upon such vacillation, as the slave Domingo of Angola learned to his cost. After having confessed his culpability on a charge of sheep-stealing, he took back his words, and subsequently made a second confession. The Court of Justice decided forthwith to inflict torture just in case Domingo changed his mind again, and they hanged him before he could give the matter further consideration. Once during the administration of Governor van der Graaff a white man was put to torture and, for the purpose of obtaining relief from his agony, professed himself guilty of an offence of which he was afterwards proved innocent, but for which he had none the less suffered punishment. This, however, was an isolated case, taking place at a time when the Cape was in a state of turmoil. Ordinarily, positive evidence was required before a suspect could be sent to the torture-chamber — "only upon such proofs as would alone amount to sufficient certainty, only that in such event nothing else is wanting but the confession of the accused, in order to convict him with sufficient certainty of the offence out of his own mouth".

This principle is illustrated by the report of a commission sent on board the ship *Mees*. She had lain for five days at Falmouth, where one man had deserted, six had died and the majority of the remainder were sick. They had been becalmed for weeks on the line, and for five weeks off the Cape. The officers maintained that several of the soldiers had planned to kill a number of their superiors and to take possession of the ship, and as a result the ship's Council had put the thumbscrews on one of these potential mutineers — "the pain of which the latter still had fresh in his memory, whilst the scar was still visible on his left thumb". When, however, the Fiscal at the Cape sent a commission aboard, these gentlemen reported that the soldiers vehemently denied the confessions which they had made to the ship's Council, averring that these had been extorted under fear of torture; and as the commission could obtain no evidence to enable them to proceed further against the men, it was decided that no justification existed for legal torture to be introduced.

There are, unfortunately, instances on record in which the officers of justice went beyond all limits in torturing and punishing their fellow-creatures — the worst undoubtedly being the actions of Petrus Vuyst, who was appointed Governor of Ceylon in 1726: the third highest position in the Dutch East Indies. No sooner had he landed in Ceylon than it became apparent that he was a man of difficult and eccentric temperament. Constantly he decried the work of his predecessors, and said that he would rule the island "with the wisdom of a Solomon and the boldness of a Vuyst". It is also said that this foolish and fanatical man's first act on landing at Galle was to clap a plaster over one of his eyes, in order to show the people of Ceylon that he did not need two eyes to rule a land of such small dimensions.

He started off by unjustly accusing a number of people of treason and sedition, and subjected twenty-nine of them, including an old man of seventy years of age, to torture. Such an evil influence did this sadistic Governor exercise over the frightened members of the Court of Justice that people said it was as though the Devil himself was reigning in Ceylon. Some of the unfortunate European inhabitants were tortured six times in succession — burning matches

THE ADMINISTRATION OF JUSTICE 151

were placed between their fingers, hot sealing-wax was poured over their lacerated backs . . . Every conceivable cruelty was practised — in fact, the Governor had so intimidated the members of the Court that the duties of prosecutor, judge and executioner virtually fell into his own hands.

Meanwhile, news that all was not well had reached the authorities and, after nineteen of the accused persons had been either broken on the wheel or hanged, instructions came from Batavia that Vuyst should return immediately, and a thorough enquiry was made into the occurrences. When the full evidence was eventually laid before the Council of Seventeen, they were horrified and deeply grieved at the shedding of innocent blood, and requested that the ex-Governor should be brought to trial without loss of time. The outcome of the case was that Vuyst was conducted to the place of execution, completely undressed and tied to a chair, and the executioner then cut his throat with a slightly curved knife. His body was thrown on a table, quartered with a chopper and finally cast into a large pot, in which it was burnt to ashes, together with his clothes, the chair, the table, the knife and the chopper. That night the ashes were collected in a bag, taken out to sea in a rowing-boat and dropped into the waters. What amazed the onlookers at the trial was the fact that Vuyst showed not the slightest sign of emotion, from the time when he heard his sentence to his last moment on earth. Seven years later the rest of these who had composed the Court of Justice — four of whom had died in confinement — were set free, as the Directors felt that no good purpose would be served by prolonging the case.

Even women, both white and black, were not exempt from torture as a method of extracting confession. When a certain European widow refused to acknowledge the alleged fact that she had ordered her slaves to kill and salt down a cow belonging to a Hottentot, which had strayed into her own herd, she was "brought to a successful confession by castigation with rods" — a measure employed also with slaves. We read, too, of a slave girl who was accused in 1750 of having murdered her master. At first she was subjected to a minor degree of torture, but when she persisted in stubborn denial the full torture was applied, and, "naar eeventjes aan de Pleije opgehaalt en wederom neergelaten te syn", she admitted her guilt. When her statement was afterwards read out to her she repudiated it, saying that she had only desired to escape from the torture-chamber. It required merely the threat of a repetition, however, to make her finally admit her crime.[101]

For sheer audacity the following case is perhaps unique: two European housebreakers denied the allegations made against them, and were sent back to their cell to think things over. They took advantage of the respite to dig a passage beneath the threshold of the door, crept through it, stole the very rope with which they had been put to torture, tied it to a gun, slid down it from the ramparts — and escaped in the darkness to liberty.

Another way of extorting confessions was to keep the prisoner in solitary confinement in the Black Hole at the Castle, on a diet of bread and water, for four to six weeks. Mentzel tells us that this treatment had such a depressing effect upon anyone subjected to it that, when brought up for examination, he would be so tired of life as to be willing to acknowledge everything, "to leave this world the more speedily". Sometimes private owners assumed the privilege of torturing their slaves themselves when they wished to obtain any confession from them, although this procedure was legally an offence. Thus, in one instance, the master of a little slave girl aged nine suspected that she had been responsible for setting his house on fire. As the youngster staunchly protested her innocence, he and his wife took her into the stable and squeezed her thumb with a pair of pincers, deaf to her cries for mercy. She then confessed, but to their chagrin retracted her words when her thumb was freed. The inhuman couple thereupon applied the pincers to her other thumb, releasing it only when she admitted having set fire to a number of houses and promised to tell the Landdrost of Stellenbosch of all her sins, providing that her mistress did not thrash her in the meanwhile. In due course the Landdrost sold her to another master, fined her original owner and forced him to pay the costs of the case in full. Beyond all reasonable doubt, he said, the little black child had had nothing whatever to do with the crime of arson; and the man who had maltreated her was severely reprimanded for having taken the law into his own hands.[102]

It will be recalled that masters were allowed by law to punish their slaves domestically without the interference of the Fiscal or the Landdrosts, but the blacks had the right to complain if they were ill-used. It was a generally accepted fact that a large number of the slaves were always inclined to dissolute conduct, and that they took no interest whatsoever in the welfare of their owners, which frequently obliged the latter, when reasoning with them or verbal correction failed, to resort to corporal punishment. One can well understand that most of the slaves preferred being privately chastised to being publicly punished under the eye of the Fiscal, and, because of this, in many families the slaves' transgressions were not brought to the cognizance of the Fiscal or the Landdrost unless absolutely necessary.

Occasionally even women owners tended to take the punishment of their slaves into their own hands. One such woman admitted having said to her slave that the Fiscal did not know as well as she how to make the black people conduct themselves properly — "de Fiscaal weet niet soo goed als ik om jou L: goed te maaken" — and thereupon beat him to death. In another case an elderly white woman's treatment of her slave brought down on her head the stern censure of the Secretary of the Council. It was a matter for astonishment, he declared, that a woman of her advanced years, whose thoughts should most certainly be turned towards higher things which would benefit her immortal soul, should contemplate instead malevolent revenge and hatred. "What is there more inhuman," he added, "than that a creature whose last grains of sand, according to the laws of nature, are already running in the hour-glass . . . should behave in such an ungodly and tyrannous way?"[103]

Occasionally the harshness of some masters — and, as we have seen, some mistresses — towards their slaves was beyond description. A certain farmer was exiled for ten years to Mauritius for having assaulted the cornet of the burgher dragoons. He managed to escape into the interior, and nine years later was back at Drakenstein, where he and his wife mishandled their slave woman in a fashion that can be classified only as bestial, and so horrible in all its ramifications that it does not bear repetition here. Among other measures, they hoisted her with chains above a fire and left her there until parts of her flesh fell off. The farmer was sentenced to four years' hard labour and subsequent banishment to Europe. When he returned to the Cape some years afterwards, he was condemned to be exiled for life on Robben Island, where in the course of time he died.[104]

In another case of extreme cruelty, for six hours on end — with occasional short intervals while certain of the onlookers and participants drank wine and smoked pipes — an unfortunate slave was beaten by his master and a numerous collection of people, including other slaves and Hottentots besides members of the owner's family. When the master relinquished the whip, he passed it over to a farm-hand with the words "T'zaa Joost, nu is het uw beurt" (Sa, Joost, now it is your turn).[105]

As a result of the inhuman treatment meted out by a few slave-owners, it was decided that from a certain date no slave should be buried without a permit from the Fiscal or the Landdrost, in order to prevent such masters from avoiding their just punishment. As it was discovered, too, that some slaves, put into chains after the commission of offences, were loaded with over-heavy shackles, a law was established which prohibited the use of chains without a similar official permit, and ordered that these should be set on the victim only by the master smith at the Castle, any free blacksmith being expressly forbidden to do this work, "as the cruelty practised in this respect exceeds all other kinds of maltreatment".[106]

Throughout the Company's régime at the Cape, the infliction privately of drastic punishment upon a slave was looked upon with considerable disapproval by the authorities, who — as the old records here and there show — deeply deplored the treatment sometimes accorded to bondsmen by wretches incapable of those feelings which elevate men above the level of the beast. In the Fiscal's Rolls for 1785 we find mention of a case brought against a burgher who illtreated his slave, one of the principal reasons being that the latter had failed to bring home the money received for some vegetables which he had been told to sell in the streets. Not only did this owner put rings and chains on the man but he also placed an iron ring round his neck and two iron horns on his head. Some inhabitants, said the Fiscal, could never be pleased by their slaves, and used these creatures with less regard than that shown to the worst kinds of animals; these poor people consequently became desperate, and committed crimes against the interests of the country; numerous proofs of his contention could be found in the records, and he himself felt that more care should be exercised generally; in this particular instance, he pointed out, the burgher's love for vengeance knew no bounds.[107]

In a certain case dealing with an offence committed by a slave, Parkat of Timor, after sentence had been passed the President of the Court addressed the members, saying that although the accused no doubt deserved the punishment which he was about to receive, in his opinion the crime had been actuated chiefly by the rough handling dealt out to all his slaves by the owner, Abraham Cloppenberg. The President therefore suggested that it would be advisable and in the Christian spirit, in view of Cloppenberg's notoriously bad treatment of those in his possession, which was a well-known fact among the inhabitants, to send two members of the Court to interview him, for the purpose of emphasising to him the dangerous results likely to follow on such behaviour, of warning him to be less uncontrolled and ill-tempered, and of cautioning him that the Government expected him in future to treat these unhappy beings in a more humane fashion. Everybody present heartily agreed with this proposal, and it was duly carried out.[108]

One of the most infamous cases on record concerning the private punishment of slaves is that implicating a shoemaker named Braun, whose home was thrice set on fire by his slaves in revenge for the unmerciful chastisement to which he subjected them. On the last occasion he was warned by the authorities that on no account was he to purchase another slave, although he was allowed to retain a slave girl owned by him on the strict understanding that he treated her properly. Previously one of his slave girls had drowned herself in a well because of his brutal ill-usage, and another slave who was learning the shoemaker's trade from him, tired of being kicked and beaten whenever his master was in a rage, had nearly succeeded in a deliberate attempt to burn the house down. The slave girl left in his possession begged Braun several times on her bended knees to sell her, but he refused; at length, in desperation, she too tried to set fire to his house, twice, and was punished in accordance with the usual sentence for arson. Braun, however, was ordered to remove himself from Cape Town, which had literally become too hot for him, and to repair to the country, where his domestic complications would be less likely to cause consternation among his neighbours, who in town were tired of helping to put out his fires and of worrying about the risk to their own houses. At the same time he was prohibited from ever again keeping a slave.[109]

Those farmers who lived in remote areas, far from the officers of justice and therefore outside the radius of due and effective supervision, often employed their own methods of punishing their slaves. Thus we read of a slave in a rural district who complained that his master was in the habit of having him inspanned, completely naked, together with a number of his fellows in the same condition, in front of a wagon with some horses, while another slave, seated on the wagon as coachman, beat them with the whip's end (*voorslag*) on their bare bodies.[110]

A further method which crops up now and again in official references was the callous one of timing a flogging by the smoking of a pipe; in other words, the duration of the punishment was determined (as was also the measuring of distances, according to the custom of those days) by the smoking of one or more pipes of tobacco. In one instance, a slave himself, in imitation of the practice of his masters, beat a Hottentot for as long as it took to smoke a pipe. Barrow describes as highly ridiculous the tranquillity and phlegm displayed by the farmer on such an occasion: "He flogs them not by any given number of lashes, but by time, and as they have no clocks . . . he has invented an excuse for the indulgence of one of his most favourite sensualities, by flogging them till he has smoked so many pipes of tobacco as he may judge the magnitude of the crime deserves . . ."[111]

We read of heavy sentences imposed upon those farmers on the remote border of the colony who treated their Hottentots and slaves harshly and unjustly, and Theal has an interesting observation to record upon this point. He says that in Ryk Tulbagh's period it had already been noticed, and was as well recognised then as at the time of writing, that the colonists found guilty of cruelty in this respect were nearly always men who either had coloured blood in their own veins or had mixed on terms of equality with the uncivilised coloured people.

Van Rheede laid it down that "no slave of a private person shall be bound to the whipping-post and flogged, by order of the Fiscal upon complaint of his master, without the previous knowledge and consent of the Commander; this consent shall, however, not be refused, provided only, that the punishment be not inflicted out of hatred, or the unreasonable caprice of harsh or cruel masters, but for an offence actually committed, and which must appear to have been committed, in order that slaves may neither become insubordinate nor be ill-treated".

Torture as part of the punishment of an offender — and by this we understand the deliberate infliction of agonising and lingering pain instead of the instantaneous death-stroke — was a legal commonplace at the Cape in early days. It was imposed on all malefactors, irrespective of race, colour or position, and included mutilation, breaking on the wheel, burning at the stake, disembowelling and other similar practices. This custom was found so harrowing by Major-General Craig when he took over the reins of government at the Cape during the first British occupation that he lodged a protest. Forcibly impressed and moved by the nature of the punishment which he saw endured by a black in a capital case, he wrote a letter to the President and members of the Court of Justice, asking them to consider the propriety of regarding loss of life as the supreme penalty in itself, and submitting that hanging and beheading should be the only methods employed. In England, he said, "the deprivation of life is considered as the extreme of punishment, in the manner of which we know no gradation; while with you the magnitude of the crime measures the severity of the mode by which the criminal is put to death".

The Court's reply, setting forth the principles by which they were guided when imposing sentences, and the reasons why they judged it unwise to mitigate the severity of capital punishment, is a most interesting and illuminating document. In the first place, they pointed out, the distinctions supposed by the General to exist between Europeans and slaves were by no means the cause of the degrees of harshness with which capital punishment was meted out to slaves at the Cape; "on the contrary, we can assure you, that in the Republic of the United Provinces, the laws and customs of which have hitherto been the rule of our criminal jurisprudence, the very same gradations of severity in punishment are observed amongst the inhabitants of those provinces in which there are no slaves, which are here equally inflicted upon free persons and slaves". The Court maintained that the rigour with which chastisement was inflicted was measured by the atrocity of the crime, "which in proportion to its magnitude demands a more striking example", and added that notice was taken of attendant circumstances which might produce some shades of difference, even in crimes essentially of the same character. The following considerations were always borne in mind:

(i) The person who committed the crime, and also the person upon whom it was committed; as when a subject murdered his Sovereign or a slave his master.

(ii) The place in which a crime was committed; for example, one who murdered a person in his own house, which ever ought to be his safest asylum, was punished more severely than one who committed murder in a place to which both had an equal right.

(iii) The quality of the fact; as, whether the instrument with which the murder was committed was generally esteemed a deadly weapon or not.

(iv) The quantity of guilt; as where the accused had murdered more than one person, or had been guilty of the same crime at any former time.

(v) The intention with which the crime was committed, as when it was followed by theft.

(vi) The motives from which the crime was committed; for instance, whether murder was perpetrated in anger or was premeditated in cool blood and in an insidious manner.

The letter went on to say that it was customary, for example, to punish more rigorously housebreaking and theft accompanied by murder than theft alone, whether committed by free people or slaves; and a wilful and deliberate murder was more strongly condemned than murder perpetrated in the heat of passion when provocation had been given: these distinctions, it was said, obtained so universally that they almost amounted to a rule of conduct for the Courts of Judicature all over Europe, and in this country they were certainly taken into account equally with free people and slaves.

"Nevertheless," admitted the members of the Court of Justice, "we cannot but observe, with regard to slaves, that the equality of punishment ceases when they commit offences against Europeans or free persons, particularly their masters: but this distinction is not peculiar to this country; on the contrary it is grounded upon analogy with the Criminal Law, according to which the distinction of persons is one of the essential points by which the degree of punishment is measured in most civilised nations, and this distinction is specially founded upon the Imperial Laws or the Roman Law, which from its exactness is not only acknowledged as Law when other Laws are silent, but it is particularly recommended as such in the Statutes which have been successively issued to the Dutch Indies, relative to slaves, and are observed here."

The document proceeded to state that the Romans considered slaves as creatures who, from their hardened bodies and their rude and uncultivated habits of thought, were much more difficult to correct and to deter from evil-doing than others who, owing to better education and better customs, measured the degree of punishment by their internal sensibilities rather than by physical pain: and this reasoning, declared the Court, could be justly applied to the slaves at the Cape, many of whom were descended from rough and wild nations amongst whom the deprivation of life was scarcely regarded as a punishment unless accompanied by such cruel circumstances as greatly aggravated corporal sufferings. Death by torture, moreover, could be abolished in the case of free people without ill effects but not in that of slaves, who would then certainly take advantage of their numerical strength and would be encouraged to revolt.

At the Cape during the seventeenth and eighteenth centuries all criminal cases were heard before the Court of Justice, which was composed of eleven members in 1686 and of twelve a hundred years later, and which combined the functions of judge and jury. Until 1734 the Governor presided over this council, but from that year he was prohibited from sitting in the Court, the presidency being conferred on the Secunde or Vice-Governor; the sentences, however, had to be submitted to the Governor for his approval, and if he withheld this he had to refer them to Batavia with his reasons for so doing. In 1713, incidentally, a resolution was carried that those who wished to appeal against a sentence of the Court of Justice should on no account be refused that privilege.

The most important functionary of the Court was the "Independent" Fiscal, who was exempt from any gubernatorial control. Among his other duties, he was appointed to regulate the administration of justice and to act as public prosecutor. It was a thankless office — the slaves loathed him with a hatred that lacked nothing in depth and sincerity, a state of mind that was cordially shared by a large number of Europeans as well.

Mentzel, for example, though a lover of the Cape — which he described as an abode of happiness and content, where a man might spend his life, literally under his own vine and fig-tree, in the utmost peace and good-will — found a serpent in this Eden in the form of the Fiscal. "This was Master Daniel van der Henghel," he wrote, "a man who loved the strictest kind of justice when it brought in any profit to himself. He had a wife who was a 'Liplapin' — that is, a woman born in Batavia — and they were both of

A Director of the W.I.C. and his black slave. In the background is Fort Delmina.

(Copyright: Ryksmuseum.)

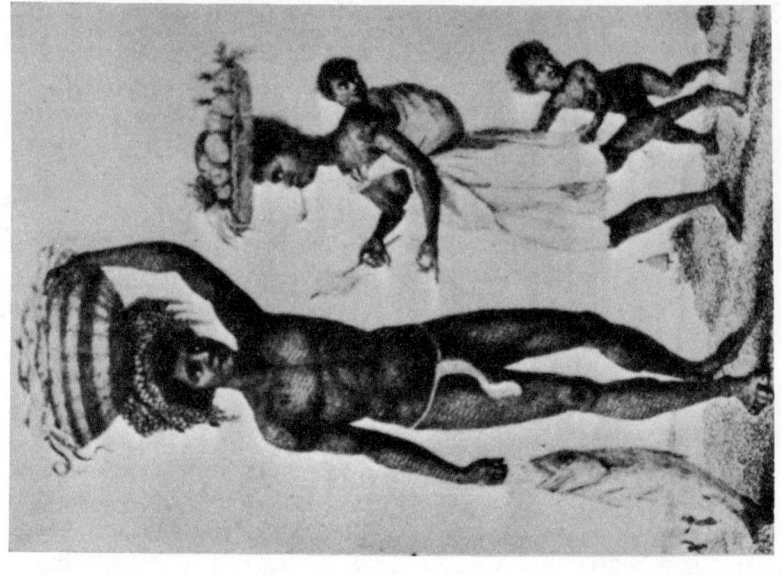

Angola slaves. (*Elliott Collection.*)

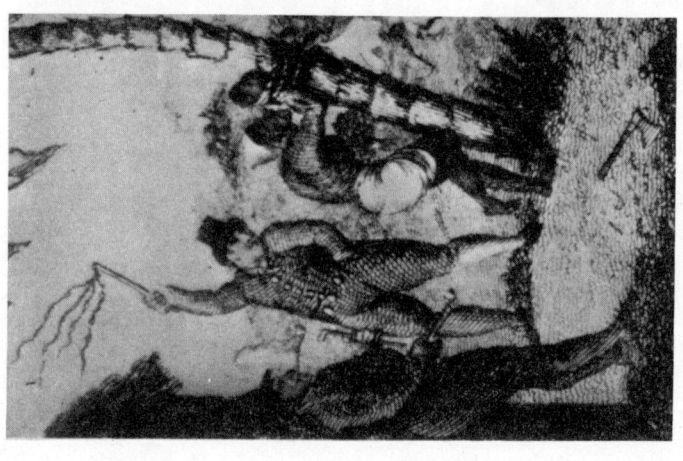

"The duration of the punishment was determined by the smoking of one or more pipes of tobacco."
(*Barrow's "Narrative".*)

them covetous and unreasonable. They would seldom pay for work that had been supplied to them . . . The barber and the wigmaker who worked for the Fiscal had not for years received a farthing from him, but if they showed the least dilatoriness in their work he used to accuse them of stealing the money out of his pockets. Since he was Fiscal . . . he had hundreds of opportunities of cheating and mortifying people. The cases he liked best were those he could push so far that they ended in the confiscation of the offender's goods." Mentzel continued by applauding the fact that this particular Fiscal had not been a contemporary of the bad Governor van Noodt, "for the two of them together would have been like Wencelaus and his Favourite". Fortunately, he added, the Governor then in office — De la Fontaine — and the councillors were upright men, and thanks to them the Fiscal often had to modify his actions "and did not dare to show his claws very much".

On one occasion a Fiscal went so far as to return to Europe in the same ship as his Governor, without leave from either the directors or the Council at the Cape. On his arrival in the Netherlands, he excused his unauthorised flight from the colony by declaring that he dared not remain there after the Governor's departure, as, deprived of the latter's protection, his life — or his limbs, at least — would have been in danger. On one occasion the Fiscal was actually attacked in a public street and badly manhandled. On another date a runaway slave threw a bundle of inflammable material, weighted with lead, on the thatched roof of the Fiscal's home — an attempt at arson which was fortunately discovered in time to save the whole town from possible destruction by fire, and whose author inspired the following ireful and eloquent description in the records : ". . . in truth such a character must be considered not as that of a human being but of a terrific monster . . . an excrement of hell".[112]

No doubt, though, we can safely infer that these much-maligned gentlemen who held the office of Fiscal were unpopular less for personal reasons than through the obligations of their position, which compelled them, *ex officio*, to tread on a good many corns. Some of them, indeed, were men of exceptional ability and integrity.

As soon as the Fiscal was notified of a crime, he set about instituting enquiries and gathering evidence, except in the country districts, where the Landdrost assumed the duties of public prosecutor, brought the prisoner to town and often conducted the prosecution himself. The testimony of slaves was received in Court subject to judicial discretion as to its credibility. On no account were criminal prisoners to be confined in gaol for any considerable length of time without trial.[113]

Although the office of Fiscal has long been abolished in South Africa, the name has been perpetuated in a somewhat unflattering simile — the white-throated, voracious shrike has become known as the Fiscal bird, because it is as much feared among the smaller birds and animals — which it ruthlessly kills and neatly impales on the long thorns of the mimosa tree — as was the Fiscal by the earlier colonists.*

Fines constituted a large portion of the Fiscal's personal revenue, and, according to Dr. Thunberg, a fine at the Cape was not in ratio to the crime of an offender but, for the most part, suited to his financial circumstances. The Fiscal, he added, therefore treated a turbulent and recalcitrant person as a physician did a plethoric patient, from whom he always drew blood in proportion to the strength of his habit. It is a significant fact that in their petition of 1779, the colonists complained that the Fiscal was frequently not interested in punishing slaves, as his pocket did not benefit as a result. It will be recalled that the slaves possessed neither money nor goods; corporal punishment was consequently the usual

---

* This general dislike of the Fiscal was not confined to the days of the Dutch East India Company. As late as 1824, we read of that official as the object of some fluent and impassioned criticism from the pen of Mr. Lancelot Cooke, who accused him of bursting into "an impertinent and intemperate declaration ... unprovoked, unjust, unlawful and unbecoming". The writer goes on to say that had the Fiscal known "to whom he addressed that impotent taunt, he would have felt it dangerous to rouse a lion that will destroy him; he would have known that I cared as little for his menace as for his persecution or himself; and that in Court — out of Court — at all times and in any place, I am, at the very, very least, his equal — taking his gown, his influence, his office, and his authority into the bargain ... he would have known that he may manacle my hands, he may shackle my feet, and he may cast my person into a cell; but I can tell him my soul bids defiance to every Fiscal; it will soar above him, it will hover over him, it will pounce upon him when and where he least dreams"!

THE ADMINISTRATION OF JUSTICE 163

means of chastising them for their transgressions; although there were cases — as in the prohibition of the purchase of clothes from a soldier — when a slave could be fined and the master forced to pay. It was the custom in a criminal case for the master to be held responsible for the expenses of the trial, and often the Company was asked to take over the slave in lieu of payment. Sometimes these requests were complied with; in other instances they met with firm refusal on the grounds that the Company, if invariably agreeable to the arrangement, would soon find itself "saddled with all the rogues and vagabonds".[114]

We know that whenever an execution took place a military display was given, and we have a description of the manner in which it was conducted. About ninety-nine men were assembled and divided into three companies of thirty-three each. Two of these groups were armed with muskets and the third, which was made up of the best physical specimens, carried pikes approximately seven yards long. The pikemen were drawn up between the files of infantry. In this formation the battalion marched to the Governor's house, to which, likewise, came the executioner and his assistants, and the members of the Court of Justice escorted by a military guard consisting of a sergeant, a corporal and twelve grenadiers. The convicted men, doomed to die that day, were brought up from the dungeon in the Castle, closely guarded by a corporal and six soldiers equipped with short pikes. The Secretary to the Court of Justice then mounted the *Kat* and read out the sentences of the condemned, always prefaced with the words "Doing justice in the name and on behalf of the High Mighty Lords, States General of the United Netherlands, as well as of His Most Serene Highness the Lord Prince of Orange and Nassauw, as Hereditary Stadtholder, Captain and Admiral-General of the Republic . . ."

After this, the troops marched slowly to the place of execution, with a band playing, and formed a ring with their pikes, each man grasping his own weapon and the end of his neighbour's at the same time. The musketeers took up a position immediately within and without this circle, with orders to keep the enclosed area free from encroachment. Then the executioner and his helpers, under strong guard, led up the criminals, whose hands were already pinioned. Next came the court messenger, bare-headed, carrying a silver-tipped thorn rod, his staff of office, and conducted by the sergeant, the corporal and the twelve grenadiers. This official, incidentally, had to see to all summonses, arrests, executions and so on, and he was obliged to assist at the latter, always wearing on his left breast his badge, in the form of a plate bearing an image of justice. His staff was bestowed on him on the day when he took the oath of office, and he had to present it when he delivered summons or performed other duties.

The clergyman, who had ministered to those condemned since the passing of the death sentence, was also in attendance to accord them final spiritual comfort — although, as one visitor remarked, it was doubtful whether many of the heathen slaves could derive much benefit from the consolations of religion, seeing that the *lingua franca* which they spoke was very poor in vocabulary, and it would be difficult for any minister, even if thoroughly versed in it, to convey through this medium an idea of salvation through the sufferings of our Lord, of the holiness of faith or of the necessity for repentance. A short prayer was offered up and then the executioner performed his grim task. When the gruesome business was over, the court messenger was escorted back to the Governor's house, where he delivered a full report of the proceedings. The troops were marched back to the Castle, the pikes were restored to the armourer and the men were dismissed to the barracks.

There were actually two main places of execution. The one, standing in the vicinity of the old Custom's House in Buitenkant Street, close to the Castle, was surrounded by a wall; steps led up to it and access was gained through an iron gate. Here the members of the Court of Justice, headed by the Fiscal, sat on a dais. The other — the so-called "outside place", where the dead bodies were exposed as a general warning to the public and were left to be destroyed by the wind, the air and the birds of heaven — was situated on an eminence at the base of the Lion's Rump, facing the Amsterdam battery. Slaves as well as Europeans were often hanged at the one place and their bodies re-hanged at the other.*

Captain Carmichael, who visited the Cape at the beginning of the nineteenth century, writes in an account that at the outside place of execution "three pillars, erected in the form of a triangle, support as many beams placed across them, and from these beams the criminals are suspended".[115] Another description is left to us by Sparrman of what he beheld at the same spot. He saw, to his horror, "above half a score of wheels placed round it . . ." and he maintained that the gallows was the largest he had ever remarked in any country, being he declared, "indeed of itself a sufficiently wide door to eternity", though "by no means too large for the purpose of a tyrannical government, that in so small a town as the Cape, could find seven victims to be hanged in chains". It was this gallows which suddenly confronted him one day, causing him to exclaim "Heus Viator!" and to pause briefly in contemplation of the uncertainty of human life.

A third description is yet more graphic: drawing near the place of execution, a traveller recorded, "we beheld a horrid spectacle. Upon the sand were erected a number of stakes and gibbets, upon which were the remains of upwards of a dozen malefactors who had been executed at the Cape at different periods. Some were suspended by the feet, decapitated; others were laid across the narrow wheel on which they had been racked, bent double and hanging down

---

* At the beginning of the nineteenth century, it was decided to build a grain magazine on the site of the place of execution which stood opposite the Castle. For various reasons it was resolved to make a movable gallows in accordance with a plan drawn up by L. M. Thibault. At first no carpenter could be found to undertake the work, but eventually it was finished — with the assistance of a large number of slaves — and comprised, besides the gallows itself, whipping- and strangling-posts and the cross for the breaking of limbs. Much satisfaction was expressed at the fact that the old ladder was still in good condition, needing merely a new coat of paint. The difficulty that arose in connection with the heating of the branding-irons on this wooden gallows was overcome by an order that an extra large *komfoor* should be made, as well as a big iron plate on which it could be placed. By these means it was possible to heat the irons properly, and not, as in former days, simply on Mother Earth — as the result of which the implements were frequently not sufficiently heated. A special place was chosen in which to house this gallows, and on those occasions when it was required arrangements were made to put it into working order, ready for use. (Cape Archives: B.R. 10 p. 87; B.R. 12 p. 2187; B.R. 13 p. 2518.—1805.)

on each side; whilst many seemed to preserve, by the attitude in which they were placed, the last writhings of pain and approaching death . . ."

That was the age, of course, of public punishment, and executions were usually witnessed by crowds of people, slaves included,*[116] many of whom must have been impressed by the offensiveness and undesirability of these events. Charles Dickens himself has left on record his opinion of these spectacles and their demoralising effect upon the minds of callous onlookers. We read that the famous novelist went to see the execution of the notorious Mrs. Manning, with the intention of watching the crowd, and he had an excellent opportunity of observing the reactions of the multitude of human beings who had collected together, studying them at intervals during the previous night and continuously from daybreak until the dreadful occasion was over.

We are told that the whole scene, inexpressibly odious and ghastly in its details, impressed him so strongly that he wrote to the *Times* in protest. "I am solemnly convinced," he said, "that nothing that ingenuity could devise to be done in this city, in the same compass of time, could work such ruin as one public execution, and I stand astounded and appalled by the wickedness it exhibits." He contended that these executions attracted as sightseers the lowest, the most depraved, the most abandoned of mankind, in whom they inspired no wholesome emotions whatever; also, that it was in the nature of things that on the class by whom these scenes were generally witnessed they should have a debasing and hardening influence. The awful sentence of death, he maintained, should be carried out within prison walls.†[117]

A Cape executioner once bitterly complained that capital punishments were often accompanied by many dis-

---

* In November 1835, an "immense concourse" of spectators, the majority being Malays, attended a public execution of three criminals at Green Point. Not until Act 3 of 1869 was passed — seventy-four years after the Cape had ceased to belong to the Dutch East India Company — was capital punishment in public abolished in South Africa.

† In the Cape, however, it was not, as in England, the custom of the authorities to rent out the space surrounding the scaffold to various enterprising opportunists, who erected thereupon grandstands, and sold the seats at different prices on the spectacular occasion of an execution. Dr. Parry, author of a book on the history of torture in England, narrates the story of Mammy Douglas,

THE ADMINISTRATION OF JUSTICE

orders, as he was unable to obtain an assistant. So the Council decided to appoint a European in this capacity, and simultaneously prescribed the rates of pay for both the executioner and his subordinate, as follows:

For the Executioner: Salary, f.18; board money, s.12; ration, 3 cans arrack, 4 loaves bread, 92 lbs. meat.

For the Assistant: Salary, f.14; board money, s.8; ration, 3 cans arrack, 4 loaves bread, 40 lbs. meat.

For the Executioner, for the following punishments

Breaking limbs	Rds. 12
Pinching with red-hot tongs	„ 4
Burning	„ 12
Decapitating	„ 8
Hanging	„ 8
Strangling	„ 6
Scorching	„ 2
Quartering and hanging up the pieces	„ 6
Transporting body to "outside place" of execution	„ 3
Torturing	„ 10
Chopping off the hand	„ 4
Scourging	„ 3
Branding with red-hot iron	„ 1
Placing a rope round the neck under the gallows	„ 2
Putting in the pillory	„ 2

The assistant received half the amount of the sums mentioned in this grisly list.[118]

The other men who helped the executioner were known

---

one of the most infamous of these people. "We have a glimpse of her in 1785," he says, "when Dr. Henesy, adjudged guilty of treason, was bumped on a hurdle in the usual way to Tyburn, there to swing off into eternity. The hanging of a doctor was not quite an everyday affair, and there was a rush for seats on the part of the crowd. Mammy Douglas, with the same discernment but with more moderation than the modern commercial man would employ, observed that the demand was greater than the supply and promptly raised the price of the tickets from 2s. to 2s. 6d. There was much grumbling about this sordid piece of profiteering, but that grumbling was nothing compared with the uproar when, having paid their half-crowns and taken their seats, the Doctor was at the last moment 'most provokingly reprieved'! In the ensuing riot, the 'pews' were reduced to matchwood, and abortive attemps were made to hang Mammy Douglas in place of the reprieved Doctor; but their praiseworthy efforts appear to have failed."

as "Caffres". Armed with iron-hilted swords and heavy clubs, they wore grey uniforms consisting of short coats with blue lapels, waistcoats and trousers. In 1720 a request came from Ceylon, asking the Cape Government to transmit four or six healthy and well-formed Caffres, but a reply was sent stating that among the Company's slaves none was available of the type required. Here at the Cape the so-called Caffres were mostly Indian exiles, and were employed to thrash Europeans as well as slaves.[119] That they did not always confine their activities to the place of execution we see from the case of the black freeman Eerst of Guinea, who prosecuted the European free burgher Steven Jansen, whose slave girl had beaten the plaintiff's wife. Jansen pleaded that the victim had been so abusive beforehand that the girl had not been able to refrain from retaliating; nevertheless, the accused was sentenced to be flogged by the Caffres before the door of her owner's house.

On one occasion a Caffre himself offended and was brought to book. It appears that a certain slave was imprisoned for having sold a sheep from Adam Tas's shed at Stellenbosch. A Caffre who served the Landdrost there waited until this official had gone to Cape Town and then broke the lock of the gaol in order to allow Coridon, his fellow-slave, to escape, after which he himself, being afraid of the consequences, absconded. He was pursued, caught and condemned to be well whipped, branded on the right cheek and riveted in chains for twenty years — a heavy penalty indeed for helping a friend out of trouble.

In 1780 the Governor remarked on the undesirability of having Cape burghers and other white men arrested by these blacks, and consequently four European constables were placed at the disposal of the Fiscal, to apprehend burghers or Company's servants. A few years later the authorities resolved to add another six constables to the ranks of the existing four, to dismiss double that number of Asiatics "and for the future prevent the danger to which one is continually exposed from such servants of Justice, as experience has so lamentably proved". In due course the remaining Caffres were to be replaced by robust and fit slaves of the Company, or other blacks suited for that kind of work.[120]

One of the most maddening habits of the slaves was that of emptying sanitary tubs into the canals, and frequently even before other people's doors, instead of into the sea. Numerous placcaats were issued forbidding this practice, and on New Year's Day, 1687, there suddenly appeared on the civic scene a bevy of night-constables in the shape of the rattlewatch. Each of them was supplied with a small salary, a large sword, a gaudy uniform and a noisy rattle. Every night at nine o'clock, when the constables went off duty, these rattlewatches would wend their weary way through the town. When the clock struck the hour they bawled out the time, sounded their rattles and, after having satisfied themselves that no loiterers lurked in the streets, proceeded on their nocturnal peregrinations. Should they notice any disturbances or evidence of "evil design" they immediately sprang their rattles and called out as loudly as possible "Murder! Thieves!" or the like. Meanwhile mothers taught their children to sing:

> "Moederlief, 'k geloof het vast
> Dat hy op de dieven past,
> Goede klepper houdt de wacht;
> Ik ga slapen — goede nacht."

Odd though it may seem, with the exception of the Fiscal none of the members of the Court of Justice was required to hold any special qualification for the position. In the reminiscences of a certain Capetonian, we are told that during the existence of the old Court many strange and diverting incidents occurred, and he relates an example which caused much merriment at the time. It was the practice of one or two of the members, he narrates, to take a quiet nap during Court proceedings, and when any case was concluded the crier roused each sleeper to give a verdict. It happened once that before leaving home a member had had a somewhat acrimonious dispute with his wife concerning the method of dressing a fine Roman fish. The lady preferred boiled fish, but her spouse insisted on its being fried. In the midst of the discussion he had been summoned to attend Court. Very soon after he took his seat, as usual he fell into a doze, during which he somnolently re-lived the recent domestic scene. Just as, in his dream, he reached a compromise with his wife in their culinary argument, the crier woke him and asked for his sentence upon the prisoner, whereupon, still dazed, he exclaimed in a loud voice "Boil his head and fry his tail!" to the extreme and understandable alarm of the accused and the amusement of the Court.[121]

Colonel C. Graham Botha has given us an interesting account of the various venues of the Court of Justice, which was established in 1656 and abolished in 1827, when its place was taken by the Supreme Court of the Cape of Good Hope. The first Court met in the "Commander's Hall", built in the centre of Van Riebeeck's earthenwork fort. After this, it assembled in the new Council Chamber in the Castle, which was approached by the blue-flagged steps in front, seen to the right as the courtyard is entered. In 1691 the courtyard was divided into two by a cross-wall, and from time to time buildings were erected on either side of this partition. Facing the first courtyard was the new Council Chamber, accessible from the beautiful blue-flagged stoep covered by a graceful balcony, the design of which is attributed to Louis Thibault, the great architect. Here the Court of Justice sat for nearly a century. From the so-called *Kat* criminal sentences and Court decrees were published, and placcaten, Government notices and advertisements, and commissions of new Governors, were promulgated to the garrison and the citizens of Cape Town, who gathered in the courtyard below after the Castle bell had tolled.

The next rendezvous of the Court of Justice was at the lower end of the Heerengracht. Court was held in a building abutting from the present Customs Office across the street, leaving a narrow passage between itself and the building then standing on the site of Lennon's corner. This passage formed an exit from the Heerengracht to the sea, and was known as Justitie Straat. On this spot a new gaol was erected in 1781 and, next to it, in front, a hall for the sessions of the

Court. It was considered that the proximity of the gaol to the Court House would be convenient when prisoners were brought to trial. A bell, placed above the Court, was rung to notify when the Court was to sit or when its decrees were to be published. Criminal sentences, however, were still proclaimed as before from the balcony at the Castle.

The verdict of the members of the Court of Justice was taken by ballot, which in the case of murder had to be decided by a majority of votes. The severity of the laws and punishments meted out by these gentlemen was commented upon by a visiting Commissioner who, as far back as 1708, recommended them preferably "to secure some alleviation and comfort to the hearts of the people, who are showing themselves somewhat dissatisfied under the cross".[122] Even earlier than this, in 1681, Commissioner van Goens, in a Memorandum for Simon van der Stel and Council, stated: "I must again call your attention to what the late Mr. N. Verburg has before said upon the dispensation of justice in the Colony; for it appears to us to have grown into a practice to pay very little attention to the formalities and the indispensable proofs in actions at law, but frequently to yield too much to the influence of the passions, and to proceed too readily to infamous punishments, banishment and pecuniary fines, which cannot be recovered — proceedings entirely opposed to the advancement of a poor Colony, which we should be glad to see encouraged; and which tend to awaken the wrath of God. We, therefore, would most earnestly impress on you this most important subject; for this it is which renders the power and character of the Company so renowned in India; and when the life, the honour, or the property of our neighbour is at stake, we should proceed with the last degree of circumspection, with the utmost fear of God before our eyes . . ."

When the English took over the Cape, it was suggested that the law itself and the constitution of the Courts should be preserved — the only change being in the number of the judges, which should be reduced to three or four, to be selected from among able jurisconsults, or professors of the universities of Leyden, Utrecht or Groningen. It was considered inadvisable at the time to form a system upon the

English model because, as the Earl of Macartney wrote to the Right Honourable Henry Dundas, "the Colony from the state of its language, manners and other causes, could scarcely be adapted to the reception of such an alteration in less than a century".

CHAPTER NINE

CRIME AND PUNISHMENT

IT seems to have been a generally accepted belief hitherto that the penalties of the law for crime were especially severe in the case of slaves. Dr. Theal, South Africa's great historian, tells us that the punishment of bondsmen for sins against the community, adjudged by courts of law, "was out of all proportion to that inflicted upon free men for the same offences . . ." This is an exaggeration; certainly the official records contain nothing to support such a statement. In the same way one can find no reason for Mentzel's allegation that the Fiscal was allowed to have his own way, more or less, with runaway slaves and other malefactors of that kind, "for if the natives were not deterred from ill-doing by the infliction of severe punishments, such as hanging, breaking on the wheel and impaling, no one's life would be safe. A European, on the other hand, must have committed a very serious crime before he is punished by death".

Professor Eric Walker, another renowned historian, tells us how in time the slave laws became fiercer and the punishments less discriminate. "In the year of our Lord 1732," he says, "a murderer was broken on the wheel and left dangling without the *coup de grace* till sunset, and alongside him hung another slave in like case for stealing a violin." In order to substantiate this statement, the Professor gives a reference in the journal for 1732. But when we turn to the pages indicated we find an entry to the effect that two slaves were broken on the wheel — "the one had violated a young girl, and the other committed burglary and murder". No mention is made in this journal, nor, for that matter, in the original records of the Court of Justice, of the theft of a violin — in fact, no goods were stolen by the burglar; and, in any event, the evidence of criminal cases shows that breaking on the wheel was strictly reserved for particularly heinous offences. How, then, did the Professor deduce the word violin? The answer seems obvious: in reading over his notes, he probably mistook "violate" for "violin" . . . Unfortunately, other writers have quoted this "example" of the severity of the punishments meted out to the slaves. In that excellent book *Towards Emancipation*, for instance, we read that "punishments were enforced with increasing rigour in the eighteenth century. Thus in the year of our Lord . . ." and the writer goes on to quote Walker *in extenso*.[123]

Slaves were punished according to the ordinary criminal laws of the day — codified and amplified by Ryk Tulbagh in 1754, owing to their insolence and wantonness having become intolerable. This code again drew attention to the clause condemning to death without mercy any male or female slave who should raise a hand, though without weapons, against master or mistress. Already at that stage it was realised that a state of slavery was inevitably accompanied by a certain feeling of enmity against masters, and that it must be regarded as uncommon to find a slave who would not rejoice at any mischief which might befall his owner. Actually, however, the authorities' bark was worse than their bite, except, of course, in serious cases. In fact, the laws were seldom enforced to the limit, the object of legislation being to lay down the maximum punishment which could be inflicted for offences rather than the ordinary penalties short of that.

In considering the question of the punishments imposed by the Court of Justice, we must bear in mind two important factors: firstly, the slaves greatly outnumbered the Europeans; secondly, many of them were a crude, treacherous species of mankind who never forgot that they had been forcibly deprived of their freedom, and who were not restrained by any moral principles from the perpetration of the most violent crimes. Those who came from the island of Celebes, and notably the Bugunese, for example, reached for their knives on the slightest provocation, and thought little or nothing of cutting the throat of a fellow creature. In other words, we must logically expect to see in the records of the Court of Justice many more sentences passed on the black man in bondage than on those — both white and black — who enjoyed their freedom.

Desertion and theft were the two crimes most frequently committed by Europeans and slaves, and they were looked upon as "most severely punishable in a well-conditioned, honour- and peace-loving government, where only charity, peace and harmony are planted and cultivated, and justice is kept pure in warding off and suppressing all evils", as the secretary unctuously expressed it. The difference in the punishment of a European and that of a slave for the offence of desertion aroused the ire of no less distinguished a person than Doctor Thunberg, in 1772. When the heathen slaves ran away and were caught, he says, they were beaten, but if Christians deserted from the Company's service and were recaptured, they were hanged! Thunberg adds that it was the money laid out in the purchase of the former that saved them from death, "but the established laws do not spare the latter".

This attitude of the contemporary Government sometimes makes amusing reading, such as in a certain instance when a drastic sentence imposed on three soldiers for theft and other malpractices was suddenly suspended. Justice had decreed that they were to be thrashed, branded, banished for twenty-five years and to have all their goods and property confiscated. But this was abruptly commuted: they were simply sent back to their posts to work without pay on promise of reformation. The reason appears a slight one: "It will be a loss to the Company to punish them, as the Company will lose the whole year's crop of meal at Clapmuts"! Just in case, however, these soldiers might misconstrue this unexpected leniency as weakness, the Fiscal assured them that the sentence could be revived at any time if necessary — in which event they would be punished with death.

From the proceedings of the Court of Justice we learn that, in early days at the Cape, fugitive slaves were chastised by being scourged: but when it was found that this measure did not impress them very greatly, the punishment was extended to whipping for the first offence and branding on one cheek; for the second, whipping with branding on both cheeks; for the third offence, in addition to the above castigation, their noses and ears were cut off. We even read of thumbs being chopped off and tongues torn out; one unfortunate man actually stood watching while his ears, having been severed from his head, were nailed by the executioner to the gallows. In later years, however, the Council decided to amend the former resolution in such a manner that "henceforth no nose or ears shall be cut off, and no branding in the face allowed, but that all branding shall be on the back". This sudden squeamishness was not for the benefit of the unlucky wretches who might be directly concerned, as one would imagine, but arose "in considering the abominableness . . . to those who see these mutilated persons"![124]

The branding-iron consisted of a long wooden handle with an iron in the form of a miniature gallows attached to it, and it was applied to both sexes without discrimination. A European widow, convicted of aiding and abetting some cattle thieves, was condemned to banishment from the Cape after having been severely whipped at the place of execution and marked with a gallows on her back, "so that this hateful, injurious and thievish propensity may once for all be eradicated from their infamous bosoms".

Periodically great variation took place in the sentences for desertion: the offenders were sometimes scourged, branded and tied to blocks; or they were put in chains and sent home to their masters after having been beaten. Often an habitual runaway was scourged at a post and then had an iron collar, with a sharp bolt protruding from it, fixed round his neck. Some were obliged to wear iron rings round their feet as well as iron collars, and in the course of time the latter each had as many as three "horns", as they were called, attached to them; on one occasion a little white youngster was brutally murdered by a slave, who pleaded in extenuation that the child had always taunted him with the term "Hoornbeest". For desertion from duty, European soldiers were frequently chained to wheelbarrows and forced to labour at the public works. In 1712 two Europeans were hanged for encouraging slaves to desert, and accompanying them in their flight; the slaves them-

Medical account, 1745, includes attention to slaves. (*Cape Archives.*)

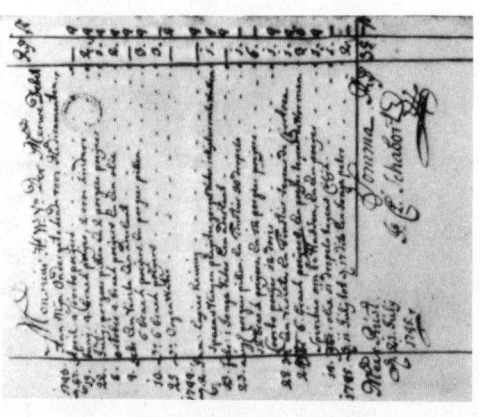

Malay quarter, Cape Town. (*Wm. Fehr Collection.*)

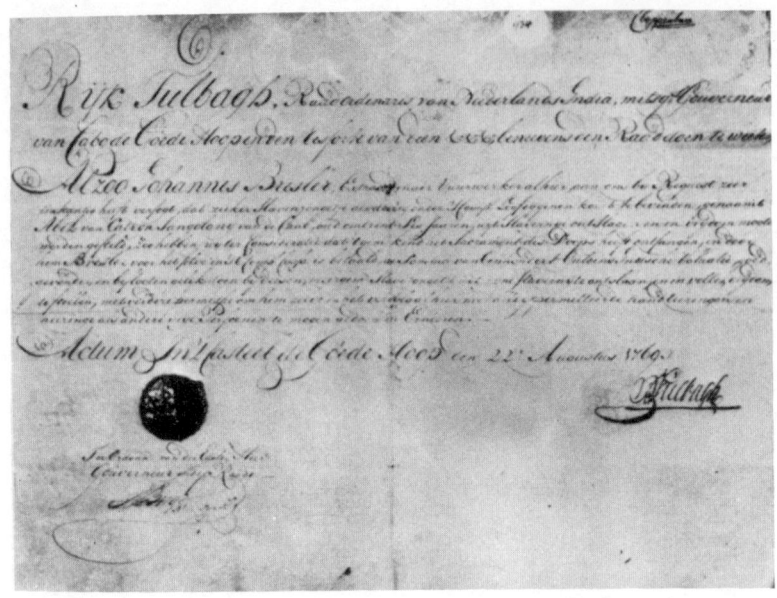

Letter of Freedom, signed by Ryk Tulbagh.
(*Cape Archives*.)

Sentences were read out from the *Kat* at the Castle.
(*Elliott Collection*.)

selves escaped the death penalty, but had their ears and noses cut off.

These punishments were imposed only when the gravity of the offences was not aggravated by murder, arson or similar crimes. Unfortunately, many fugitives perpetrated acts of violence which cried out for vengeance, and, in accordance with contemporary usage not only at the Cape but also in most other parts of the world, barbarous and ruthless retribution was visited on those found guilty. Only a callous-hearted reader can peruse the judicial records with anything approaching enjoyment, and it would certainly serve no useful purpose to recapitulate here all the lurid details of the methods of execution, often accompanied by horrible bodily mutilation. It will suffice to repeat two cases — the one of a slave guilty of a cruel murder, and the other of a European deserter who led a petty insurrection.

The slave was first of all bound naked to a cross at the place of execution near the Castle. The executioner was instructed to nip ten pieces of flesh from his body with red-hot pincers, at lengthy intervals. After this the right hand had to be hacked off and thrown in his face, and the criminal was quartered. The mutilated portions of his body were finally dragged through the streets of the town to the outside place of execution, where they were secured by chains to a pole, on the top of which his head was set, while his hand was nailed to the bottom. There they remained until destroyed by decomposition and predatory birds. The punishment of Etienne Barbier, the turbulent French sergeant in the service of the Company who, after deserting, stirred up ill-feeling against the Government, was almost exactly similar. After he had been bound to a cross, the executioner chopped off his right hand, then his head, and quartered him. The severed members were exhibited on a pole in the Roodesands Kloof, while the remaining parts of his body were set in conspicuous places exposed to beasts of prey — a gruesome reminder to any other malcontent who might contemplate attempting a rebellion against the Government. Some time later the Landdrost wrote to the Governor that the pole to which Barbier's trunk was attached had been accidentally burnt; within a few days, however, with what seems to us a zeal for duty little short of ghoulish, he complacently announced that the matter was not serious after all, as portion of the body was still there and could be placed on another pole.

Equal zeal for duty, incidentally, was displayed in a different case altogether, when a slave, Ary of Bengal, who had attempted arson, was sentenced to spend the rest of his life on Robben Island. The Governor gave strict instructions that on no account were the slave chains and block to be removed from this dangerous criminal. Within two years, in 1708, the delinquent died, and the superintendent of the island wrote to inform the Governor of the event, adding virtuously that he had "had him, naturally, buried in that same uniform"! The Governor was highly incensed at this over-literal interpretation of his orders. Surely, he said, the chains would have been found serviceable for another prisoner — why bury them with the black boy? The superintendent, though contrite, stuck to his point. He would be the last man, he protested, to act contrary to the Governor's wishes. With the utmost respect, however, he would like to refer to the strict injunction of Governor Willem Adriaan van der Stel to the effect that the slave was never to be released from his bonds — in fact, he added as an afterthought, he still had the written order!

In dealing with the question of desertion, one must mention another kind of offender in this respect, who was invariably much frowned upon by the Court — namely, the woman who left her husband. One unhappy wife was so ill-treated by her spouse that she dressed in male attire and tried to desert in a departing ship. Unluckily she was caught, tied to a pole, severely scourged and compelled to toil at the public works for fifty years.

Hanging and shooting were sentences which appear to have been generally, if not exclusively, reserved for the white man in the days when the Cape was in its infancy. Jan Jans, a European sailor, fled from the settlement in company with two free burghers, intending to make for Portuguese territory. They were not guilty of any violence, but in order to facilitate their flight they stole some horses and prevailed upon a slave to join them. At first the sailor refused to confess, but he changed his mind when brought to torture. He was thereupon hanged.

In another instance a group of European soldiers, when the usual signal to resume work was given by the tolling of a bell, gathered together and asked for their board money and rations of rice which, according to custom, were issued to them on the first day of the month. The Governor regarded their behaviour as rebellion, and four of them were condemned to draw lots for life or death: the two who drew the lots for life were scourged and sent to labour at the public works for a considerable number of years, while the second pair, to whom death fell by lot, were hanged. This drawing of lots at the place of execution was not an uncommon sentence, as far as the Europeans were concerned; but the records fail to reveal any case of the same method being applied to slaves. A sailor who drew his knife upon and wounded his officer was sentenced in this manner: if he drew the lot for death he would be hanged; if the lot for life he would be flogged, branded and placed in chains on Robben Island for twenty-five years.

One must remember, of course, that the old mode of execution by hanging differed from the modern rapid and expeditious operation. In those days the criminals had to mount a ladder, and we read in a report of the sentence carried out on two Europeans hanged at the end of the seventeenth century that one of them, when pushed from the ladder, fell from above to the ground, the cord having snapped. "He cried for mercy, but no attention was however paid to it, and he was hanged a second time alongside the other." Apparently the men of those days considered it hardly chivalrous to expose the limbs of a woman to the indignity of swinging in the south-east wind at the end of a rope, so out of gentle courtesy they strangled or burned her instead. In fact, they occasionally combined the two processes, as in the case of a European woman who arrived at the Cape from Holland with her husband, nicknamed "Schurfde Frans" (Scurvy Frank), and who was later an accomplice in his murder. She was condemned to be half-throttled, after that to be scorched and finally strangled to death.[125]

An incendiary, white or black, was either burned alive, gradually strangled while the hangman's assistant, somewhat appropriately, waved a flaming bundle of reeds about his face and before his eyes, or was otherwise half-strangled and killed on a slow fire. In 1686 a European guilty of arson was strangled to a degree short of death, scorched with fire and then completely throttled; in 1712 a slave was burnt alive for the same offence; in 1724 a slave convicted of arson combined with attempted murder had his right hand cut off before being half-strangled and then despatched on a slow fire; and in 1767 a slave girl who had twice set fire to her master's house was burned to death. This girl's sentence shows clearly how the nature of execution in that epoch depended upon the character and implications of the crime: the punishment inflicted upon her was one of calculated severity, for all knew well how easily such an act as hers could have laid the whole of the little town in ashes. She was taken to the place of execution, an iron ring was set round her neck and she was chained in an upright position to a pole standing in the middle of a pile of wood, which was then ignited. The charred remains of her body were carefully collected and put into a pot, which was carried to the outside place of execution and there exhibited on a pole as a warning to others.[126]

The slave mentioned in the records as having been burned to death in 1712 was actually seen in his sufferings by Peter Kolbe. This writer says that the man was secured to a vertical post by a chain long enough to enable him to make one turn around it. "Then was kindled a fire round about him," continues Kolbe, "just beyond the stretch of the chain; the flames rose high, the heat was vehement, he ran for some time to-and-again about the post, but gave not one cry. Being half-roasted he sank down, and said (speaking in Portuguese) Dios mios Pays (O God, my Father) and then expired." Several years later, in 1768, Stavorinus was another eye-witness at the punishment of a slave for arson. The proceedings, he recorded, lasted a full quarter of an hour. The criminal, who had been convicted of setting a house on fire, was broken alive on the wheel, after the flesh had been torn from his body in eight different places with red-hot pincers. This man, too, showed endurance almost beyond human belief; throughout the whole barbarous execution he gave not the slightest sign of pain.

However, one needs but to read the history of punishments in other lands to realise that those imposed at the Cape in the seventeenth and eighteenth centuries were comparatively mild. England, Scotland, France, Spain, Italy . . . for thoroughness and ingenuity in torture and chastisement, these countries of the Old World were far in advance of the embryo South Africa. We are told that for witchcraft alone seven thousand suspects were burnt at Treves, and four hundred in a single mass execution at Toulouse: at the end of the eighteenth century the law of England inflicted the death penalty for over two hundred crimes, including that of stealing property to the value of five shillings . . .

In a dispatch of the Council of Seventeen dated 23 July 1701 the attitude held in those days concerning retributive justice is plainly manifested: ". . . The people in this evil world (God better it) are so constituted that they are kept from crime more, yea, almost entirely, by the fear of punishment, and by no means through love of that which is good". This was the motive, of course, behind the carrying out of executions and punishments in public.

Numerous witnesses beside Kolbe and Stavorinus left on record their amazement at the fortitude of many of the slaves when enduring the most terrible chastisement. Cornelis de Jong mentions in his book an invitation which he received to attend the simultaneous execution of several of these blacks. Two of them were first broken on a cross, where they were left awaiting decapitation while five others were hanged and a number whipped and branded. To the spectators, says De Jong, the scene was awesome and harrowing; only the victims themselves remained impassive. Not a complaint, not a cry, not even a sigh reached his ears. The lion-heartedness of these people was beyond description, he declares; he himself overheard an argument conducted in strong voices and firm tones between the pair who had already been broken on the wheel, and who were therefore almost *in extremis,* and those who were climbing the ladder to the scaffold. Doctor Sparrman made similar observations. He said that the Bugunese slaves were reported to be capable of bearing the cruellest torments with wonderful hardihood, as though they were entirely devoid of feeling, and he added that there were instances known of their not having uttered the least cry or complaint when impaled alive, or broken on the wheel.

Even the official records contain many references to the brave — and sometimes callous — hearts that beat beneath black skins. On one occasion we find the secretary writing regretfully of a slave who had brutally murdered his mistress, aged eighty-two years, a very active woman who had always been of a kindly and happy disposition. When the authorities spoke of God to the criminal, he replied without the least perturbation that he knew neither God nor Devil, that by descent he was a Malabar, that he was only to be given good food and drink to be satisfied, and that he would readily submit to death.[127]

A notable case was that of a runaway slave, Francis of Batavia, found guilty of participating in certain acts of violence and ultimately caught on the slopes of Table Mountain, whence he was removed to the prison. He spoke good Dutch, showed dauntless courage and voluntarily prepared himself for death. The Lord's Prayer and the Articles of the Christian Faith he could repeat without faltering; and he begged for a minister to strengthen him in his belief — a request which was immediately granted. By sentence of the Court he was broken alive on the wheel. This brave man bore his punishment with more than ordinary steadfastness. From the place of execution he exhorted all male and female slaves to take an example from him and to serve their masters loyally, and he showed great repentance for his crimes, "praying to the Almighty God to be merciful unto him as He was to the murderer on the cross, and to receive his soul into the Eternal Glory".[128]

Another instance — though the protagonist was not a pious slave this time — mentioned in the records is that of Titus of Bengal, paramour of a white woman and murderer of her husband. He was condemned to be impaled (held in position by an iron prong thrust through his body) and to remain so until death. For two days Titus lingered on in his misery. Four hours after his impalement he received a bottle of arrack, from which he drank freely and heartily. When advised not to take too much lest he should become drunk, he retorted that it did not matter, as he sat fast enough and there was no fear of his falling. Whilst surviving "in that deplorable state" he often joked, and scoffingly said that he would never again put his trust in woman! The secretary wrote in his journal that the whole affair was "something horrible to think of", and concluded his entry with the following phrase: "a way of dying, lauded by the Romans, but damnable among Christians".[129]

Paradoxical though it may seem, once criminals approached the death agony they were shown many little acts of kindness. Sometimes they were given water, often mixed with a small quantity of wine. Thus in 1693 Jan of Sofala, when lying broken on the wheel, "after having previously partaken of some water with wine, and smoked a pipe of tobacco, gave the last gasp . . ." It happened, too, that friends might quietly steal at night to the place of execution to help an unfortunate wretch out of his sufferings. A slave named Tromp, impaled for some offence, was found strangled the next morning; "he had received some linen from a kind friend during the night for the purpose . . ."[130]

It is interesting to notice that the sentence passed for unnatural vice never varied: young boys and old men, white, black or yellow, one and all were condemned by the Court of Justice to be conveyed on board a vessel in the bay and there delivered to the executioner, in order to be cast into the sea, with weights attached to them, and drowned. In one case, two slaves were tied back to back before being thrown overboard. Sometimes, to avoid the assembling of crowds of inquisitive young sightseers, the Fiscal was asked to remove the malefactors inconspicuously in a boat, and not to throw them into the sea until the sun had set.[131]

Several types of punishment were imposed for murder. A sailor who committed this crime with a knife was hanged, with the knife suspended above his head; a certain slave, for having attempted to kill his mistress, had his right hand cut off and placed on his head and was then hanged. In another instance a sailor, who had murdered a man with an axe, was condemned to be beheaded with a similar weapon; this sentence, however, was subsequently modified, on the intercession of the minister and on account of the honourable parents of the evil-doer, and he was shot instead. In the case of vicious premeditated murders the punishment was made to fit the crime even as to details, with little modification. With the actual knife which he had used to commit a dastardly murder, Alynea of Boegis had his stomach ripped up at the place of execution; he was then disembowelled and his entrails cast into the sea. Quaint punishments were devised for theft. A thief who stole a fruit-tree was scourged with the tree dangling over his head; those who purloined some cabbages were whipped, with a number of these vegetables tied round their necks; a slave was placed in the pillory with cabbages above his head; and a few days later a European woman underwent the same correction with a sack of rice above her.

Infanticide and suicide were also looked upon as heinous offences. A female slave who strangled a half-caste child was tied up in a bag and consigned to the cold waters of Table Bay; and a slave girl who hanged herself was ignominiously dragged by a donkey to the gallows and there, "as a loathing of such abominableness, placed with her head in a fork, and hanged between Heaven and Earth". Sometimes the bodies of the self-slain were "dragged over the high road" towards the scaffold, where they were suspended by the legs; sometimes their bodies were placed in a porcupine's hole; a European soldier was even buried underneath the scaffold as a caution to others. An interesting case occurred in Stellenbosch when a slave, in a fit of jealousy, seriously wounded a slave girl with whom he was in love. He then fled and, on being pursued, inflicted upon himself a mortal wound by ripping open his stomach with a knife. The Landdrost recorded that he could find no trees or wood on which to hang him by the legs, so justice had to be observed merely by the man's being dragged by the feet into the veld. More often than not, the cause of suicide among slaves was the fact of their having been torn away from their native countries, rather than any ill-treatment from their masters; such a desperate act as self-destruction was more commonly due to their unhappiness at being removed from their natural environment than to their actual enslavement.

If a person guilty of infanticide was brought to justice through the agency of a slave, this informer was manumitted, besides receiving a reward of two hundred rixdollars, and he was also exempt from any punishment even if he had assisted in carrying out the crime. While dealing with the subject of infanticide — considered throughout the history of South Africa as a sin of the first magnitude — one may perhaps mention the amazing credulity of some folk in this respect. Shortly after the English had taken over the reins of government at the Cape, a man by the name of R. B. Fisher (younger brother of the then Bishop of Salisbury), who described himself, probably quite correctly, as a "poor and insignificant individual", felt impelled "by a sense of duty to my country, and a charitable and Christian disposition" to write to William Wilberforce of the plight of slaves at the Cape. "The murder of infants," he stated, "generally passes by unregarded; and I have instanced the report made to me by an officer of very respectable character in the 93rd regiment, of having himself seen the bodies of no less than thirteen infants lying exposed on the beach, and no inquiry made . . ."!

In the same letter the writer vehemently refused to concede the point so often asserted that the slaves of the Cape were better treated by their masters, underwent fewer hardships and were altogether more fortunately placed than those of the West Indies — although he admitted that there were only a few cases of the murder of slaves, "because being considered as a valuable property, a man will no more kill his slave than he will kill a horse, while he has strength to work. But when a slave is no longer able to work, his condition becomes dreadful in the extreme. He is left almost literally to starve"! There were also, according to this highly imaginative gentleman, a number of people whose only means of subsistence were the wages of their slaves earned while out on hire. Female slaves, he amplified, were let out by their mistresses on weekly terms to Europeans for the sole purpose of cohabitation — indeed, he believed that there still lived in Cape Town a woman of great consequence "who could be seen every day parading to church, attended by slaves, with her books, stool and cushion", and who was visited by all the superior people, although she derived "a very considerable income from this most shocking and infamous trade".

This letter to Mr. Wilberforce was published in England, with the result that the Governor of the Cape was duly asked to investigate the matter. Although the Secretary of State felt that the document was bristling with inaccuracies, and was personally inclined to pay but little attention to Mr. Fisher's unsupported assertions, he was nevertheless obliged to request the Governor to ascertain whether the crime of infanticide was in actual fact as prevalent at the Cape as the writer alleged. The official reply was most reassuring. "From the perusal of the very extraordinary work Mr. Fisher has put forth," the Governor wrote promptly from the Cape, "I can only conceive that some mischievous individuals have from mere wantonness imposed upon a credulous and weak mind . . ." From the united testimony of all the authorities, from the indignation aroused by so foul an accusation, and from his own observation of the strictness with which crimes, when they unfortunately did occur, were impartially prosecuted, he continued, he had no hesitation in pronouncing Mr. Fisher's allegations gross and unfounded misrepresentations, utterly devoid of foundation.[132]

One of the harshest laws of the Company which existed was that concerning the confiscation of the property of delinquents. Women, children and other relatives were often left destitute as the result of a man's being compelled to forfeit all his belongings. It was only after 1779 that neither the whole nor any part of a criminal's property could be confiscated. Already it had been decided that in cases where slaves were condemned to death and executed, even though the verdict stated "with costs and expenses of justice", no fees should be accepted from those inhabitants — who were all, of course, responsible for their slaves — for whom it would be difficult to pay costs, besides losing the value of their bondsmen.[133]

CRIME AND PUNISHMENT

The Court itself had resolved to settle the fees due to the messenger and the secretary in respect of all condemned slaves who were privately owned. It was the secretary's duty to prepare the documents relating to each case. An amusing incident implicating this worthy official is recorded in the journal for 22 April 1689. It appears that a man had to be executed, but that the secretary of the Court was unable, through drunkenness, to write out the sentence properly, so mutilating the document instead that it was unfit to be signed. The Governor "gave him some blows with his stick" and afterwards threw a cushion at his head -- with what effect, salutary or otherwise, we are not told. Perhaps one should be glad that it was the secretary and not the executioner who had erred, or else we might have had at the Cape a repetition of a scene that took place in Hereford, England, in 1738, when two housebreakers were executed: at the tree the hangman, who was under the influence of alcohol, imagining that there were three to be executed, insisted in his inebriated state that one of the ropes should be put round the parson's neck as he stood in the cart, "and was with much difficulty prevented by the gaoler from so doing".

With regard to the punishment of Europeans at the Cape, there were certain offences for which white people, but not slaves, were severely corrected. Bigamy and adultery were two of these. One ill-fated burgher, charged by the Landdrost of Stellenbosch with adultery, was deprived of his civil and military offices and prerogatives, declared unfit ever to assume either again and ordered to be locked up for a month on a diet of bread and water, with a fine of a hundred rixdollars for the benefit of the Landdrost.

The slaves, of course, were exempt from military duties, and were therefore not liable to all those punishments which usually accompanied any transgression of the rules. Perhaps some of them enjoyed witnessing the carrying out of the sentence against a number of burghers who, as a result of reluctance or cowardice, failed to take part in a raid on the Hottentot Captain Klaas, and who stayed at home without the permission of their officers. These offenders were required to kneel on the ground in front of their respective flags, before everybody, with folded hands and bare heads, praying for forgiveness for their reprehensible behaviour. In addition, they were each fined fifty gulden; if any one of them did not wish to pay this amount, he was formally to be declared infamous and, with a well-placed kick ("met een voetschop onder sijn billen"), chased away from his flag.

Perhaps, too, the slaves relished watching the discomfiture of a certain slanderer, a woman who had spread calumnious reports about another of her sex; as a precautionary measure against this feminine practice, she was forced to stand exposed on the place of execution for an hour, with a paper on her breast bearing the word *Achterklapster* (Backbiter) for all to read. And undoubtedly they must have been puzzled and impressed on another occasion, when a large assembly of Commissioners and others solemnly looked on while the hangman ceremoniously burned at the place of execution a written libel on the good fame of the Government officials and various citizens.

Instances are recorded of Europeans being broken on the wheel, although apparently this form of punishment was reserved in the Cape almost exclusively for slaves. Thus we read that at Fort Lydsaamheid, Delagoa Bay, sixty-two men — comprising one-third of the total garrison — conspired to rebel and desert. The Commander learned of the plot in time, and he had the men arrested and put into close confinement. Owing to the circumstances of the case, the whole trial was held in a state of panic: there was no opportunity to send the conspirators immediately to Cape Town, so more than half their number were sentenced to death, while some were allowed to draw lots for their lives, with a long term of hard labour in chains included. Twenty-two of the Europeans were executed, some of them being bound on crosses and having their bones broken before their heads were cut off, and others were half-suffocated and then beheaded. Another instance occurred when sixteen European soldiers and sailors, accused of mutiny on board the *Duynenburg*, were brought to the place of execution in Table Valley and one of their number, Jean Baptist Paradys, was tied to a cross and broken alive, before being strangled to death.[134]

It was an ancient law at the Cape that slaves who were ill-treated by their masters, or inadequately supplied with food or clothing, were entitled to lay their complaints before the authorities; and, if these could be verified, they would be sold to other owners not related to the accused. Malicious slaves frequently took this chance to defame the names of their masters. Once a slave of Martin Melk's accused him of a very grave crime, of which, however, not the slightest evidence could be found when the Landdrost and two Heemraden instituted immediate investigation. These officials then cross-examined the slave, who broke down and confessed that he had told lies. Consequently he was chained to a wheelbarrow and sent to Robben Island to work there for the rest of his life.[135]

It is surprising to note how often incidents of this kind occurred during the history of slavery at the Cape. At a later date, another episode took place in a country district when a slave named Azor, from Mozambique, went to a field-cornet with allegations against his master. The latter was summoned at once to appear before the Court, and Azor stated that he had not provided him with sufficient clothes and that he had made him work too hard; he had been employed by this master for ten years, and in other respects he had no reason for complaint. Being asked from whom he had received the garments he was wearing — a Kersey jacket and a blue-checked shirt, both whole and in good condition — he admitted having been given them by his owner. He was then stripped and examined for marks left by blows or other ill-usage, but of these there were no signs at all; on the contrary, he was "thick and fat", bearing every external symptom of having been well-treated in his situation. For additional confirmation a second slave, who had accompanied Azor and who belonged to the same master, was interrogated, and he declared that he believed no person had any cause for complaint against their owner, the defendant. It was thereupon resolved, in consequence of Azor's false and calumnious assertions, to give him a beating not exceeding twenty strokes of a switch, in the presence of his master. During its infliction the latter, touched by the penitence professed by the slave at the fifth stroke, requested that the business might end there and then.

Unfortunately not all owners mentioned in the records were equally innocent of the complaints laid against them, and in instances when they were guilty of inhuman severity in dealing with their slaves they received rigorous retribution from the law. In 1702, a certain master, instead of administering ordinary correction to a slave for some misdemeanour, actually ripped his skin open with a currycomb. On another occasion a slave was accused of theft: in the first place his owner tied him to a ladder and beat him with a thick cane; then a servant continued until he was tired, when he passed his birch, made of three or four thatch yarns bound together, to another slave; this man, having given the miserable culprit about forty strokes, passed the birch on to a fourth, who was in his turn succeeded by the owner's wife, his children and other slaves. Some hours later the victim died. The Court of Justice regarded the case as one of plain murder committed with more than barbarous cruelty. The owner was condemned to be brought without delay to the place where criminal sentences were carried out, and to be handed over to the executioner; with his eyes blindfolded he was forced to kneel before a heap of sand while a naked sword was waved over his head; after this he was sent for life to Robben Island *ad opus publicum,* and all his goods were confiscated. A European farmer, for a similar crime, was taken to the place of execution, severely thrashed on the bare back, branded with a red-hot iron and consigned to Robben Island to serve a sentence of ninety-nine years in chains.[136]

For the same type of offence, one of the French refugees, Jean de Thuilet, actually received the death sentence. It appears that he suspected one of his slaves and a Hottentot of having appropriated and hidden his keys. He caught and bound them, hoisted them by their hands to a beam and thrashed them grievously with an ox-thong. He continued as long as he was able, and then with threats compelled another European to give the wretched sufferers about three blows each with the same implement. Afterwards, his rage not yet abated, De Thuilet endeavoured to kick them, but was restrained by a visitor, who urged him to take them instead to Stellenbosch and charge them there. Through the kindly intervention of this man, the brutal master untied the two blacks, but when the caller had gone he strung them up again by the feet with their heads hanging downwards, beat them all over their bodies and left them suspended in that state for about an hour. This almost incredible chronicle of human savagery concluded with his taking down the pair and trampling and kicking the Hottentot so severely that he expired on the spot, the slave dying a few days later.

At last realising the enormity of his conduct, the criminal lost no time in taking to flight, but the Court of Justice found that his was a crime "most drastically punishable" under a Government where "justice is kept pure in warding off and suppressing all licentious offences, limitless excesses and all other evils". De Thuilet was condemned to be shot as soon as he fell into the hands of the law, and meanwhile the whole of his property was confiscated. But he was never caught: it would seem that he managed to escape in one of the ships, for his name does not again appear in the Cape records.[137]

In concluding the subject of punishments imposed upon Europeans, one may quote an interesting example which occurred when a white man had wounded a slave with fatal effects. The malefactor in this instance was not an owner but a sailor. The executioner bound him to a pole, his sword was broken at his feet and, "with the utmost terror of death", a bullet was fired over his head — a particularly unnerving experience when a seventeenth-century gun was the weapon used. After this he was branded crosswise on the back with a red-hot sword, and was finally banished for life as a convict to Robben Island, all his property and pay, for good measure, having been confiscated as well. Criminals, incidentally, who were found guilty of excessive crimes were confined in the Black Hole at the Castle pending their trial. In a famous episode which took place when Willem Adriaan van der Stel was Governor, the Heemraad of Stellenbosch, Jacob van der Heiden, was put into the Black Hole together with a slave convicted of arson, with whom he shared his food and to whom he taught the Ten Commandments, the Articles of the Christian faith and the Lord's Prayer.

It must be borne in mind that for many years the Cape was regarded as a convict station: Europeans and others were often sent here from the East, and the treatment which they received certainly left a great deal to be desired. Towards the close of the Dutch East India Company's régime, the Reverend J. P. Serrurier, clergyman of the Cape Town congregation, found early one morning on his stoep a letter addressed to him in faulty French on the outside, although the actual contents were couched in the Dutch language. The communication was so disturbing that he submitted the whole matter to the Governor. Translated, the letter ran:

"Sir and Worthy Servant of Jesus Christ on Earth,—The unhappy European slaves who sigh in their chains assure you of their humble respect. They beg of you to look with compassion on their unfortunate circumstances; we pray you, Sir, as being a servant of Jesus Christ on earth to have pity on us, for although we have brought punishment on ourselves through our bad behaviour, yet we do not deserve eternal condemnation. The misdeeds of which we are guilty consist merely of a form of punishable desertion. We can go to no one but you to look for any alleviation of our sorrow. It is only in the sanctuary of Religion that we can pour out our tears and desires. We throw ourselves in your holy arms in the hope that you will ask the Governor to forgive us our false steps. Never in Africa has it happened that Europeans had to live in chains for so long a time, nor found themselves mingled with heathens who not only are guilty of the most unprecedented crimes but also are born slaves . . . it is a shame and a blot on Christians that we should be mixed with them and treated in such a brutal manner.

Among all European powers and even among the Roman Catholics the prisoners are visited by a comforter who consoles them in their sorrowful state and prevents them from forgetting the principles of religion. We are deserted by God and man; no one has mercy on us. It is as though the rattle of our chains hardens the hearts of men . . . It is therefore alone to you, who takes the place of Jesus Christ on earth and who is always the support of the unfortunate, that we apply ourselves with the respectful request that you will try to soften our fate that we may be separated from the heathen sects with whom we have to mingle.

Kindly take note that the majority of us committed our crimes in our youth, and that time, which matures one's judgment, has caused us to repent.

In former wars all European slaves were released and sent back to their fatherland . . . we do not doubt that through your mediation we could enjoy the same privilege . . . Have mercy on the unhappy European slaves, who number thirty-two . . ."

As it was impossible at the time to send these men to Robben Island, a suggestion was made that those Europeans exiled to the Cape should at any rate be separated from the Hottentots and slaves.[138]

Many of the Indian exiles were political prisoners of royal blood and high position: the Rajah of Tambora, the King of Madura, the Pangerang (Prince) Loring Pasiir, Sheik Joseph and divers others of their class were banished to the Cape, in many cases accompanied by a number of followers. Thus Sheik Joseph arrived here with his two wives as well as fourteen friends and several servants — forty-nine persons altogether. The tomb of this Javanese Mohammedan, at Zandvliet, Faure, is to this day a place of pilgrimage for those of his faith in South Africa. In 1682 he took a very active part in the Bantamese civil war, being a leader on the side opposing the Dutch, who were ultimately the successful party. In 1683 he surrendered to the Dutch forces, and for some years was kept in India as a prisoner of state. So great was the veneration felt for him by the Mohammedans, however, that the Batavian authorities felt it advisable to remove him to a distance, and in 1694 he was sent to the Cape with his retinue; here he was provided with a residence at Zandvliet, where he died and was buried in 1699. It is not certain that his body remained at this spot, because his countrymen wished it to be removed to Java, and the authorities directed the Cape Government to close its eyes if any attempt were made to transfer it there quietly.

We gain from the records a clear impression of the

general character of the Eastern type of prisoner. "Their Honours at Batavia have sent us some Ternaten great men, who had taken up arms against the Company and been made prisoners-of-war," runs an entry in 1682, and another during the following year notes the arrival of a certain exile, "a Bantam Javanese of high family, but an arch rogue, whom the Bantam King requested to be sent away . . ." Men such as these were little disposed to moderate their lavish style of living, as far as was possible in banishment, and sometimes they had to be severely taken down, as in the case of the Prince of Ternate. This potentate and his slave, "whom he uses as a pointer to find his game", were sentenced to be thrashed by the Caffres and afterwards relegated to Robben Island, there to work for their food. The Prince had been guilty of admitting to and harbouring in his house, by day and by night, Europeans as well as slaves of both sexes, for "gambling, whoring and other irregularities". Exile in a foreign settlement was by no means to the taste of these oriental aristocrats, and we read of at least one strenuous — though, as it turned out, unsuccessful — attempt to avoid this fate: a political prisoner by the name of De Rottij offered no less than one hundred slaves in lieu of himself if the Company would grant him his freedom.[139]

From early days the advent of these Eastern people had been viewed with disfavour in the colony, a fact acknowledged in a tacitly apologetic dispatch dated 1681: "Though you do not like to be burdened at the Cape with many convicts, and we shall act as sparingly as possible in this matter, the service of the Company and present circumstances have demanded from us to send you a considerable number of exiles and evil spirits, who, for reasons, dare not be trusted in this country or left here . . . Among this lot are Princes, etc. . . . and Assang and Jare, slaves in Crani Lambeengy's service. Crani was sent out as an exile . . ." In fact, so many Malays, both exiles and slaves, from various parts of the East came to the Cape that strict orders were issued to the Governor and Council of India prohibiting the dispatch of any more. Then, too, a placcaat was issued dated 28 September 1767 by which all authorities or anybody else leaving India were strictly forbidden to take with them any

Eastern male slaves to the Cape, either for sale or in execution of orders received, or otherwise. Described as "dier gevaarlyke creaturen" (these dangerous creatures), Eastern slaves were confiscated if imported into the Cape on the sly, and those responsible were heavily fined. According to a resolution of the Council of Policy, it was considered that the settlement was also becoming too full of European convicts who, after their term of imprisonment had expired, remained here free, "competing with the poor whites of European descent in procuring their livelihood, and consequently very injurious to the latter"; the authorities at Batavia were therefore asked for permission to send the white convicts back to the places whence they came, after the completion of their terms of banishment.

An additional reason why neither the Malay slaves nor the Malay exiles were welcome in the colony was their terrifying habit of running amok: without any apparent cause, on these occasions, they would rush into the streets armed with short-handled *krisses* or knives, crying out "Amok, amok!" and slashing, hacking, cutting at every person they met until they themselves were overpowered or killed. When this dreadful cry went echoing through Cape Town, women fainted and men took to their heels as fast as they could. And no wonder! To these Malays, amok-running was the national and honourable way of committing suicide; the recognised avenue of escape from difficulties; the heroic method of revenging themselves upon mankind.

Towards the end of the year 1750 a tragic scene was enacted in the shadow of Table Mountain. One of the exiles armed himself with a poniard and a sharp *kris*, and dashed out into the streets of Cape Town. Within a few minutes he had stabbed to death two night-watchmen and a slave. He then ran on, bloody *kris* in hand, hacking at everyone whom he encountered. A few feet away from the Governor's house, situated in the Company's garden, he murdered the sentry on duty, annexed his bayonet and attacked another sentry who was on his way to relieve his comrade. When the Governor heard of these onslaughts, he selected his strongest slave, provided him with a sword and told him to fetch the surgeon. *En route* to the latter's residence, the slave met the amok-runner and a stand-up fight ensued. For many minutes they thrust and struck at each other, but without inflicting any wound, until at last the Malay fled. That night, heavily armed soldiers and burghers patrolled the town and warned the citizens to be on their guard. Next morning a reward of one hundred rixdollars was offered to anyone who caught the criminal, dead or alive, and a large commando was sent to the outskirts of the city to prevent him from escaping into the interior.

Meanwhile the amok-runner had found a hiding-place in the mountain, where he was discovered by a burgher and six of his servants. Called upon to surrender, he refused. They fired on him and the would-be suicide rushed madly forward, bayonet in hand, fighting with maniacal fury. He wounded four men, one of them fatally, and was attacking the burgher himself when a servant suddenly seized a tremendous stone and hurled it at his head. The amok-runner fell instantly, with a smashed skull. In due course the Court of Justice pronounced sentence. First of all, every bone in his body was broken, then his right hand was cut off, his head severed and his trunk quartered and dragged through Cape Town. Finally each quarter was exhibited at a different cross-road. When the authorities counted those killed and wounded by this desperate criminal, they found that there were eighteen victims, several of whom were buried the following morning.

One or two early travellers mention cases of amok-running which they witnessed. We are told of a Malay who, being justly chastised by his master, suddenly drew a knife and stabbed him to the heart, after which he rushed out of the house, his weapon dripping with the blood of the unfortunate victim. In Strand Street he met a handsome slave girl, seventeen years old, into whose face he dashed the dreadful weapon. Luckily a country farmer was at that moment passing in a wagon. Quick as lightning he seized his loaded gun and shot the maniac dead on the spot.

That hardy adventurer and traveller, Christopher Frycke, had a narrow escape in similar circumstances. He narrates that no sooner had he landed from his ship than an amok-runner, "who had done a great deal of mischief, and put the people in an uproar, came running by me, and by good fortune did me no harm", although he killed a youth just a few yards away. At last the man was shot in the head, and so despatched. "Nothing saved me," says Frycke, "but the corner of the street, by means of which, as he ran so furiously, he overshot me, and got past me before I could get aware of him; and so, God be praised, I was safe, but ever since I was always upon my guard at turnings and crossings of streets."

Another case is recorded in which an aged Malabar slave showed both courage and resourcefulness. Having beheld the murders perpetrated by an amok-runner, this man, a woodcutter, waited outside a doorway through which he expected the criminal to rush, and when he did so smote him on the head with his axe, killing him instantly. As a reward the old man received one hundred rixdollars and his freedom.

Chapter Ten

THE GIFT OF FREEDOM

FROM the city of Amsterdam there arrived at the Cape one day a letter of freedom together with a note addressed to a young slave woman called Bintham and her child called Primus, born at Naarden. Translated, the note reads:

"Bintham:

Freedom   Equality   Fraternity

"I promised to write to you and now I am fulfilling that promise. I arrived in England hale and hearty and will shortly leave for Holland. As soon as I am at home with my wife and children, I shall write to you again.

In my pocket book I came across some paper money which I am sending you: purchase with it whatever you will.

I trust that you will always bear in mind your promise to me — to look after yourself well and to behave yourself as becomes a respectable person, faithfully and honestly serving Mr. and Mrs. Hohne, neither neglecting yourself nor associating with unprincipled people or 'zwarte jongens'.

You are now *Free*! I feel that I have done everything in my power for you. Were I to hear that you are behaving yourself, I shall not forget you, nor shall I ever neglect to provide for you; and when I return to the Cape, you must again come to me. With the first opportunity I shall send you something.

Now, Bintham, I have no time left to write more. I have written to Mrs. Hohne. Ask her to write direct to me and also suggest to Myntjie that she should write a short note for you to me. Brother Gees, to whom I have also written, will come and talk to you. Adieu, Bintham! Farewell! Look after yourself well, care for your little child well and live respectably. Be faithful. Be honest. Never neglect yourself. And always bear in mind your good friends and your Master, who will never forget you.

Jan Valkenburg."[140]

Like Bintham, hundreds of slaves received their freedom from those whom they had served loyally — although it must be admitted that sometimes good conduct proved in itself an obstacle to emancipation, because a slave's pecuniary value increased in proportion to the satisfaction given by his behaviour. In the seventeenth and eighteenth centuries, Christian men and women at the Cape showed great kindness towards their slaves, in accordance with the exhortation of the Apostle Paul: "Remember those that are in bonds, as if bound with them; (and) those that are cruelly treated, as being yourselves also in the body". Some slaves were emancipated by will, others by their owners for faithful service, others again by relations or friends already free who purchased them for the express purpose of manumission, and quite a number bought their freedom themselves from their masters with money obtained in various ways. Sometimes slave girls were emancipated by owners who wished to marry them, or by whom they were with child.

Naturally enough, many of these slaves, as soon as they had received letters of freedom, wished to return to their native lands, and, on condition that they paid the full double passage, no objection was made. Sometimes, when the applicants were too poor to pay, they were allowed to work their passage overseas.[141] These letters, or acts of emancipation, incidentally, had particularly to contain the information whether freedom had been bought or otherwise acquired. Children of a female slave born previously to the time prescribed for liberation, or pending the fulfilment of the condition, were to be considered slaves. This circumstance caused much heart-burning amongst those women whom it affected, and it is noticeable how many of them, through the course of the years, managed in some way to obtain the freedom of their offspring.

We can still read the statement taken down in one

instance by a notary from a slave woman who laid various complaints about her former owner: towards the end of the deposition, she says "My cruel master had advanced through all the gradations of power and honour ... I am christened, and allowed to approach the altar of my Maker, whilst my heart is rent with the knowledge that my children are denied this blessing. They are obliged to follow their mistress on each Sabbath; they are bound to wait in the street until the service is concluded, when they bear back the proud mistress's stool and the blessed Book, the record of our Lord's humbleness".[142]

In the early days, proprietors of aged or sickly slaves were sometimes anxious to be rid of them and therefore gave them their freedom, with the result that in the course of time these unfortunate mortals became a public burden, and caused a severe drain on the relief funds in charge of the deacons of the Reformed Church. Even the Government itself was not guiltless of throwing on the mercy of the country slaves who could scarcely be expected to fend for themselves. Thirty years after the first importation of slaves, a note appeared in the journal to the effect that the Council of Policy had unanimously decided to manumit some male and female slaves, at their own request, as they had served well and faithfully for many years, and as they were now "old and worn-out and no longer able to be of any service". This loose method of freeing bondspeople, however, ceased in 1708, when Commissioner Simons established a law that no owner could emancipate his slave without first producing the names of two guarantors who would stand security that the freed man or woman would not become an incumbent upon the poor funds within ten years, as laid down in the Statutes of Batavia.

Nevertheless, as time went on more and more slaves were emancipated, and thus a progressively greater number came to rely on the funds of the Dutch Reformed Church for support. Already in 1753 the Batavian Government had resolved that the payment of ten rixdollars should be exacted from the owners for every slave emancipated — an order which was brought into force at the Cape twelve years later. Later again, after 1777, it was made a *sine qua non*, generally speaking, that anyone when freeing a slave should pay the sum of fifty rixdollars to the funds — the Council reserving the right to exercise their discretion when required — as well as supplying the usual security that the liberated individual would not develop into a burdensome pauper for a period of ten years.[143]

The fact that the Dutch Reformed Church received this amount for every slave enfranchised caused dissatisfaction among the members of the Lutheran Church, who pointed out in a petition that if a freed slave became an adherent of the Lutheran confession, and if he happened to be reduced to poverty, the Lutheran Church was obliged to maintain him. They therefore naturally requested that their Church might share the privilege with the Reformed Church in regard to enfranchised individuals proving themselves to be of the denomination. At the same time they referred to a regulation laid down concerning the christening of children, to the effect that in a family where one parent was Protestant and the other Lutheran, a son had to be baptised in the church to which the father belonged and a daughter in the mother's church. They requested that an amendment should be made enabling the parents to follow their own choice in the matter.

In spite of the conditions imposed, kind-hearted owners were not deterred in their eagerness to bestow freedom on certain of their slaves. In 1783 the Governor personally and deliberately decided to oppose the excessive number of manumissions and to make the process more difficult thenceforth — "ten eynde diergelyke meenigvuldige vrygeevingen van slaven zo veel moogelyk tegen te gaan en voor het vervolg bezwaarlyker te maken" — by increasing the term during which the guarantors had to hold themselves responsible, if necessary, for the sustenance and alimentation of any freed slave from ten to twenty years.[144] This Governor's attitude might well have been inspired by Milton's couplet penned in the previous century:

"Licence they mean when they cry Liberty;
For who loves that, must first be wise and good."

Meanwhile, even in Mentzel's time, the poor fund of the Church was in an extremely flourishing state: the collection plate returned a considerable sum annually, and at Communion the wealthier burghers unobtrusively slipped whole piles of ducats under the napkins that covered the vessels. Donations were made from outside sources as well, such as the generous amount of five thousand gulden left by Ryk Tulbagh on his death to the poor fund, on condition that the trustees would undertake to support those of his slaves who were infirm, the rest of them being emancipated.

After many of the Company's aged slaves had been liberated it was realised that not a few of them, through one cause or another, were unable to make ends meet. A resolution of 1682 stated that from time to time a number of such slaves, male and female, had been manumitted in order to maintain themselves as freemen, "and some others have now appeared before the meeting also asking for their freedom, but as it has been found that some of them have afterwards fallen back on the hands of the Company, not knowing how to earn a living", it was decided that such slaves should no longer be set at liberty, and that all those who had previously obtained their freedom but who might yet appeal to the Company for support should again be made and considered slaves, "as it is but fair that if the Company must maintain them that they should return to their former servitude".[145]

Even private slaves who had been set free, if guilty of certain crimes, could easily find themselves sold back into bondage. Thus Flora of Bengal, manumitted under the will of her late master, was both impoverished and guilty of scandalous crimes — so much so that she had been whipped and branded on the cheek — and the authorities ordered that she should be re-sold into servitude notwithstanding the provisions of the will, as it was regarded as improper and contrary to the established laws that such a person should enjoy freedom to the annoyance and detriment of others. In any case, it was significantly added, she was not a Christian.[146] This attitude was by no means confined to the case of slaves. On numerous occasions European servants of the Company who had received their letters of freedom, and who subsequently abused the privilege, were simply taken back into the Company's service. For instance, a free fisherman bearing the nickname of Pieter de Noorman was again received into official service as arquebusier, in order that he might be sent to work on Robben Island and so be prevented from tyrannizing over his wife.

In some cases emancipated slaves voluntarily sought to be taken back into ownership, finding their freedom, with the consequent obligation of providing for themselves, a burden rather than a blessing, even though, when possible, they were often assisted by their former masters and mistresses and their friends. An interesting instance is quoted by Dr. de Haan, of a slave girl, Elizabeth of Bengal, whose master liberated her and her two children. Left to her own resources, she soon discovered that in her previous state as a slave she had been in a more enviable position, and so she asked for the letter of emancipation to be repudiated and the necessary documents drawn up to place her once again under the "yoke" of slavery.

The great kindness shown to many of the privately-owned slaves by their masters is illustrated in the wills of early colonists, who well knew the difficulties which would confront these dependants when deprived of protection through the death of their owners. Repeatedly we find evidence that these good people made ample provision for the maintenance of their slaves. One widow, for example, willed that on her decease her slave girl, Lena, and all her children should be given their freedom at the expense of her estate. A small house, fully equipped with furniture and effects, was to be purchased for Lena, to whose eldest child, moreover, the mistress's large Bible was bequeathed as a token of remembrance, with the precautionary rider that it "zal nimmer mogen werden verkogt" (must never be sold). All the other slaves in the household were provided for as well; all were to receive clothing and further necessities.

Freed black men and women, never forgetting the days when they too had been slaves, were responsible for a relatively tremendous proportion of emancipations, and for this commendable chapter in our history we must give them full credit. A notable case was that of Maria of the Cape, aged two years, who was not only manumitted through the agency of a freed slave woman but was also actually left 3,000 gulden by her benefactress so that she should not become a charge on the diaconate.

From even a cursory perusal of the wills, one soon realises that there were indeed many families as well as individuals who cherished feelings of genuine attachment towards their slaves. A burgher of Stellenbosch, Van Rheenen, declared in his will that, upon his decease, his faithful slave boy, Karel of Bengal, should not only be immediately set free but should also be made the sole heir to everything he possessed. Pieter Hanssen was another owner who bequeathed all his belongings to his slave, but unfortunately this testator, through forgetfulness, omitted to make arrangements for his heir's emancipation. The Council, however, appreciated without question that this had been the late master's intention, on account of the slave's loyal services, and they therefore had no hesitation in handing him his letter of freedom; they also excused him from paying the usual amount to the poor fund and from finding two sureties.

It often happened that certain conditions were laid down by owners before manumission could be granted. Sometimes a slave was required to reach a stipulated age before permission was given. Captain Rhenius made a proviso when leaving his slave girl to his brother that she should be emancipated if she behaved herself properly and was desired in marriage by a respectable person. As his brother soon applied for her manumission, we must presume that she became a happy bride. It is interesting to observe that in her case Mr. Rhenius gave the names of two free blacks as sureties. One or two of the inhabitants displayed a somewhat more parsimonious spirit when awarding freedom to their slaves. A certain widow expressed her willingness to emancipate her slave boy on the following conditions: firstly, that he would always provide for her maintenance; secondly, that he would bear the expenses of her funeral and honest burial; and thirdly, that he paid for the mourning dresses, the church duty and the costs.

Kindly, courteous old Simon van der Stel desired that two of his slaves — Hendrik Constant, aged thirty-six years, and Lena, aged forty — should be emancipated after his death in consideration of their long term of faithful service;

it was his express wish that they should marry each other and that they should always show respect towards his descendants. Anna Rebecca of Bengal, a freed black woman, willed that immediately after her demise her slave April of Ceylon should receive his freedom, together with his little daughter Johanna — on condition that he did not desert the child but cared for her until she was old enough to earn her own living. She also left the girl one hundred rixdollars and all her gold and silver jewellery. Even those colonists who were in poor circumstances often tried to reward their slaves who had served them faithfully during their lifetime. There is pathos in the will of a burgher who mentions in that document that his slave girl Dorinda of Bengal — whom he had been forced to pawn on one occasion, and who was subsequently redeemed by his two sons with the contents of their money-boxes — was never to be sold, neither she herself nor her sickly, deformed son. He trusted that she would be looked after by his children, whom he requested to allow her to work and earn money so that she could support her child.[147]*

Amongst applications for permission to liberate slaves, one frequently comes across those sent in by heirs who inherited from their parents slaves as well as property. Many of them had grown up in the company of these black people, who had perhaps even been their playmates in the days of their youth. It was a golden opportunity for them, as owners, to repay in some measure all the little acts of kindness and attention which they had received from the slaves.

Occasionally slaves were sold on condition that they were never to be emancipated. One slave girl arrived at

---

* Sometimes one comes across in the records such an interesting and rare document as the will of an actual slave. The last testament of Kitjiel, the slave of Johan David Piton, for instance, is worth mentioning; he left all his possessions to "zijn byzit de Vrye meyd Flora" — his concubine the freewoman Flora — and their children begotten together, Primo, Silvia, Fredrik and Hannetje. Now and again, cases in which children benefited showed how scattered a single family of slaves could become: Alie, a free black woman, bequeathed her belongings, which formed quite a considerable estate, to her seven children, Rachel, Lea, Filander, Chrisje (who received an ex ten rixtradollars on account of her unselfish and devoted service to the testatrix on her sick-bed), Vlooitje, April and Alida; all of these worked for different masters, some at Paarl, one at Swellendam and another at Worcester.

the Cape from Batavia whose deed of sale stipulated that she was not to be permitted ever again to set foot on that island; if at any time the present owner wished to re-sell her, that condition was to be expressly observed. Sometimes slaves were sold with the proviso that if they saved enough money to buy their freedom (usually the amount for which they were purchased), this privilege was not to be withheld from them. The memorials for 1721 include an uncommon one from Leander of Malabar, a slave, who said that in the year 1717, at a sale on Mr. Samuel Elsevier's farm, he was bought by the Prince of Ternate, for two hundred and one rixdollars. The Indian exile had promised to give him his liberty if he refunded that sum to him. Accordingly Leander worked hard, and within four years had amassed the required sum. He then paid it to the Prince, who, after having received it, refused to comply with his part of the arrangement. The petitioner therefore asked the Government to compel the Prince to manumit him, and attached the receipt for the money, with the Prince's mark on it.[148]

At times complications arose in connection with the purchase and the emancipation of slaves, and the Government felt impelled to administer a sharp rebuke. "To our great surprise," the authorities once announced, "we have noticed that a number of the inhabitants, despite the Statutes of India, with the purchase and sale of slaves neglect to inform the Secretary of the Council, with the result that a great deal of confusion arises; many slaves are also given their freedom by wills, etc., without the knowledge or consent of the Government." If this state of affairs continued, the poor fund would again be encumbered, and so the colonists were ordered not to manumit slaves without first obtaining the necessary permission and supplying the required guarantors. Neither were any slaves to return from Holland with the impression that they could simply settle down forthwith at the Cape as freemen; here again the Government's sanction would have to be sought. According to the Statutes of Batavia of 1669 and 1784, no slaves were to be transferred otherwise than before the Secretary of the Council, or notary and witnesses, and even then only after each slave concerned admitted that he was the property of the man wishing to dispose of him. If this admission were not made, no document could be drawn up, and notice had to be given to the Fiscal for investigation.[149]

Hudson tells us in his diary that instances frequently arose in the colony of slaves saving sufficient money to purchase their freedom. Those permitted to work on their own account toiled very hard and took their usual allowance to their masters regularly every evening, reserving for themselves the surplus, which was sometimes considerable. He adds that tradesmen, particularly, had plenty of opportunity to put aside savings — in fact, on the Sabbath, which was a free day for them, an expert workman among the slaves "earns as much from his leisure hours as many country tradesmen in England do the whole week" — and, having collected together small sums, were able to turn them to advantage, often assisted by those of their fellows who were already at liberty. Several inhabitants, finding that their slaves possessed this industrious tendency, encouraged it by numberless acts of generosity and interest, and set a low price upon their freedom as a further incentive to their exertions.

He also relates that a slave once liberated seldom forgot the family to which he had formerly belonged, and was still considered one of the household, claiming their advice and sometimes their assistance to enable him to carry out his little mercantile concerns, and on New Year's Day — the principal festive occasion amongst the Dutch — receiving some trifling present from his ex-master or ex-mistress as a remembrance of his satisfactory conduct.

An explicit example of how an industrious slave could improve his position is described in the diary in a vivid pen-picture of a Malay named Frank, "a singular character now living in Cape Town . . . a strange mixture of good nature and folly. This man was formerly a slave, but by dint of good behaviour and a determination to shake off the trammels of slavery he bargained with his master for a certain price for his freedom, and was indefatigable till he had hoarded up the sum agreed on. He then with the small sum left became a fruit dealer and fish seller, till in a few years he had saved sufficient to purchase him two slaves and a boat, and to furnish his home as Malay houses generally are furnished. Business increased, and when the English established themselves in this Colony in 1795 old Frank was in high esteem with the captains upon the station, who recommended him to the crews as an honest good fellow — sometimes receiving several thousand rixdollars at a time. Admiral Sir Roger Curtis was his warm friend . . . He has become rich and really deserves his honest gains. When Frank purchases a slave, he makes the condition with him that 'if you serve me faithfully for so many years you are then free, and I shall give you sufficient money to begin for yourself. If you act otherwise, I shall sell you'. And he invariably keeps his word unless he can gain a proselyte to his faith, then emancipation is the consequence. Several have received from this humane creature the blessing of Liberty, and with a liberal hand he gives them sufficient to begin the world as free men . . .

He procured from the Dutch Government a grant of land upon the side of the Lion Rump as a burying-place for those of his persuasion, and you will see old Frank with his boys working all the leisure hours he has from other employment erecting a wide wall round this sacred spot that the remains of his friends may not be disturbed by the cattle that are constantly grazing upon the side of the mountain . . . Frank some time ago informed me his intention was to leave the Cape; that he had made over all his property to his wife and adopted children, and that he was determined to visit the Tomb of the Prophet, and several applications have been made to the captains of vessels going to India for a passage, but hitherto without effect . . ."

Sometimes an owner found difficulties in the way of his liberating a slave immediately, and he would arrange to do so at a later date. For instance, a certain slave was once transferred for a period of two years on condition that the new master would look after his welfare, provide him with the necessary clothes and food and see that he did not perform any arduous agricultural work, such as labouring with the spade, and that on the expiration of the stated period he could not be sold, but was to be given his freedom. In many a case such a strong bond of mutual understanding and affection existed between a slave and his master and a slave girl and her mistress that they were liberated on the decease of their respective owners, and often at the same time the rest of the household slaves were handed over to these favoured ones to be their own servitors. Occasionally even privately-owned slaves who were allowed to earn their own living purchased servants to assist them. Nevertheless, we can well imagine the surprise of the authorities in January 1756, when they discovered that a Company's slave, residing in the Slave Lodge, had died and left a slave named January of Boegis actually belonging to himself! Such a problem had no precedent at the Cape, so without delay they took counsel together, referred to the Statutes of India and decided that in the circumstances January was the lawful property of the Company, and as such should be appropriated, so this measure was accordingly taken.[150]

When the Company gave letters of freedom to its slaves, it was on condition that they had reached a certain age, had been baptised and were thoroughly proficient in the use of the Dutch language. Such slaves were never required to give securities or to donate sums of money to the poor fund. Frequently they were taken into the Company's service at fixed salaries. Jacob of Madagascar, emancipated because of his long servitude, was appointed as sailor to be employed as interpreter in the slave trade with his native island; while another man who had worked steadfastly and well for the Company for twenty years, as mason, received both his freedom and further employment in that capacity at ten gulden per month. In rare instances it occurred that the Company attached a proviso to emancipation, such as in the case of a slave who was a highly skilled cook; with reluctance the authorities handed him his letter of freedom, and expressly stipulated in so doing that when the General or Councillors of India arrived at the Cape, or when any public dinner was given, he would be obliged to cook for the Company.[151]

It sometimes happened that a slave woman in the Lodge married and then requested the manumission of her children born previously out of wedlock. Griscella of the Cape, wife of a white free burgher, applied for the emancipation of her son, still a slave in the Lodge, so that he could be properly educated, and she offered in exchange a healthy male slave. Shortly afterwards she sent in a similar petition on behalf of her daughter Maria, aged seven years, and some months later yet another applying for the freedom of her youngest child, four years old.

Occasionally inhabitants who particularly wished to own slaves already in the Company's possession asked for permission to take them over, in exchange for others whom they could offer. This practice had been forbidden in principle by Commander Goske in 1671, and the local authorities found it convenient to refer to these instructions whenever they desired to refuse a request of this nature. On the other hand, it was quite often allowed — in fact, a memorial exists, written by the overseer of the Lodge to Lord Macartney shortly after the English annexation of the Cape, asking that a certain Capetonian might be permitted to manumit a female slave, over fifty years of age, belonging to the Government. He wished to make her his heiress, and would give in exchange an eighteen-year-old male slave, valued at six hundred rixdollars. Is there a hint of disingenousness, one wonders, underlying the unctuous rectitude of the words in which the old hand discreetly prompts newly-installed authority not to miss such an advantageous offer — "such changes, tending at once to the benefit of Government and to the happiness of a poor slave, were very usual under the former Government"!

The Lord of Mydrecht left instructions that Company's slaves who had been imported could be given their freedom after thirty years' faithful service, while those born at the Cape were eligible for this privilege as soon as they attained the age of forty, provided that they knew the Netherlands language and professed the Christian faith. His motives were that the Company's slaves should not be worse off than those owned by private individuals, and that they should not be compelled to "sigh under constant slavery". He trusted that this regulation would tend to stimulate their interest in good conduct, "for except in this way, there is no hope open to them".

The principle of compulsory manumission was not unknown at the Cape. To encourage fidelity in slaves towards their owners, any of them who saved their masters or mistresses from murder or other violence, or those who risked their own safety and did their utmost in attempting to save them, were to be emancipated immediately — and, in the latter instance, were on no account to be sold by their owners' executors or administrators. As late as 1807 we find a request for the emancipation of a slave who had preserved the life of his master at the peril of his own, "at the time of the horrible murder committed by an Eastern exile in the evening of the 25 September, 1786".[152]

Freedom was also frequently offered to a slave by the Government as a reward for the discovery of a crime, the Court of Justice in such cases fixing the appraisement. An interesting example occurred in 1760 when a bondsman, at the greatest danger to himself, managed to escape from the hands of a band of fugitive slaves who had taken him prisoner, and at once reported the whereabouts of their hiding-place, with the result that they were arrested. So pleased were the members of the Council of Policy with the initiative and resourcefulness of this slave that, having first given his master as compensation two hundred and twenty-five rixdollars collected privately amongst themselves, they manumitted him, as an inspiration to other slaves to do their duty.[153] Sometimes acts of conspicuous bravery and service were performed by women slaves as well; one of the earliest on record occurred on 25 September 1658, when W. C. Mostert and a number of his slaves were cutting some wood near the Fort. Suddenly they beheld a large leopard pounce on a foal, not four yards away from Mostert. A female slave, seeing the foal under the leopard's feet, approached the brute with an axe and "cut it so thoroughly in the head and neck that it remained dead on the spot".

Special premiums were paid to European soldiers or sailors who assisted in the capture or destruction of enemy ships; to slaves who participated in this type of work freedom had to be awarded.[154]

In Holland, of course, slavery did not exist, and therefore, in the seventeenth century at any rate, slaves taken across to the fatherland were automatically free as soon as they set foot on its soil.[155] This fact sometimes led to complications. Amongst the records of the Court of Justice for 1813 is a letter from the Fiscal to the President of the Court, giving details regarding the case of a certain Saronie of Batavia who, he said, had accompanied her then master, G. van Grol, from Batavia to Holland nearly thirty years before. There she remained in his service for two and a half years, first in the city of Utrecht and afterwards at Zwolle, where she was brought to bed of a son, to whom was given the name Pieter. After this, she and her son were handed over by Mr. van Grol to an officer, to be transported by him to the Acting Fiscal at the Cape, who took them into his service as slaves, and later sold them to separate masters. In the course of time, both she and the boy were sold again to different people, until at last, at the time of the Fiscal's letter, she was a slave in the service of a Mr. During, and her son in that of Mr. van der Spuy.

Strangely enough, stated the Fiscal, Mr. van Grol happened just then to be at the Cape, although he was preparing to depart for Batavia. He therefore asked him for a clarification of the position, which Van Grol gave in writing from the ship as she was leaving the bay. As a result of his investigations, the Fiscal felt that the present owners of Saronie and her son could not be prosecuted, as they had bought them in good faith; nevertheless, as Saronie had been in Holland for two years she must be freed, and as her son had been born on that soil he must obviously be considered a free man. Therefore it behoved all concerned to see to it that Saronie and her son received every possible help in rehabilitating themselves without delay as free people. He also asked the Court to grant them their liberty without any expenses; even their letters of freedom should be issued *Pro Deo* and without the usual stamps.[156]

In the records one often comes across cases in which free individuals were sold as slaves. Although nominally for the crime of "menschenroof" — stealing of people — the penalty was death, to be dealt out to those "who transport or steal people out of the Company's possessions", there were among those exiled to the Cape a number of offenders who had stolen children and then attempted to sell them. One of these was Jerla, of the Caste Toeloewa Wellala and an inhabitant of Nagapatnam, who received a sentence of twelve years' banishment for kidnapping, on the grounds that he "had not hesitated to decoy with sugar into a house a girl four years old, named Erritz, in order to sell her as a slave, telling the women of the house to look for buyers, and that he had six months ago bought her at Tranquebar".

As early as 1681, J. Marquart was sued before the Court of Justice by C. Stevens for the recovery of the price paid for a free person who had been sold to him as a slave. Marquart lost the case as he was unable to produce the necessary documents, and he had to repay the amount in addition to the Court charges. Even long after the days of the Dutch East India Company at the Cape, memorials were received from men and women claiming that they were unjustly detained in servitude. Sameda, in 1819, wrote to the Governor, demanding her freedom and that of her children. She asked him to consult the records of 1790 in order to ascertain in what capacity her mother and herself had been received on board the ship that brought them from Ceylon; as she pointed out, the transportation of slaves from Ceylon into the colony was prohibited, and the Government's permission was required before slaves or freemen could be taken as passengers into any Dutch ship.[157]

"It is the general opinion," wrote Sir John Cradock in 1814, "that there are very many persons in this colony in a state of slavery, who are not under any just or even legal claims in that unfortunate situation," but he added that any remedy in the existing circumstances could scarcely be hoped for. "From the earliest period," he explained, "this colony has been the resort of strangers of every description from all parts of the world; they have brought with them persons in their service from India, Java, Ceylon and many other places, upon whose original lot, time and distance, deception and avarice have thrown impenetrable mystery. Every reasoning and supposition may be in their favour, that they were not slaves, but it seems impossible at this hour to overcome the obstructions even in the course of justice."

To stress his point Sir John enclosed a petition from

Classina, a Bengal woman, who now claimed her freedom, as well as that of her numerous descendants, after a lapse of sixty-five years. In this document Classina said that during the 1740's she had been brought to Cape Town together with her father and mother, free people from their native Bengal, by the Governor, the Honourable Zigterman, in order to proceed with the same to Holland. As she was then yet a child, the Governor recommended her remaining at the Cape in good hands while both her parents went with him to Holland, where afterwards her mother died and whence her father returned to Bengal. She was baptised in 1746 in the Dutch Reformed Church, "and whereas the Petitioner as a Christian for the clearing of her conscience before God as well as her children, in her decrepit age, and before her death could wish to know from whence the state of slavery of her children has its origin", she requested that relevant enquiries should be made. The Court of Justice expended much trouble and thought upon the matter. "I am persuaded, and so is the Public," wrote Sir John Cradock, "that she is not a slave; but the difficulty lies in the obligation to prove it . . . If through the force of feeling this woman had been declared free, her progeny, to a great extent indeed, would have participated in her emancipation", and so the petitioner and her offspring had to continue in a state of slavery.[158]

By the Batavian Regulation dated 10 April 1770 it was enacted that no slaves who had been catechised and confirmed in the Christian religion should be sold; and, of course, the inhabitants of the Cape were included in the duty of obeying to the letter the provisions of that humane enactment. Although, strangely enough, it does not appear in any of the local placcaats, this regulation was observed at the Cape: after that date and up till 1812 no testamentary document was considered valid unless the notary had introduced into the body of the will a clause purporting that he had informed the testator of the existence of this law . . . "And I, the notary, having acquainted the Testator with the order of the Supreme Government of India, that, namely, slaves who have been confirmed in the Christian Religion may not be sold . . ."

The preamble to this admirable law contained a statement that the enormity was fully realised of the act of taking slaves who had made profession of their Christian faith and selling them together with heathens, at a public auction or in any other manner. It gave to those in bondage an abhorrence of Christianity, and would certainly not encourage them to become Christians. It had therefore been decided, it was said, to make a law which would prevent this, and which at the same time would not deprive the owner of the services of the slave. Owners of slaves were consequently enabled to arrange that in the event of their death or departure from the country any of the following measures could be taken:

(*a*) their slaves would be emancipated;

(*b*) they would be bequeathed to relations or friends, on the understanding, however, that they would never be sold;

(*c*) they would be handed over, for a nominal amount to be fixed by competent authorities, to any persons whose Christian principles or love of mankind would render them prepared to give these people their freedom;

(*d*) the slaves would be allowed to purchase themselves free, either at their original purchase price or for an amount to be decided by taxation.

The usual sum which was payable for letters of freedom would in these instances be waived.

Certain officials of the Company were entitled to have one or two slaves to assist them. To the sergeant of the Fort was relegated a youth from the Slave Lodge to look after his children. In the course of time the youngsters became so attached to this little slave that the sergeant wrote to the Company, saying that they could not bear the thought of ever parting with him, and offering to give in exchange a fine, healthy male slave. This request, however, was refused. When the Honourable van Goens was at the Cape he was allotted a small slave boy called Toontje. During his illness the slave had smeared and rubbed him, and now Van Goens felt that he owed his recovery "next to God" to Toontje, whom he accordingly wished to take away with him. This was permitted. A tiny slave, Paul of the Cape, aged eighteen months, whose father and mother were owned respectively by a free burgher and by the Company, received his full freedom, as it was taken into account that since his birth he had been maintained by his father in the burgher's house, and also that it would cost the Company a great deal before little Paul could be of any service.

The care of aged and infirm slaves was always a problem to those who were in the evening of their lives. It was obviously of little use to emancipate those no longer able to earn their bread and butter. Numerous owners realised that many freed slaves were leading a lazy, aimless existence, living from hand to mouth, putting nothing aside for a rainy day and, more likely than not, depending on the poor funds for assistance in times of illness or necessity. Fortunately, there were always compassionate people to be found who were willing to look after these slaves, as, for instance, in the case of Rudolph Siegfried Alleman's blind slave, who was given a home and assured of food and clothing. Johannes Mulder and his wife, in their will, jointly undertook and individually promised each other that whichever of them lived longer would care for those of their slaves who were too old to fend for themselves but whose faithful service was never to be forgotten.[159]

Longevity amongst slaves was by no means unusual. Lichtenstein mentions the cases of one or two of them who lived well over a hundred years. On one occasion this traveller came across a slave who must have been nearly one hundred and twenty; although he himself could not tell his age, from many circumstances it could be calculated almost to a nicety. He remembered perfectly that when he left his native country, Java, the name of the Governor of Batavia had been Van Oudtshoorn. In addition, when he went on the morning of 1 January 1801 to offer his best wishes to his master upon the dawn of a new century, he remarked that it was the second time he had performed this ceremony. A hundred years before, he said, he and all his fellow-slaves at the time had presented themselves before their owner "at the Cape Town, to offer him the like good wishes", and it was only by his having done so that he could on the second occasion instruct his comrades in their duty, since it was a piece of courtesy which they were not aware ought to be practised. This old man, incidentally, spoke with great warmth and gratitude of his master, who, he declared, took such excellent care of him, although he was unable to work any longer; and these praises were unanimously echoed by the other slaves.

"We saw here another remarkable instance of longevity among this class," recorded Lichtenstein, "in the person of a Malay slave now a hundred and seven years old."

The word "slave" so often conjures up in one's mind a mountain of injustice; and in the foreground we visualise the unhappy creatures being beaten mercilessly with sjamboks and knotted ropes. Actually, however, it must not be forgotten that, as Commissary General de Mist said, the life and condition of a slave at the Cape very much resembled that of a cattle-herd, shepherd or farmhand on the Westphalian borders, with this distinction, that the latter were so-called freemen who could change from one master to another at will, while the former could not. "There is a great difference," he stated, "between the treatment of these slaves and that meted out to those who are yearly shipped to America from the Congo and Angola. At the Cape they are, in the majority of cases at least, looked upon as permanent family servants . . . The abundance of the necessaries of life and the comparatively easy work of fetching and carrying wood, herding cattle, tilling the fields, labouring in the vineyards or attending to the daily housework, make their lot in life quite tolerable, and if, at times, some inhuman wretch is found who ill-treats his slaves, nowhere is there a better opportunity of obstructing and altogether preventing this ill-treatment by means of good laws than at the Cape."

An Englishman who arrived in the colony soon after the Dutch East India Company had ceased to function has fortunately left an interesting record of his impressions of slavery at the Cape. He writes: "The number of slaves in the service of each family is a cause of some surprise, and particularly as there are so many women and children. This is indeed a burthen imposed by an honourable aversion to sell those who have been born under their roof. The history of slavery is in general a mournful recital of oppression and sufferance; but detestable as is the usage, still the condition of the slave is not at the Cape Town a subject of reproach to the master. Here, and here alone perhaps in the world, are the slaves treated with a mildness that would merit the admiration of a Howard. No rigorous toil excites compassion or indignation, no melancholy plaints pierce the heart of the passenger. The little children are even caressed by their proprietors with as much kindness as if they were the offspring of relations, and if they be not born in freedom they are for years unconscious of their shackles. They are associated in every amusement, they share every act of tenderness with the white children, and although the European mother prefers her own race she would think herself unworthy to be a parent if she could neglect an infant or not treat it with kindness because it was the offspring of a slave. This indulgent conduct towards infants born in a state of reprobation does surely more honour to these people than any imitation of those refinements in other colonies that too frequently render the heart insensible to offices of humanity . . ."[160]

This kindly attitude of owners towards slave children often attracted the attention of visitors who called at the Cape. The author of *Gleanings in Africa* tells us of an incident which made an indelible impression on his mind. It appears that he stayed overnight with a private family, and while at supper he noticed the good-hearted treatment accorded by the host to his slaves. A young child was brought in that had lately lost its mother; but the kind and endearing assiduities of the family soon made it forget its bereavement. As the poor little black creature was about to be led away, both master and mistress blessed it with a parting kiss for the night.

In the diary of Hudson, we read an actual description of his own attitude towards his slaves: "I treat them as my children and they return it with gratitude and affection. I have had repeated proofs of this when I have been confined to a sick-bed, unable to assist myself. My slaves have been indefatigable in their attendance, and when I have suffered a momentary pang from the acuteness of my disorder the big drops have chased each other down their sooty cheeks and their very looks expressed the thousand terrors that assailed them . . . Let those preach for ages upon the want of feeling in this race of man. I have had proof that would put all this sophistry to flight and convinces me that they are alive to all that sensibility which the white inhabitants of colder climates are so unwilling to allow them . . ."

However, generally speaking, one observes how in many ways the attitude of the European towards the slave class gradually hardened with the progress of the eighteenth century. A great number of the emancipated slaves failed to earn an honest living; they were indolent, and showed little enthusiasm to make good use of their freedom. A letter from the Burgher Council at the beginning of that century sheds a significant light on the manner in which the white men regarded the free blacks. It appears that the Governor deeply deplored the dirty condition of the streets, and put the question to the Burgher Council whether it would not be advisable to adopt the same measures as those employed in Europe, by having the rubbish daily removed in carts, for the upkeep of which a tax of one or two skillings per month could be levied. The Councillors replied that most of the filth lying in the streets and between the houses was thrown there by free blacks and Chinamen, who were too lazy to carry it away to the appointed places. It would therefore be unjust, they argued, to tax the law-abiding residents for such a purpose. The evil could easily be prevented, they continued, if the newly-formed Company of Free Blacks, from whom the malpractice emanated, took the refuse away in wheelbarrows and kept the streets clean. They should have no objection to doing this work, as they were excused from all expeditions and guards, which duties devolved upon the burghers, though "at the same time, like all burghers", complained the Councillors, "they, the Free Blacks, have every civil benefit and liberty".[161]

Other slaves again made strenuous efforts to place themselves on a social level with the Europeans. But when the authorities saw that there was a growing tendency among the freed females, as far as clothes were concerned, not only "to consider themselves the equal of respectable burghers' wives but actually to surpass that standard of apparel indulged in by them", they decided to put a stop to "this exceedingly annoying practice". Thenceforth the female slaves were prohibited from wearing "coloured silk dresses, crinolines, fine lace, trimmings on bonnets, hair that has been curled, also earrings, whether made of imitation or of precious stones". Only garments of chintz could be worn, but, provided these women conducted themselves well, they were permitted on their bridal days, and certain other ecclesiastical occasions, to don as a special privilege black silk gowns.[162]

In a letter to Viscount Melville, written towards the end of the eighteenth century, Lady Anne Barnard describes her arrival at Waggonmaker's Valley (now Wellington), and the arrangements made by her party to sleep at the house of Mynheer Wegg (probably Benjamin Gottlieb Weigt), formerly a soldier in the service of Frederick the Great and therefore possessing, according to her, a little more *savoir faire* and sophistication than most of the other farmers. His wife was a hale, oldish woman, full of hospitable frankness. "We found at Waggonmaker's Valley," the narrative runs, "what is universal in this country, a constant drinking of coffee going forwards. It is to be found boiling on the table over charcoal all day long. Wine handed about half a dozen times in the course of the evening, pipes filled and smoked by the gentlemen, and the room filled with slaves — a dozen at least. Here they were particularly clean and neat. The vrouw sat like Charity tormented by a legion of devils, with a little black baby in her arms, one on each knee, and three or four larger ones round her, smiling benignly on the little mortals, who seemed very sweet creatures, and devilish only in their hue. She and her husband have (for a wonder) no children of their own; so they mean to leave their slaves free, and to give amongst them all their fortune . . ."

It was Lady Anne, too, who in another place mentions that at the Fiscal's dwelling she came across a small clean house kept by a black woman, wife of the Landdrost's coachman, who in her own turn kept a slave, a mother of

THE GIFT OF FREEDOM 221

eight "little naked mice" that ran about the gardens and offices "just as they came into the world, without being ashamed . . ."

Those who have made a superficial survey of the life of the slave will perhaps form a mistaken opinion of slavery as a whole. It must be remembered that one cannot conclude simply from the court cases on record that the majority of slaves, and of masters, were bad. When considering, broadly, the relationship between owners and bondsmen, one should always bear in mind that those cases of oppression or violence which gained unpleasant notoriety related to a small minority of unusually harsh masters or exceptionally unruly slaves. By far the greater number of the colonists lived in peace and harmony with the blacks under their control. After all, there were in 1795 no less than 17,000 slaves at the Cape and an almost equal total of Europeans: comparing this figure with the number of cases that came before the Court of Justice, we see that the latter was almost infinitesimal.*

This truth was stressed by Semple. After saying that the slaves were well cared for, he impressed on his readers the fact that if now and then an instance were found to the contrary, it did not affect the general character: "A man at the Cape may use his slave ill, but the slaves at the Cape are well treated; or he may lodge him badly, but the slaves at the Cape are well lodged; or he may half clothe or half feed him, but the slaves of the Cape are well clothed and fully fed". The Englishman Hudson, too, deplored the attitude of the numerous people who judged slavery "from the futile horrors of their diseased imaginations". He admitted that upon his first advent in the settlement his feelings had been wound up to such tension that he determined never to purchase a slave. It was only after he had resided among the Dutch inhabitants for ten years, and had observed their treatment of the slaves, that he began to realise "that those tales of woe and cruelty appeared only as chimeras to amuse children", and added that although it would be wrong to say that every slave met with humanity

---

* See Population Figures: Reference No. 162.

and tenderness, experience had taught him that they were "better fed, clothed and have a more comfortable bed to rest their weary limbs on than half the peasantry of our boasted land of freedom . . ."

Not only were these colonists on the whole kindly disposed towards their slaves, but they also possessed the ability to elicit from them the best service of which they were capable. In his observations made at the Cape during a stay of six weeks on his return journey to Europe in 1771, Bernardin de St. Pierre, the author of *Paul et Virginie*, drew attention to this capacity: after stating that the situation of these negroes was preferable to that of the peasants of Europe, if there were any compensations for the lack of liberty, and after acknowledging that their liberal and humane treatment at the Cape had a profound influence upon their behaviour, he went on to say that "their zeal, activity and fidelity are amazingly great". And then came a compliment: "Yet these are the very same islanders of Madagascar, who are so inattentive to their masters in our colonies". Another observant visitor, Sir Joseph Banks, recorded at about the same time some similar impressions. He declared that the Malay slaves at the Cape behaved much better towards their masters and mistresses than did those in Batavia. Here they were "much quieter, honester, and more diligent, and less wicked than in that place".

Prudence, tact, forethought — these were some of the qualities required of the owner if he wished to handle his slaves satisfactorily and keep them in proper subjection. Those who were allowed excessive indulgence very soon abused it. Whereas an oppressed slave was abject and cringing, a pampered one often became insufferably insolent, obstinate and difficult to manage.

If the demoralising effects of slavery upon both master and slave were powerful, the economic effects were worse. So much capital was invested in the purchase of slaves that nothing was left for those requirements essential for the growth and development of a young country. As a matter of fact, this freezing of capital in slave labour was recognised and discussed by the Council of Policy in 1786. They were disturbed because the inhabitants vied with one another in acquiring more and more slaves, spending all their profits in the process, and forgetting that if lean times came these dependants still had to be fed, and that during the comparatively frequent epidemics they died in numbers and thus brought ruination upon their owners. Then, too, there was the insidious softening effect upon those Europeans able to command and rely upon unpaid labour; almost inevitably they degenerated into habits of sloth and ease, extravagance and waste.

For nearly forty years after that day in September 1795 when the troops of the Dutch East India Company laid down their arms and surrendered as prisoners-of-war to the English, slavery continued to exist at the Cape. It still required as much time as that for people to realise that such an institution was contrary to the laws of God and the rights of man; but enlightenment did finally dawn, and on 1 December 1834 the ignoble title of "slave" was erased for ever from the annals of the Cape of Good Hope. By far the majority of our coloured folk to-day have slave blood in their veins: to their credit be it said that many of them have become useful citizens of the great and beautiful country whose children they are. And just as their forefathers volunteered to go forth, armed with assegais, against recalcitrant Hottentots nearly three hundred years ago, so in our times we know that when their services are needed against a common enemy they will be ready and willing, as they have so often shown in the past, to shed their blood for the land of their birth.

PRINCIPAL SOURCES CONSULTED

1. ARCHIVAL SOURCES

A. — PUBLISHED

Dagverhaal van Jan van Riebeeck — Deel i, Utrecht, 1884; deel ii, 's-Gravenhage 1892; deel iii, 's-Gravenhage, 1893.

Jeffreys, Kathleen: Kaapsche Archiefstukken 1778-1783, Cape Town 1926 — 1938.

Leibbrandt, H. C. V. — *Précis of the Archives:*

Journal 1651 — 1662, 3 vols.	1897
„ 1662 — 1670	1901
„ 1671 — 1674, 1676	1902
„ 1669 — 1732	1896
Resolutiën 1652 — 1662	1898
Letters Received 1649 — 1662	1898
„ „ 1649 — 1662	1899
„ „ 1695 — 1708	1896
Letters Despatched 1652 — 1662, 3 vols.	1900
„ „ 1696 — 1708	1896
Requesten or Memorials A-E	1905
„ „ „ F-O	1906
„ „ „ P-Z (In Manuscript, Cape Archives)	
Defence of W. A. van der Stel	1897
Rambles through the Archives — Cape Town	1887

Molsbergen, Dr. E. C. Godee: Reizen in Z.A. — Linschoten Vereniging, 's-Gravenhage, 1922.

Moodie, Donald: The Record i, ii and iii, Cape Town 1838

Ryks Geschiedkundige Publicatien: Beschryvinge van O. I. C., 's-Gravenhage, 63, 68, 74, 76.

Theal, G. M.: Belangryke Historische Dokumenten, Vols. 1 and 2, Cape Town, 1896, 1911.

Records of the Cape Colony, Vols. 1-15.

Van der Chys, J. A.: Nederlandsch-Indisch Plakaatboek, Vols. 1 — 11, 1602 — 1811.

Van Riebeeck Society Publications:
1. Reports of De Chavonnes and his Council, and of van Imhoff, 1918.
2. Mentzel, O. F.: Life at the Cape — 1919.
3. De Mist, J. A.: Memorandum — 1920.
4, 6, 25. Mentzel, O. F.: A Geographical-Topographical Description — 1921, 1924, 1944.
5. Collectania: Ovington, Beeckman, Dampier: .... Joan Simons — 1924.
10, 11. Lichtenstein, Henry: Travels — 1928-1930.
14. Dapper, Ten Rhyne, de Grevenbroeck: Early Cape Hottentots, 1933.
19. Duminy Dagboeke — 1938.

B. — UNPUBLISHED

(a) *Raad van Politie* (C)

C. 1 — 112	Resolutiën, 1652 — 1795.
C. 120 — 222	Bylagen tot Resolutien, 1716 — 1795.
C. 223 — 290	Requesten en Nominatien, 1715 — 1791.
C. 291 — 325	Memorien en Rapporten, 1710 — 1791.
C. 326 — 408	Attestatien, 1652 — 1791.
C. 409 — 477	Inkomende Brieven, 1649 — 1795.
C. 493 — 582	Uitgaande Brieven, 1652 — 1791.
C. 583 — 649	Dagregister, 1652 — 1794.
C. 666	Dagregister van Commies Holtsappel nopens Madagascar Slaven Handel, 1773 — 1774.
C. 667	Journaal van Hoeker de Snelheyd, 1773 — 1774.
C. 680 — 687	Origineel Placcaat Boek, 1652 — 1795.
C. 689 — 691	Brieven van Nederburgh en Frykenius, 1792 — 1793.
C. 692 — 697	Verslag en Bylagen van Nederburgh en Frykenius 1792 — 1793.
C. 698 — 699	Brieven en Papieren, A. J. Sluysken
C. 700 — 707	Memorien en Instructien, 1657 — 1795.
C. 708	Instructien voor Com. S. van der Stel door Van Rheede, 1685.
C. 709	Instructien van Com. Steeland, 1713.
C. 710 — 711	Instructien
C. 712 — 715	Statuten van India, A — Z.
C. 716 — 716 (a)	Placcaaten en Statuten van India.
C. 717	Instructien uit Holland en India ontvangen 1655 — 1765.
C. 735	Rapport van Gouverneur Van Plettenberg over Burger Memorie, 1781 — 1782.
C. 741 — 741 (a)	Burger Bezwaren, 1784 — 1790.
C. 742 — 745	Kaapsche Geschillen, 1779 — 1785.
C. 798	Gemengde Stukken — Slaven, 1687 — 1780.
C. 800	Burgerbesware en Kom. van Ondersoek, 1742 — 1796.

(b) *Verbatim Copies* (V.C.)

V.C. 1 — 35	Dagregister, 1652 — 1789.
V.C. 36	Rapporten der Commissarissen, 1657 — 1764,
V.C. 38	Journaal van Hendrik A. van Rheede, 1685.
V.C. 58	Wilson's Description of the Cape.
V.C. 59	Rapport — Colonisatie van de Caap, 1717.
V.C. 65 — 73	Brieven en Bylagen, Sluysken
V.C. 77 — 79	Notulen, de Mist.

(c) *Raad van Justitie* (C.J.)

C.J. 1 — 77	Oorspronklike Regsrolle en Notule, 1652 — 1795.
C.J. 123 — 168	Klad Regsrolle en Notule, 1756 — 1795.
C.J. 281 — 458	Criminele Proces Stukken, 1654 — 1795.
C.J. 661 — 724	Minuut Criminele Proces Stukken, 1654 — 1795.
C.J. 780 — 797	Kriminele Vonnisse, 1652 — 1798.
C.J. 822 — 897	Oorspronklike Regsrolle, 1728 — 1795.
C.J. 1022 — 1231	Civiele Proces Stukken, 1708 — 1795.
C.J. 2485 — 2492	Inkomende Brieven, 1729 — 1795
C.J. 2562 — 2568	Bannelingen, 1722 — 1789.
C.J. 2569 — 2579	Uitgaande Brieven, 1720 — 1795.
C.J. 2597 — 2685	Testamenten, 1691 — 1793.
C.J. 2686 — 2824	Prokurasies, 1702 — 1795.
C.J. 2870 — 2913	Kontrakte, 1692 — 1790.
C.J. 2914 — 2948	Vendu Rollen, 1688 — 1794.
C.J. 2952 — 2954	Konfessies en Interrogatien, 1652 — 1685.

C.J. 3173   Annotatie Boek van Justieele visitatie — Kwetseren, 1757 — 1766.
C.J. 3175   Dokumenten re Verongeluktes, 1765 — 1792.
C.J. 3188   Bandietrolle, 1728 — 1795.
C.J. 3189   Lysten der ter Robben Eyland gecondemneerde, 1758 — 1802.
C.J. 3635 — 3647 Diverse Processtukke, 1688 — 1794.

(d) Weeskamer (M.O.O.C.)

M.O.O.C. 6/1 — 6/8   Doodregisters, 1758 — 1797.
M.O.O.C. 7/1 — 7/40 Testamente, 1689 — 1795.
M.O.O.C. 8/1 — 8/21 Inventarisse, 1673 — 1795.
M.O.O.C. 9/1 — 9/6   Koopkondisies, 1697 — 1796

(e) Accessions (Acc.)

Diaries of S. E. Hudson (1796-1798): (Copy made by Mr. A. C. G. Lloyd, in the S.A. Public Library. Other Hudson diaries are in the Cape Archives, placed with Accessions.

(f) Stellenbosch Archives. (St.)

St.					
1/1 — 1/47	Notule van Landdros en Heemrade	..	..	1691—1795
3/8 — 3/13	Verklaringe in Kriminele Sake	..	..	1702—1796
8/1	Skouaktes en Lykskouings	..	..	..	1731—1799
18/40 —18/48	Kontrakte	..	..	..	..	1689—1793
18/195—18/196	Lyste van Ingeboekte Baster Hottentotte	..	1787—1824
22/127—22/128	Transporte van Slawe	..	..	..	1793—1804

(g) Swellendam Archives. (Sw.)

Sw. 1/1 — 1/ 3   Notule van Landdros en Heemrade   .. 1747—1798
    3/10 — 3/17 Algemene Verklarings   ..   ..   .. 1746—1795

(h) Graaff-Reinet Archives. (G.R.)

G.R.					
1/1 — 1/2	Minutes of Landdrost and Heemraden	..	1786—1802
3/16 — 3/18	Judicial Declarations	..	..	..	1786—1802
15/1 —15/5	Notarial Deeds	..	..	..	..	1786—1801
15/43	Contracts of Service	..	..	..	1786—1795
17/30	Transfers of Slaves	..	..	..	1781—1795

II. BIBLIOGRAPHY

Barrow, John: An Account of Travels — 2 vols. London, 1801-4; A Narrative of Travels .... London, 1802.

Beyers, C.: Die Kaapse Patriotte, 1779 — 1791, Kaapstad, 1929.

Blommaert, W.: Het Invoeren van de Slavernij: Archives Year Book, Vol. 1, 1938.

Bogaert, A: Historische Reizen .... Amsterdam, 1711.

Bontekoe, W. Y.: Memorable Description .... East Indian Voyage, 1618-25, (Broadway Travellers), 1929.

Bosman, D. B.: Oor die Ontstaan van Afrikaans — Amsterdam, 1927.

Bosman, W.: A New and Accurate Description of the Coast of Guinea. — London, 1721

Botha, C. G.: The Cape Supreme Court, S.A. Law Journal, November, 1932; Public Archives of S.A. — Cape Town, 1928.

Cape Colonist: The Cape Malays — an Essay .... Cape Town, 1883.

Cook, J.: A Voyage .... Round the World, 1772 — 5. London, 1777.

Cory, G. E.: Rise of S.A., Vol. III, London 1919.

Cowley, Captain: Voyage Round the Globe, 1683 — 6. London, 1687.

Cruse, H. P.: Die Opheffing van die Kleurlingbevolking, 1652 — 1795 .... Kaapstad, 1947.

Dampier, Wm.: A New Voyage Round the World, 1679 — 1691 .... London, 1697.

De Haan, F.: Oud Batavia — Bandoeng, 1935.

Dehérain, H.: Le Cap de Bonne-Espérance au XVIIe Siècle — Paris, 1905.

De Jong, C: Reizen Naar de Kaap, 1791-7 (3 vols.) — Haarlem, 1802.

De St. Pierre, J. H. B.: A Voyage to ... The Cape of Good Hope — London, 1775.

Du Plessis, I. D.: The Cape Malays — Cape Town, 1944.

Du Toit, P. J.: Afrikaansche Studies — Proefschrift — Gent, 1905.

Du Toit, P. S.: Onderwys aan die Kaap, 1652 — 1795 — Cape Town, 1937.

Edwards, I. E.: Towards Emancipation — Cardiff, 1942.

Encyclopaedie van Nederlandsch-Indië: Vol. III — 's-Gravenhage, 1919.

English Officer: Gleanings in Africa .... With Observations .... State of Slavery — London, 1806.

Falconbridge, A: An Account of the Slave Trade — London, 1778.

Fouché, L.: The Diary of Adam Tas, 1705 — 6 — London, 1914.

Franken, J. L. M.: Catrinha Kel: Tydskrif vir Wetenskap en Kuns — June, 1927; Vertolking aan die Kaap in Maleis en Portugees — „Die Huisgenoot", 23.5.1930, 27.6.1930, 18.7.1930; Die Taal van die Slawekinders en Fornikasie met Slawinne — Tydskrif vir Wetenskap en Kuns, September, 1927; Huisonderwys aan die Kaap 1692-1732 — Annale van Universiteit, Stellenbosch, July, 1934.

Fryke, C. and Schweitzer, C.: Voyages to the East-Indies — Seafarers' Library, 1929.

Hesseling, D. C.: Het Afrikaans — Leiden, 1923.

Hickey, W.: Memoirs .... 1749—1775. Edited by Alfred Spencer — London 1913-1925.

Hoge, J.: Personalia of the Germans — Archives Year Book, 1946; Privaatskoolmeesters aan die Kaap — Annale van Universiteit, Stellenbosch, July, 1934 and June, 1937; Rassenmischung in Sudafrika im 17 und 18 Jahrhundert — Stuttgart, 1938.

Jeffreys, K.: Malay Tombs of the Holy Circle: Cape Naturalist: Vol. 1, No. 1, 1934, Vol. 1, No. 5, 1938, Vol. 1 No. 6, 1939.

Kindersley, Mrs.: Letters from the ... Cape of Good Hope — London, 1777.

Kolbe, P.: Naauwkeurige Beschryving van de Kaap. 2 Vols. — Amsterdam, 1727.

Le Valliant, M.: New Travels into the Interior, 3 Vols. — London, 1796. Travels into the Interior, 2 Vols. — London, 1790.

MacCrone, I. D.: Race Attitudes in S.A. — London, 1937.
MacMillan, W. M.: Cape Colour Question — London, 1927.
Malherbe, E. G.: Education in South Africa — Cape Town, 1925.
Marais, J. S.: The Cape Coloured — London, 1939.
Marais, M. M.: Armesorg aan die Kaap — Archives Year Book, 1943.
Maurice, E. L.: History and Administration of the Education of the Coloured Peoples, 1652 — 1910, Vol. I (Thesis, University of Cape Town).
Miller, T.: Consideration on the Exact Position of Slave Question — Cape Town, 1831.
Molsbergen, E. C. G.: De Stichter .... Jan van Riebeeck. — Amsterdam, 1912.
Ovington, J.: A Voyage to Suratt . . . Cape of Good Hope — London, 1696.
Paterson, Wm.: A Narrative of Four Journeys, 1777-9 — London, 1789.
Percival, R.: An Account of the Cape — London, 1804.
Pettman, C.: Africanderisms — London, 1913.
Resident at the Cape: Remarks on Demoralising Influence of Slavery, by a Resident at the Cape — 1828.
Rogers, W.: A Cruising Voyage, 1708-1711 — London, 1712.
Semple, Robert: Walks and Sketches — London, 1803.
Sparrman, A: A Voyage to the Cape, 1772-1776 — London, 1786.
Stavorinus, J. S.: Voyages .... at the Cape of Good Hope 1768-1778 .... London. 1798.
Tachard, Guy: Voyage de Siam des Péres Jésuites — Paris, 1686; Second Voyage du Pére Tachard — Paris, 1689.
Theal, G. M.: History and Ethnography — Before 1795. 3 Vols. London 1909-1910.
Thunberg, C. P.: Travels in Europe, Africa — 1770-1779 — London, 1795.
Valentyn, F.: Beschryving van .... Kaap — Amsterdam, 1726.
Van Rensburg, A. Janse: Die Toestand van die Slawe — 1806-1834 — Tesis, Universiteit van Kaapstad, 1935.
Walker, Eric A.: History of S.A. — London, 1935.

REFERENCES

[1] C. 584: Dagverhaal, 16 Nov. 1658.

[2] L. C. Vryman: Slavenhalers en Slavenhandel, Amsterdam, 1937; I. Murray: Article in "Africana Notes & News", Vol. I, Note 4 — Johannesburg, 1944.

[3] C. 702 p. 5: Instructiën 19 June 1686; C. 702 p. 97-110: Instructiën 17 July 1694; C. 594 Dagverhaal 19 July 1694; Compare C. 587 Dagverhaal 5 Mar. 1673: "God Almighty has also let fall into our hands the (English) sloop... with 240 slaves on board... will come in very handy here...."

[4] C. 44: Resolutiën 4 April 1752; C. 704: Memorien en Instructiën 29 April 1775.

[5] Ryks Geschiedkundige Publicatiën 68 pp 653-670.

[6] V.C. 154 p. 25: Dagverhaal van Joan van Hoorn in het schip „de Vryheid", 30 Nov. 1676.

[7] Theal since 1795, Vol. iii p. 32; see also C. 605: Dagverhaal 3 June 1719. Another mutiny amongst the slaves occurred in the „Slot ter Hoge": C. 469: Inkomende Brieven, India, 5 Oct. 1784.

[8] V.C. 5: Dagverhaal 28 Nov. 1667.

[9] C. 460: Letter from Soetendals Valley 7 Mar. 1766. C.J. 390: Criminele Proces Stukken 30 Oct. 1766.

[10] C. 702: Memorien en Instructiën 17 July 1694; C. 508: Uitgaande Brieven 15 June 1705.

[11] C. 704 p. 117: Instructiën 2 May 1776.

The following table gives a rough indication of the value of the coins used:

	s.	d.
Duit	0	$\frac{1}{8}$
Stiver (st.)	0	1
"Dubbeltje"	0	2
Skilling (sh.)	0	6
Guilder (Cape) (f.)	1	4
Guilder (Dutch)	1	8
Rixdollar (Rds.)	4	0
Silver Ducaton	6	6
Golden Ducaton	8	9
Guinea	22	0
Doubloon	80	0

Other coins such as the Spanish dollar or Real of Eight, worth about 5s., the piaster (4s. 6d.) and the rupee (2s. 6d.), although not in circulation amongst the inhabitants, were often used for trading purposes, especially with regard to the slave trade.

[12] "Some Historical Accounts of Guinea" by Anthony Benezet, London, 1738.

[13] C. 416 p. 2: Inkomende Brieven 24 Jan. 1685; C. 591: Dagverhaal 13 Nov. 1686.

[14] C. 605 Dagverhaal 22 Feb. 1720.

REFERENCES

[15] V.C. 13: Dagverhaal 14 June 1694; Ryks Geschiedkundige Publicatiën No. 68, p. 655.

[16] Ryks Geschiedkundige Publicatiën, No. 68 p. 668: Orders van de XVII voor den Slavenhandel; C. 179 p. 15, Bylagen 1778; C. 416 p. 315: Inkomende Brieven 22 Nov. 1685; C. 451 pp. 102, 103: Inkomende Brieven 29 Nov. 1747; C. 444 p. 309: Inkomende Brieven 16 Oct. 1733.

[17] C. 505: Uitgaande Brieven, Amsterdam, 23 Jan. 1696.

[18] C. 428, p. 537: Inkomende Brieven, Middelburg 22 Aug. 1705; C. 508: Uitgaande Brieven, Amsterdam, 31 Mar. 1706; E. C. Godee-Molsbergen's "Jan van Riebeeck", p. 156.

[19] Theal's Records of the Cape Colony Vol. XXVII p. 91: 30 June 1826.

[20] C. 220 pp. 115, 399: Bylagen Jan.-April 1795; C. 222 p. 571: *Ibid* May-Sept. 1795.

The following were the heads of the Cape Government from 1652 to 1795:
Jan van Riebeeck, Commander, 1652-1662.
Zacharius Wagenaar, Commander, 1662-1666.
Cornelius van Quaelberg, Commander, 1666-1668.
Jacob Borghorst, Commander, 1668-1670.
Pieter Hackius, Commander, 1670-1671.
Albert van Breugel, Acting Commander, 1672.
Isbrand Goske, Governor, 1672-1676.
Johan Bax, Governor, 1676-1678.
Hendrik Crudop, Acting Commander, 1678-1679.
Simon van der Stel, Commander, 1679-1691; and Governor from 1691-1699.
Willem Adriaan van der Stel, Governor, 1699-1707.
Johan Cornelius d'Ableing, Secunde acting as Governor from 1707-1708.
Louis van Assenburgh, Governor, 1708-1711.
Willem Helot, Secunde acting as Governor, 1711-1714.
Maurits Pasques de Chavonnes, Governor, 1714-1724.
Jan de la Fontaine, Secunde acting as Governor, 1724-1727.
Pieter Gysbert Noodt, Governor, 1727-1729.
Jan de la Fontaine, Secunde acting as Governor, 1729-1730, and Governor from 1730-1737.
Adriaan van Kervel, Governor, 1737.
Daniel van der Henghel, Fiscal Independent acting as Governor, 1737-1739.
Hendrik Swellengrebel, Governor, 1739-1751.
Ryk Tulbagh, Governor, 1751-1771.
Joachim van Plettenberg, Secunde acting as Governor, 1771-1774; Governor from 1774-1785.
Cornelius Jacob van der Graaff, Governor, 1785-1791.
Johan Isaac Rhenius, Secunde acting as Governor, 1791-1792.
Sebastiaan Cornelius Nederburgh and Simon Hendrik Frykenius, Commissioners General, 1792-1793.
Abraham Josius Sluysken, Commissioner-general, 1793-1795.

[21] C. 81 p. 131: Resolutiën 9 Feb. 1787.

[22] C. 412: Inkomende Brieven 21 Oct. 1676; Moodie's Record of the Native Tribes ... p. 344; C. 63 p. 167: Resolutiën 16 April 1771.

[23] Archives Year Book 1948, Vol. ii: Die Kompanjie se Besetting van Delagoabaai, deur C. J. Coetzee.

[24] C. 590: Dagverhaal 24 Jan. 1684; C. 591: Dagverhaal 23 April 1686.

[25] C. 413: Inkomende Brieven, Colombo, 20 Jan. 1677; see also C. 588 Dagverhaal 26 Mar. 1677; C. 494: Uitgaande Brieven 1662-7 ... "en een eenige

slaeff die by nacht met een canootie aen boort gecomen was, en sich selffs vrywillich aen d'onse overgegeeven hadde".

[26] Sara Dreyer (widow Bresler) of Cape Town purchased for 230 rixdollars a slave who had originally been sold by his mother in the East Indies when he was twelve years old, "mits dringende armoede en gebrek van Leevens middelen" . . . on account of desperate poverty and lack of subsistence: Cape Archives, Miscellaneous Collection.

[27] V.C. 7: Dagverhaal 30 Nov. 1676; C. 587 Dagverhaal 12 Mar. 1673; C. 596 Dagverhaal 27 Feb. 1697 and 15 Mar. 1697; C. 591: Dagverhaal 13 Dec. 1686.

[28] C. 588: Dagverhaal 22 Dec. 1677; C. 589: Dagverhaal 21 Jan. 1679.

[29] V.C. 5: Dagverhaal 23 Dec. 1669 and 22 Jan. 1670; C. 589: Dagverhaal 28 July 1679 and 19 Aug. 1679; C. 27 p. 188: Resolutiën 12 June 1732, C. 10 p. 371: Resolutiën 16 Mar. 1716; C. 11 p. 463: Resolutiën 30 Mar. 1717; C. 536: Resolutiën 14 Sep. 1751; C. 521 p. 101: Uitgaande Brieven 4 Mar. 1733; V.C. 5: Dagverhaal 23 Dec. 1669 and 22 Jan. 1670; C. 521 p. 101: Uitgaande Brieven 1731-2; C. 4: Resolutiën 27 April 1679. The building, now known as the Old Supreme Court, still stands.

[30] Theal's Belangrijke Hist. Doc. Vol. I pp. 24-27; C. 19: Resolutiën 11 Dec. 1725; C. 608: Dagverhaal 9 Aug. 1728; C.J. 10 pp. 49-51: Criminele Regts Rollen 7 Aug. 1728.

[31] Quoted by Dr. Anna Boëseken: Archives Year Book 1944, p. 65.

[32] C. 210 p. 539: Bylagen 1793.

[33] C.J. 663 p. 58: Criminele Proces Stukken 1736-7: "Ja, Ja, Baas, dit is goed soo, ik heb lang genoeg met mijn hongerige buyk voor jouw gewerkt, ik kan dog nu niet meer. . . ."

[34] B.O. 50 p. 378: Letters Despatched within Colony 1797-8.

[35] C. 509 B: Uitgaande Brieven, Amsterdam, 6 June 1709; V.C. 5 Dagverhaal 25 June 1670; C. 587: Dagverhaal 13 Mar. 1673; C. 10: Resolutiën 31 Mar. 1716; C. 420 p. 476: Inkomende Brieven 1692-3.

[36] Dr. C. Beyers: Kaapse Patriotte, p. 129; Leibbrandt's Requesten V.-Z. p. 494.

[37] C. 728 p. 59: Diverse Vrybrieven en Billieten.

[38] In 1783, when prices were high, a slave was sold for 1,551 rixdollars: Kaapsche Geschillen Vol. IV p. 26; C. 686 p. 291: Original Placcaat Book 1787-1792. The tax was imposed three years later: C. 88 p. 126: Resolutiën 9 July 1790; C. 695 p. 362: Report of Nederburgh 24 July 1793.

[39] C.J. 2533 p. 45: Requesten 25 June 1789; Records of Cape Colony Vol. IX p. 160.

[40] C. 16: Resolutiën 3 Mar. 1722; C. 18 Resolutiën 6 July 1723; C. 85 p. 534 Resolutiën 1789.

[41] C. 600: Dagverhaal 27 Nov. 1708.

[42] Leibbrandt's Memorials F-O pp. 771, 772.

[43] C.J. 363 p. 328: Crim. Proces Stukken 15 Aug. 1754.

[44] C. 596: Dagverhaal 5 April 1697; C.J. 317 Crim. Proces Stukken 12 June 1713; C.J. 322 No. 73: Crim. Proces Stukken 1718; C.J. 349 p. 91: Crim. Proces Stukken, Vol. 1, 1744.

[45] Small pieces of wood each with two supports underneath and a wooden knob on the upper side; the *kaparang* is easily put on, and has a very slight fastening, as the knob fits between the first two toes.

[46] Jacob Wallenberg's "Min son pa Galejan": Quarterly Bulletin of the

S.A. Library Vol. 2, No. 2 (Dec. 1947); C.J. 794 No. 17 Crim. Proces Stukken, 1780.

[47] Dated 1789 "Lyst van Sodaenige s'Comp Leijfeijgen" Slave Office 7/34 No. 1; also C. 214 p. 151: Bylagen 1794.

[48] C.J. 2905 No. 67: Contracten 23 Dec. 1772; C.J. 2896 No. 51: Contracten 2 Feb. 1760; C.J. 3037 No. 33: Notariële Documenten 11 Feb. 1755.

[49] C.J. 2894 No. 36: Contracten 2 Feb. 1756.

[50] C. 70: Resolutiën 20 Jan. 1778; Cape Town Municipal Records 12/1: 13 April 1763.

[51] C.J. 395 p. 806a: Crim. Proces Stukken 1768; C.J. 398 p. 627; Crim. Proces Stukken, 1770; C.J. 363 p. 383: Crim. Proces Stukken, ". . . met een negotie bak langs de straaten is rond gegaan en zijn goederen publiquelijk by uijtroep aan haar uijtgeveijlt heeft"; C.J. 380 p. 56: Crim. Proces Stukken 1763; V.C. 17 p. 459: Dagverhaal 11 May 1706; V.C. 5: Dagverhaal 1 July 1670; C. 683 p. 275: Placcaat 28 Jan. 1749.

[52] C. 286: Requesten en Nominatiën 1789, No. 187.

[53] C. 409: Inkomende Brieven, India, 13 Dec. 1658;

[54] C. 436: Inkomende Brieven, 24 June 1716; V.C. 59 p. 1 et seq; Rapport over vryen in plaats van slaven... 1717. Van Riebeeck Society, Vol. 1 p. 137.

[55] C. 90: Res. 15 Feb. 1791 and Res. 3 Mar 1791; C. 104: Res. 22 Nov. 1793; C. 214 p. 147 Bylagen, 31 Dec. 1793.

[56] Van Riebeeck Society Vol. 1 pp. 49 et seq; V.C. 59 p. 178: Rapport over vryen in plaats van slaven . . . 1717.

[57] Leibbrandt's "Rambles" p. 32.

[58] V.C. 5: Dagverhaal 31 Mar. 1669; C. 584: Dagverhaal 10 Oct. 1658; C. 584: Dagverhaal 15 Oct. 1658; V.C. 13: Dagverhaal 25 Nov. 1693.

[59] C. 508, p. 624: Uitgaande Brieven aan XVII, 30 Mar. 1705; C.J. 397 p. 234: Crim. Proces Stukken 1770; V.C. 7: Dagverhaal 17 Dec. 1676.

[60] C. 38: Resolutiën 10 May 1746; C. 35: Resolutiën 13 Aug. 1743; C. 596: Dagverhaal 24 Jan. 1697.

[61] C. 589: Dagverhaal 12 April 1679; C. 587: Dagverhaal 16 Nov. 1672: Dagverhaal C. 587 19 Nov. 1672.

[62] C. 600: Dagverhaal 17 Dec. 1707; C.J. 782: Sententien 16 Dec. 1707.

[63] V.C. 20: Dagverhaal 7 Feb. 1714; C.J. 318 p. 94: Crim. Proces Stukken 1714.

[64] C. 584: Dagverhaal 19 Oct. 1658.

[65] C.J. 663 p. 23: Minuut Criminele Proces Stukken 4 Jan. 1737. Water and brandy were often carried in calabashes, or even in ostrich eggs: C.J. 662 p. 4 Minuut Criminele Proces Stukken 1712.

[66] C. 202 p. 167: Bylagen 18 Sept. 1792.

[67] C. 13: Resolutiën 5 Sept. 1719; V.C. 6: Dagverhaal 7 Jan. 1671; see also E. C. Godee-Molsbergen's "Tydens de O.I.K." p. 30; Placcaaten 11 Feb. 1762 and 11 Mar. 1763: Kaapse Plakkaat Boek Vol. iii, 1754-1786, by S. D. Naudé — Cape Town, 1949.

[68] Captain Carmichael: Article in Good Hope Literary Gazette, 1 Oct. 1832.

[69] Cape Times 31 Mar. 1923: Cape Argus 10 July 1928.

[70] C.J. 328 p. 338: Crim. Proces Stukken 1724.

[71] C. 700 p. 551: Memorien en Instructiën, 15 July 1685.

[72] C. 5 p. 669: Resolutiën 10 Sept. 1685; C. 429 p. 385: Inkomende Brieven

5 Jan. 1707; C. 592: Dagverhaal 19 and 21 June 1687; C.J. 293 pp. 553, 555, 557: Crim. Proces Stukken 1690.

[73] C. 513 p. 539: Uitgaande Brieven 24 Mar. 1722.

[74] C. 97 p. 327: Resolutiën 27 April 1792.

[75] C. 591: Dagverhaal 9 and 11 July 1685.

[76] C. 493 p. 810: Uitgaande Brieven 1658.

[77] Molsbergen's Reizen Vol. ii p. 236; Government Gazette 24 April 1802 et seq.

[78] V.C. 58 p. 31: Wilson's Description of the Cape.

[79] Deeds Office, Cape Town: Transporten No. 1.

[80] C. 600 Dagverhaal 22 May 1705; 4 June 1705, 8 June 1705. See Hoge's "Rassenmischung... im 17 und 18 Jahrhundert".

[81] V.C. 20: Dagverhaal 16 July 1714; V.C. 6: Dagverhaal 25 July 1671.

[82] C. 588: Dagverhaal 9 Dec. 1678; V.C. 9: Dagverhaal 27 Nov. 1681.

[83] C. 326 No. 183: Attestatien 19 Dec. 1660; C.J. 1 p. 83: Oorspronklike Regsrolle en Notule, 4 Sept. 1660.

[84] C. J. 327 p. 690: Crim. Proces Stukken 1723.

[85] Archives Year Book 1943 p. 26.

[86] C. 173 p. 361: Batavia Resolutiën 17 Jan. 1772, Bylagen tot Resolutiën.

[87] C. 6 p. 84: Resolutiën 1 July 1686; C. 6: Resolutiën 20 Dec. 1686; C. 591: Dagverhaal 20 Dec. 1686.

[88] C.J. 404 p. 679: Crim. Proces Stukken 1773; C. 602: Dagverhaal 26 Feb. 1710.

[89] V.C. 13: Dagverhaal 1 June 1695; C.J. 795: Sententien 23 Nov. 1786; Prof. Franken in "Huisgenoot" 18 July 1930; C.J. 317 p. 79: Crim. Proces Stukken 1713.

[90] V.C. 13: Dagverhaal 23 Jan. 1693; C.J. 344 p. 347: Crim. Proces Stukken 1739; C.J. 417 p. 31: Crim. Proces Stukken, 1782; C.J. 324 p. 46: Crim. Proces Stukken 1720; Van Riebeeck Society, Vol. 8 p. 98.

[91] C.J. 373 p. 51a: Crim. Proces Stukken 1760.

[92] C.J. 297 p. 818: Crim. Proces Stukken 1694.

[93] C. 702 p. 273: Instructiën 1 Dec. 1700.

[94] C. 3: Resolutiën 2 Oct. 1677.

[95] Cape Town Municipal Records 7/7: Kassa Rekening.

[96] C.J. 415 pp. 979, 997: Crim. Proces Stukken 1781; Fouche's "Diary of Adam Tas", p. 75.

[97] C. 47: Resolutiën 21 June 1755.

[98] C. 424, p. 661, Inkomende Brieven, Batavia, 27 Nov. 1699; for cases of torture see C. 595: Dagverhaal 2 April 1696; C. 595: Dagverhaal 17 Sept. 1696; C. 596: Dagverhaal 4 June 1697; C. 596 25 July 1697; C. 596 3 Aug. 1697; C. 596 24 May 1698. For fiscal's views on torture see C.J. 122, Fiscaals Rollen: 19 May 1785.

[99] V.C. 33: Dagverhaal 16 Feb. 1782. Unfortunately this sketch could not be found amongst the archives at the Cape or at the Hague.

[100] C.J. 20 pp. 115, 121: Crim. Regts Rolle, 1738; C. 601: Dagverhaal 13 Sept. 1708.

[101] C. 587: Dagverhaal 2 Sept. 1673; C.J. 358 p. 34: Crim. Proces Stukken, deel I, 1750.

REFERENCES

[102] C.J. 23 p. 21: Crim. Regts Rolle, 1741.

[103] C.J. 381 p. 33: Crim. Proces Stukken, 1764; C.J. 400 p. 176: Crim. Proces Stukken 4 April 1771.

[104] C.J. 314 pp. 225-285; Crim. Proces Stukken, 1710; C.J. 321 No. 41, Crim. Proces Stukken 5 Aug. 1717.

[105] C.J. 780 p. 263: Sententien 13 April 1697.

[106] C. 682 p. 440: Origineel Placcaat Boek: 10 July 1731.

[107] C.J. 122: Fiscal's Rollen 1785.

[108] C.J. 349 No. 99: Crim. Proces Stukken 1744; C.J. 26 p. 16: Crim. Regts Rolle 1744.

[109] C.J. 107, pp. 180-188, Crim. Rollen 1767.

[110] C.J. 2537 No. 36: Requesten 1792.

[111] C. 600: Dagverhaal 23 July 1707; Barrow 1. p. 145; compare C.J. 2962 p. 36: Minuut Justitieele Attestatien, 1707.

[112] Theal's History (before 1795) Vol. iii p. 189; C. 594: Dagverhaal 19 May 1694; C. 10: Resolutiën 15 Oct. 1715.

[113] C. 422 p. 359: Inkomende Brieven, Amsterdam, 14 July 1695.

[114] Beyers's Kaapse Patriotte p. 16; C. 11: Resolutiën 26 May 1716; C. 21: Resolutiën 19 Nov. 1726.

[115] Article in Good Hope Literary Gazette 1 Oct. 1832.

[116] Cape Government Gazette 27 Nov. 1835.

[117] "*Charles Dickens, His Life, Writings and Personality*" by F. G. Kitton.

[118] C. 74: Resolutiën 5 Feb. 1782.

[119] C. 74: Resolutiën 5 Feb. 1782; Mentzel: V.R.S. 6 p. 124; C. 587: Dagverhaal 17 Nov. 1673.

[120] Leibbrandt's Memorials A-E p. 22.

[121] Random Reminiscences of the Cape, by E. L. Kift (Wilmot and Chase's History of the Cape Colony).

[122] C. 702 p. 507: Instructien 19 April 1708.

[123] Theal, Before 1795, Vol. iii p. 35; Walker, p. 88.

[124] V.C. 7: Dagverhaal 23 Nov. 1674; V.C. 19: Dagverhaal 21 Sept. 1709; C. 22 p. 103: Resolutiën 4 Mar. 1727.

[125] C.J. 318 p. 336: Crim. Proces Stukken 1714; V.C. 20: Dagverhaal 1 Sept. 1714.

[126] C. 591: Dagverhaal 13 Sept. 1686; C. 602: Dagverhaal 4 June 1712; C. 605: Dagverhaal 12 Feb. 1724; C.J. 392 p. 432: Crim. Proces Stukken 24 Sept. 1767.

[127] V.C. 12: Dagverhaal 13 Mar. 1692.

[128] V.C. 12: Dagverhaal 24, 25, 27 and 29 Sept. 1690.

[129] V.C. 20; Dagverhaal 3 Sept. 1714: "een wijse van sterven by den Romeynen gepresen, dat onder de Christen ten hoogste verdoemlyk is".

[130] V.C. 20: Dagverhaal 7 and 8 Feb. 1714.

[131] V.C. 7: Dagverhaal 17 July 1674; C. 606: Dagverhaal 15 Feb. 1725; C.J. 394 p. 449: Crim. Proces Stukken, 1768.

[132] Theal's Records, Vol. XI pp. 176-183; 188; 344-349.

[133] C. 685 p. 27: Placcaat Boek 1776-1786; C. 601: Dagverhaal 31 July, 1708.

[134] C.J. 791 No. 28: Sententien 2 Oct. 1766.

[135] C.J. 790 p. 18: Sententien 30 Sept. 1762; Theal's Records of Cape Colony, Vol. viii p. 328.

[136] C. 598: Dagverhaal 19 Jan. 1702; C.J. 314 pp. 225-285: Crim. Proces Stukken, 25 Sept. 1710.

[137] C. 601: Dagverhaal 7 July 1708.

[138] C. 106 p. 355: Resolutiën, 30 May 1794.

[139] C. 17: Resolutiën 24 Nov. 1722; C. 496 p. 415: Uitgaande Brieven 9 Feb. 1673.

[140] MOOC. 14/215, Fragmentariese Boedelpapiere, 1790-1799; MOOC. 14/90 No. 34, Bylae Boedelrekeninge, 1798-1799.

[141] C. 511: Uitgaande Brieven, Batavia, 19 April 1715; C. 502, p. 337: Uitgaande Brieven, Middelburg, 15 April 1689; C. 512: Uitgaande Brieven, Colombo, 23 April 1718.

[142] Quoted by Wilmot and Chase, p. 239.

[143] V.R.S. 5 p. 9; C. 702; p. 556: Instructiën 19 April 1708; C.J. 3077 No. 58: Obligatien Transporten van Slaven, 1724-1725; C. 167 p. 197: Bylagen 10 Dec. 1765; C. 168 p. 465 Bylagen 27 July 1767; C. 69: Resolutiën 3 June 1777.

[144] C. 75 p. 609: Resolutiën 23 Sept. 1783. C. 289 p. 1069: Requesten 1791.

[145] V.C.9: Dagverhaal 8 April 1682.

[146] C. 14: Resolutiën 31 Oct. 1719.

[147] C.J. 3024 No. 22: Obligatien 24 Oct. 1706; MOOC. 7/4 No. 159: Testamenten 1726-1735; MOOC. 7/22 No. 18: Testamenten 1775.

[148] C.J. 3039 No. 66: Notariële Documente 1 Aug. 1759; C.J. 3037 No. 25: Notariële Documente, 26 Sep. 1754; Leibbrandt's Memorials F-O p. 665.

[149] C. 682 p. 204: Original Placcaat Book 29 Sept. 1722.

[150] C.J. 3023: Transport, Obligatien en Procuratien 8 April 1699; MOOC. 7/55 No. 30: Wills filed in 1808; C. 48: Resolutiën 7 Jan. 1756.

[151] Van der Chys, Vol. IV p. 684; C. 6: Resolutiën 26 June 1686.

[152] Placcaat 20 June 1766 (Order of Council in India) filed in C. 168 p. 48: Bylagen 1777; C.O. 3861 No. 7: Memorials 1807; see also Leibbrandt F-O. p. 572.

[153] C. 52 Resolutiën: 10 June 1760 and 19 Aug. 1760.

[154] Kaapse Archiefstukken: 1782, Vol. ii pp. 58, 59.

[155] C. 436 p. 57: Inkomende Brieven, Amsterdam, 28 Sept. 1715. See also C. 511: Uitgaande Brieven, Amsterdam, 28 Mar. 1716: "... we can assure you that on their return they have never again been sold, but considered as free people"; see also C. 87 Resolutiën 2 Mar. 1790; C. 87 Resolutiën 23 June 1790.

[156] C.J. 2558: Requesten 17 Feb. 1814.

[157] C.J. 2 pp. 144, 146, 156 Oorspronklike Regsrolle en Notule, 6 Jan. 1681-10 Feb. 1681; Leibbrandt's Memorials S-T p. 278.

[158] Theal's Records of the Cape Colony Vol. X pp. 4, 45-60.

[159] C.J. 2666 No. 23: Testamenten 1762-1763, Raad van Politie; MOOC 7/4 No. 117: Wills 1726-1735.

[160] Lt.-Col. Robert Wilson: V.C. 58 p. 19.

REFERENCES

[161] C. 17: Resolutiën, 9 Feb. 1723.
[162] C. 684 p. 313: Originele Placcaat Boek 12 Nov. 1765.

EUROPEAN AND SLAVE POPULATION AT THE CAPE: 1701-1793*)

Year	Europeans	Slaves
1701	1,334	891
1706	1,769	1,107
1711	1,870	1,771
1713 (small pox)	1,699	1,794
1718	2,145	2,436
1723	2,364	2,922
1728	2,835	3,873
1733	3,191	4,703
1738	3,748	5,757
1743	4,096	5,361
1748	4,589	4,922
1753	5,533	6,045
(small pox)	—	—
1758	5,676	5,932
1763	6,877	7,215
1768	7,818	8,207
1773	8,554	9,902
1778	9,802	11,107
1783	11,064	11,950
1788	12,704	14,810
1793	13,842	14,747
1795 (End of D.E.I. Co.'s period)	14,927	16,839
1797	21,746	25,754

*) From figures in Beyers's „Kaapse Patriotte", Theal's Records, Barrow's Travels.

INDEX

Adultery	187
Alleman, R. S.	216
Aloes	133
America	217
Amok-runners	195
Amusements	86
Angola	30, 81
Appeal Cases	160
Auctions	42
Back, E.	101
Baptism	109
Barbier, E.	108, 177
Barnard, Lady Anne	220
Bergh, Dr.	135
Bergh, E.	68
Bigamy	187
Black Hole	80
Bloodletting	131
Borcherds, Memoirs of	96
Branding-iron	176
Braun	155
Bull-fight	98
Burial	144, 154
Caffres	168
Caledon Baths	84, 136
Cape Hangklip	83
Capitein, J. E. J.	14
Carpius, Alexander	102
Church, Dutch Ref.	109, 201
Church, Episcopal	107
Church, Lutheran	107, 201
Christmas	104
Cloppenburg, A.	155
Clothing	39, 41, 49
Cock-fighting	86
Comets	128
Complaints by Slaves	38
Constables, European	168
Convicts	40, 192
Cook, Captain	137
Corn Farms	66, 70
Court Messenger	164
Court of Justice	160, 170, 171, 187
Courtship	113
Cowper (Poet)	148
Cowley, Captain	115
Curtis, Admiral Curtis	208

Dancing	93
De Chavonnes, D. P.	63
De la Fontaine, Governor	161
Delagoa Bay	33, 188
Delmina Factory	14
De Mist, Augusta	92
De Mist, Com. General	217
Desertion	71, 175
Dessin	124
De Thuilet, J.	190
De Wet, O.	68
Dickens, Charles	166
Drakenstein	106
Duminy, F.	31, 32, 88
Duminy, Mrs.	84
Eastern Slaves	194, 195
Economic Effects	222
Education	100
Emancipation	198, 223
Engelgraff, D.	101
„Erasmus"	81
Evidence of Slaves	162
Execution, Display at	163
Execution, Places of	164
Exiles, Indian	193
Fines	162
Fiscal	48, 101, 120, 153, 155, 157, 160, 169, 212
Fisher, R. D.	185
Food	38
Fort Lydsaamheid	188
Free Blacks	219
Fugitives	71, 175
Funerals	141
Gambling	90
Ganzekraal	46, 68
Gaol	170
Garden, Company's	97
Gom-Gom	96
Gordon, Col.	95
Goske, Commissioner	114
Guillotine	147
Hanssen, P.	204
Hanging, Method of	179
Heerengracht	69
Herbs	132

INDEX

Hickey, William	 95
Hope Mill	 92
Hospital ..	.. 35, 137, 141
Hottentots	.. 13, 115, 124
Huilebalken	 141
Hyneman, F.	 41
Ill-treatment, Complaints	.. 189
Immorality	 121
Incendiaries	 180
Infanticide	 184
Inns ..	 88
Interpreter	 25
Johnson, Samuel	 16
Joseph, Sheik ..	 193
Joubert, Jacob ..	 82
Justice, Administration	.. 146
Justitie-straat ..	 170
„Kat" ..	 170
Klaas, Captain	 187
„Knechts"	 62
Klavervalley	 94
Knives, Fighting with ..	.. 98
Komfoor	 55
Languages	 51
Laws Regulating Slavery	113, 173, 174
Le Boucq, E. F. Rev. ..	.. 108
Libel ..	 188
Lodge ..	36, 37, 102, 104, 114, 119, 120, 124, 139, 140, 210
Longevity	 216
Lots, Drawing of	.. 35, 45
Madagascar	.. 22, 32, 78, 82
Malays	53, 94, 143, 194, 222
Malay grave	 208
Marriage	.. .. 114, 209
Medicine	 130
Meerlust	 88
Meermin	 19
Melk, Martin	 189
Money — see Ref. II	
Menagerie	 98
Military Duties, Exemption	.. 187
Mostert, W. C. ..	 211
Mulder, J.	 216
Musical Instruments	 91
Mutinies	 18
Myburgh, Johannes	 106
Needlework	 61
New Year's Day	96, 169, 207
Nurses ..	.. .. 137, 139
O*pslag* and *Afslag*	 45
Orang Bharu	 89
Oranglammen ..	 89

Orangezicht	 95
Pass ..	 78
Pasqual, Jan	.. .. 102, 103
Pipe (Punishment by) ..	.. 156
Pirates ..	 27
Poor Fund	200, 201, 204, 206
Population: See Ref. 162	
Price Paid	 44
Property, Confiscation of	.. 186
Quakers	 67
Rattlewatch	 169
Return Fleet	 89
Religion ..	 107
Robben Island ..	40, 154, 178, 189, 190, 191, 194, 203
Roman Catholics	 107
Roodezand	.. .. 106, 177
Sales ..	.. .. 42, 44, 47
Sanitary Tubs ..	 169
Schabort, Dr. ..	 134
Schools ..	 100
Scurvy ..	 30
Serrurier, Rev. ..	 192
Slanderer	 188
Slave Code	 174
Slave Owns a Slave	 209
Small-pox	 139
Smith, Adam	 64
Snakebite	 134
Snakestone	 134
Snakewood	 135
Suicide ..	.. .. 184, 195
Sundays, Work on	 61
Superstition	 126
Stellenbosch	 106
Strombom, I. ..	 31
Strykgeld	 41
Swellendam	 106
Table Mountain	 95
Tas, Adam	 142
Ternate, Prince of	.. 194, 206
Thibault, L. M.	.. 165, 170
Torture ..	.. 146, 153, 157-160
Tropsluiters	 141
Tulbagh, Governor Ryk	.. 202
Tutucorin Slaves	 33
Valkenburg, J. ..	 199
Van de Graaff, H.	 61
Van der Heiden, J.	 191
Van der Henghel, D. ..	.. 160
Van der Meer ..	 70
Van der Stael, P.	 100
Van der Stel, Simon	72, 104, 122, 129, 171, 204

INDEX

Van der Stel, W. A. 178
Van Imhoff, Baron 65
Van Noodt, Governor .. 161
Van Rheede, Com., Lord of
   Mydrecht 37, 102, 105, 112, 114,
   117, 119, 120, 157, 210
Van Riebeeck, A. .. 18, 92
Van Riebeeck, Jan 16, 65, 74, 75,
   77, 80, 81, 97, 120
Van Ryneveld, Daniel 58
Vergelegen 53
Vissershok 46, 68
Voyages, Mortality 28
Vuyst, Petrus 150

Wagon-drivers 58
Walker, E. 173
Water-pumps 54
Wallenberg, J. 56
West India Coy. 30
Wet-nurses 61
Wheel, Breaking on 188
White, John 37
Wilberforce, William 185
Wills of Slaves 205
Wine 68
Wine Farms 66, 70
Witchcraft 127

Zwartland 106